WOMEN AND ECONOMIC DEVELOPMENT

Local, Regional and
National Planning Strategies

BERG/UNESCO STUDIES IN DEVELOPMENT THEORY AND POLICY

S. Jay Kleinberg (ed.), *Retrieving Women's History Changing Perceptions of the Role of Women in Politics and Society (forthcoming)*

WOMEN AND ECONOMIC DEVELOPMENT

Local, Regional and National Planning Strategies

Edited and with an Introduction by
Kate Young

Berg / Unesco

lished in 1988 jointly by
g Publishers Limited
Morrell Avenue, Oxford, OX4 1NQ, UK
Fifth Avenue / Room 400, New York, NY 10010, USA
:dalbingerweg 14, 2000 Hamburg 61, FRG and
sco, 7 Place de Fontenoy, 75700 Paris

Part of this work was published as *Women's concerns and planning: a
methodological approach for their integration into local, regional and national
planning (Socio-economic studies 13)* by Unesco, Paris, 1986
© Unesco 1988

Unesco ISBN 92-3-102549-X
British Library Cataloguing in Publication Data

Women and
    economic development : a critical assessment
    of local, regional and national planning.
    1. Women and economic policy
    I. Young, Kate
    338.9   HC79.W6
    ISBN 0-85496-091-0

Library of Congress Cataloging-in-Publication Data

Women and economic development : a critical assessment of local, regional,
and national planning strategies / edited and with an introduction by Kate
Young.
    p.   cm.
    Originally published as: Women's concerns and planning.
    Bibliography:
    ISBN 0-85496-091-0 : $30.00 (U.S. : est.)
    1. Women in development—Case studies.   2. Economic development
projects—Planning—Case studies.   3. Economic development—Social
aspects—Case studies.   I. Young, Kate.   II. Title.
HQ1240.W665 1988
305.4'2—dc19   87-35927 CIP

Printed in Great Britain by Billings of Worcester

Contents

List of Tables

Preface

All the papers in this volume were commissioned by Unesco's Division for Socio-Economic Analysis as part of its on-going programme of work on devising adequate methodologies to capture data on social processes and economic change in both developed and developing countries. The programme was particularly concerned with identifying useful socio-economic indicators for development planning. The papers were given a first airing at a Unesco workshop held in San Marino in July 1985, and were then edited for publication in Unesco's Socio-economic Studies series. A list of publications in this series is given in the annex to this book together with the recommendations from the San Marino meeting for sensitising planners and incorporating women's concerns in national planning.

The method used by Unesco to stimulate reflection at the national level on the issues of women's needs, appropriate indicators and national planning, was to ask a number of groups (research centres, women's organisations) in 5 different countries to organise a national seminar on the topic of women's present level of incorporation in development and the steps that needed to be taken to enhance this in the future. In some cases this led to original research being undertaken at the national level (in Togo for example the group carried out a national level survey of women), in others to a synthesis being made of a number of meetings on similar topics (for example in Ecuador) in addition to a national level seminar.

The papers then reflect both the ways in which data was gathered on women's participation and the factors inhibiting or encouraging such participation, as well as Unesco's request that recommendations be put forward on the ways in which women's concerns could be more systematically dealt with by planners.

The Introduction to the book is a substantially rewritten version of that originally published in the Unesco publication (Socio-economic Studies No. 13).

REFLECTIONS ON MEETING WOMEN'S NEEDS

Kate Young

The question of the situation of women in developing countries has been on the agenda for over 20 years now. Literature on the subject is voluminous yet while we have learned a great deal about women in a wide variety of countries and differing situations, there is still little consensus as to the nature of their fundamental difficulties, the solutions to be sought, or indeed the impact that economic change has on them. So the question of how to meet women's needs, raises a prior question: that of the need for a clear-cut framework by which to identify, assess and prioritise needs. This in turn may indicate what set of agents or agencies should be charged with meeting such needs once identified. In this article I will first address the question of the framework and distinguish between types of needs; I then turn to the question of whether planning and planners should be privileged agents of change and whether the State itself should also be enlisted and if so in what ways.

What is the Cause for Concern

A preliminary approach to this question might be to adopt the useful distinction between *the condition and the position of women*.[1] By *condition* I mean the material state in which women find themselves: their poverty, their lack of education and training, their excessive work burdens, their lack of access to modern technology, improved tools, work-related skills, etc. By *position* is meant wo-

---

1. This distinction was originally suggested to me by Shireen Huq who developed it in her work with Naripokko (a women's organisation) in Bangladesh.

men's social and economic standing relative to men.

The condition of women is the subject of much of the development literature on women, and indeed it can be said that a major part of development practitioners' concerns centre on finding ways of improving women's condition by targetting ameliorative resources to them rather than by radically changing underlying structures. This forms an important body of literature.[2] Through a whole range of detailed studies the particular conditions of women in different occupations has been highlighted. Initially interest focused on rural women, then industrial workers took centre-stage, more recently urban informal-sector workers. Over time the collective focus has also shifted from women in general to poor women, to the poorest or even the poorest of the poor. Additionally, over the 20-year period the specific concern has shifted from women as mothers and carers of children, to women as economic producers.

This literature to some extent addresses the question of whether women's condition has improved with the integration of developing countries into the market system and the modern world socio-economic system. The general response is that women's condition has worsened; they are poorer, live in increasingly hazardous environments, and have lost the supportive mechanisms of the past. Such findings can appear somewhat contradictory given that studies on the impact of modernisation suggest that in many countries general improvements in health, hygiene, housing, transport, etc., have until recently facilitated improvements in women's levels of health, education, life expectancy, etc. In part this may be an effect of the WID (Women In Development) focus on the poorest since there is considerable evidence to show that they have not benefited equally from general improvements. But in part the conclusion may derive from contrasting assessments of women's condition with that of their position. Thus while conditions may have improved in general for both men and women, in relative terms women may have benefited less. The emphasis on women's condition has had two consequences. Firstly, from the prescriptive point of view there has been a tendency to emphasise women's practical and day-to-day needs and thus to focus on ameliorative measures — giving women greater access to credit, special training schemes, better domestic technology. Secondly, the approach makes it difficult for structural

2. The literature is vast and selecting a few representative texts indivious. I am therefore taking it for granted that readers will know at least some of the literature I am referring to.

issues concerning women's position to be raised. It inhibits posing the question of whether women's condition is related to their structural position, and/or whether any serious and sustainable improvement in their condition is possible without structural change. As a result while women's needs as mothers, producers, etc. are highlighted, their interests as women are not.

The structural issues are the central concern of the (less abundant) literature on women's position.[3] This suggests that the social position of women, whatever their class, has worsened as a result of the integration of developing countries into the market, regardless of whether or not women's condition has improved. There is however less consensus on what the key structures are that have shaped this unequal outcome. A number of different explanations are put forward. Firstly that colonial powers destroyed the political organisation of their subject nations, including those of women, to replace them with more pliable political forms in which women were notably absent. Secondly that the structuring of the economy was deliberately male centred to create a similar basic social and economic unit — the nuclear family — as is found in the West, and which is deemed an essential social-economic component of the market system. Thirdly that economic and other necessary inputs were targeted largely to men in conformity with Western stereotypes, women's needs as producers being ignored, thereby exacerbating their dependence on men.

There is yet another strand in the literature which contests the treatment of women as a unitary category. For some writers the heart of the problem lies in the inequality of social groups, whether this is structured by class, race, ethnicity, religion or some other factor. From this perspective, the differences between men and women's life chances within the same group/class/category are less important than the differences between groups of men and women. Writers in this vein point to the ways in which some women oppress of exploit other women (mothers oppress their sons' wives, (white) employers exploit their (black) maids), and the ways in which class position creates oppositional interests. This viewpoint informs much of the writing on women and development: it leads to the assumption that either all women cannot have the same needs, or the interests of differing categories of women are opposed. In other words, the concept of common women's needs or interests

---

3. Much of this literature focuses on women's *status*.

has no meaning because there is no valid category 'women'; in every case the term has to be modified by other social signifiers, class (middle or working class), age (young or old), civil status (married or unmarried), race (black or white) and so on.

In contrast much of the feminist literature starts from the premise that all women share a common experience of oppression and subordination which is founded on two separate social facts: (1) the sexual division of labour which allots to women the bulk of the domestic tasks of reproducing (including maintaining) current and future generations and yet excludes them from enjoying social value or exercising social power; (2) the organisation of sexuality and procreation which permits individual appropriation of women's generative and sexual capacities, and limits their autonomy and freedom of action. Although all women are believed to share this common fate, few feminists nowadays would suggest that the forms in which oppression is experienced are identical between cultures, or even within societies.

Despite pinpointing sexuality and the sexual division of labour as critical elements, the structures underlying women's subordination to men are still very poorly understood, as is the dynamic of that relation. In part this is precisely because the forms that subordination takes vary widely both in terms of history and in differing cultures. Lacking a general theory of gender inequality, it is difficult to cut through the mass of contradictory empirical data — the diversity of forms of subordination, deeply rooted convictions as to the appropriateness of such forms — to the underlying bedrock of gender differentiation and inequality from which women's interests, as a gender category, could be derived.

As a result the prescriptions for improving women's position are varied: some writers stress interpersonal relations, particularly within marriage and family, while others emphasise culture or ideology; some give priority to laws, institutions (inheritance, the professions, education), others to the productive relations typical of market economies. What they share is the concern to go beyond the condition of women, in many cases to the more profound structures, and in the latter case, to insist that structural changes are required in order to improve women's social and material conditions.

The Problem with Needs

The importance of being clear about our aims — are we concerned with women's condition or their position — and our assumptions — is class oppression more onerous than gender oppression or does class exploitation embody gender oppression — is that they inform both policy and strategy. Most of the papers in this collection recognise that men and women have rather different life chances, and that society is structured in such a way as to produce a pervasive set of disadvantages for women. However, given the prevailing and painful situation of poverty and lack of economic dynamism in the countries concerned, most of the papers emphasise the salience of economic differentiation. As a consequence the intention behind the focus on meeting women's needs remains ambiguous. Is it the condition of women that appalls, or is this seen as a major stumbling block to provision of family welfare or to development efforts themselves? Is it women's unequal position in society which acts as a drag on development projects? Must women's condition be improved before their position can be changed?

In other words, when discussing women's needs we should be clear as to what end these should be directed. Maxine Molyneux (1985) identifies two forms of women's needs. She differentiates between the needs of women as occupiers of particular social roles, predetermined and sustained by custom, practice and ideology, and the interests of women as a social category with unequal access to socially valued resources (both economic and social) and political power. As a result she differentiates between practical and strategic gender interests. (Molyneux, 1985).[4] In our own thinking about this division we have found it more useful to talk about practical needs and strategic interests and will use this terminology throughout this piece.[5]

---

4. See also C. Moser, 1985, who uses the distinction to discuss planning.
5. In some of the papers in the book a parallel distinction is made between short-term or immediate needs and long-term needs (see for example the paper on Ecuador). While it is easy to conflate short-term and practical and long-term and strategic, none the less Molyneux's distinction is a conceptual one — between empirically verifiable wants or needs and theoretically deducible interests.

Practical Gender Needs

Women's *practical gender needs* derive from the necessity of fulfilling the roles allocated to them by the traditional sexual division of labour: care and education of children, maintenance of the household, care of the elderly and the infirm, servicing of husband and his relevant kin, maintenance of the network of familial ties, servicing of the community (which in turn enables women to carry out their family based tasks). Many of these needs are short term, but not all. Most of the papers in this volume focus on women's practical needs in their struggle to provide a livelihood for themselves and their families: access to water, land, housing, land, employment, appropriate technology, credit. Their urgency in many LDCs (Less Developed Countries) derives largely from the dislocations caused by the structural changes taking place as these societies are impelled to embark on the transition to economic and political structures based on the market and the State. In the transitional period, traditional demands are made of women without the conditions which enabled their foremothers to fulfil their obligations in the past. In these societies, almost all women have great unmet needs, but these differ according to the women's differing social positions.

Some writers, however, emphasise the different practical needs of women of the same class which are imposed upon them by life cycle changes; thus older women's practical needs often relate to questions of (ill)health, housing and general physical security, or financial security (especially access to conjugal property in the case of widowhood); while younger women's concerns relate to their childcare responsibilities, and to their need for safety from physical violence, sexual assault and so on. The paper from Italy (pp. 87f.) touches on younger women's need for a less restrictive education and for better preparation for the labour force. It recognises too that older women may also have need of vocational training and guidance. Both groups need a system of management of the labour force (and the economy) which enables them to put their training and talents to good use both for society and themselves. In our terminology most of these needs address the condition rather than the position of women, and Molyneux's terminology practical rather than strategic interests.

The Ecuador paper (pp. 31f.) also addresses questions of longer-term needs: those of women factory workers which derive from their marginalised political position — a position which they share in part with the men of their class but none the less the differences between them can be striking. Women workers' needs centre around political education and training, so that they can learn to promote more successfully their demands for better working conditions and pay. The problem of representation is not merely that of women's lack of experience. They also have to surmount their male colleagues' indifference, even hostility, to their demands. Yet if women are to be successful in their attempts to enter work-based political organisations, whether these be cooperatives, trade unions or other political institutions, they need male workers' support. The paper argues that in the longer term, women workers need to be encouraged to take part in the political process as voters and decision makers. For women to be heard they must organise themselves within pressure groups, political parties, or sector and occupation based groups — and put themselves forward as political leaders. But this requires an openness at the highest levels to a greater democratisation of society itself, and, in essence, to a strengthening of the institutions of civil society. This point is discussed further on page 27 of this Introduction.

Women who are involved in informal work situations may also have similar organisational and educational needs. A number of the papers argue that women not only need better education but an education which does not prepare them merely for traditionally 'feminine' occupations (e.g. papers from Togo, Egypt and Italy in this volume). Suggesting that women should strive to equip themselves to enter non-traditional occupations does not necessarily mean that one has left concern with women's condition in favour of concern with their position. It depends on what exactly non-traditional occupations means: it can mean occupations that are new to the society rather than those which were formerly restricted to men. In the former case, it is possible for women to take up these new economic activities, particularly if they share some of the characteristics of their old ones, without any questioning of their position. Even in the latter case, if men have moved into new and more lucrative positions, those tasks formerly associated with them can be reallocated to women without any change in their relative positions. Probably more important is the ideological justification of such new endeavours: do they support women's traditional roles or undermine them in any way?

Strategic Gender Interests

So far this discussion has focused on women's needs as occupiers of predetermined roles and as bearers of certain predetermined social responsibilities and obligations, largely toward the immediate family and local community. These practical gender needs may be short or longer term, and may differ between classes as well as between women of the same class. But some of them, such as the need of women workers for greater political agency and say in trade-union organisation so as to have their practical needs reflected in union demands, could also be categorised as *strategic gender interests*, if we follow Molyneux's categorisation (ibid). These, in contrast to practical needs, arise not from women's attempts to fulfil traditional, or even modern, obligations imposed by the sexual division of labour, but from women's growing recognition that the age-old structures of male dominance and privilege are not sacrosanct, nor indeed given in the genetic inheritance, but are social impositions, and as such amenable to change. This recognition has been impelled in many countries by changes in the traditional economic and political system whether brought about relatively peacefully or by means of revolutionary or nationalist struggle. It has also been enhanced in recent years by the pressures exerted by international agencies on national governments (as shown in the Ecuador paper), and the growth of an international women's movement which has changed and enlivened the discourse about women's position in society. How are strategic gender interests to be identified?

> Strategic interests are derived in the first instance deductively, i.e. from the analysis of women's subordination and from the formulation of an alternative, more satisfactory set of arrangements to those which exist. These ethical and theoretical criteria assist in the formulation of strategic objectives of overcoming women's subordination, such as the abolition of the sexual division of labour, the alleviation of the burden of domestic labour and childcare, the removal of institutionalised forms of discrimination, the establishment of political equality, freedom of choice over childbearing, and the adoption of adequate measures against male violence and control over women. (Molyneux, 1985, p. 232)

In other words, women's strategic gender interests come into focus when women's position in society is called into question. Any critical analysis of the way in which relations between men and women are organised involves making ethical and moral judgements about such social arrangements, the nature of equity and social justice. Almost by definition such an analysis will be shaped by an alternative vision of what such relations could be and their placement within wider political and economic relations. This poses the problem, as all reformers or revolutionaries have found, of constructing a vision of the future which satisfies — or even inspires — the majority of potential supporters. In the case of gender relations, given the great variability in forms of subordination and their cultural and ideological elaborations, reaching a common and universal vision requires a long-term process of consciousness-raising, discussion and vision-building. But over the past 20 years the outlines of such a vision have been appearing, and almost every international gathering of women adds further elements.

Strategies and Priorities

Hand in hand with vision-building goes the question of strategies and priorities to be adopted. Should the main thrust be towards changing laws (particularly those concerned with inheritance and ownership of valued resources), or opening up all branches of education to women, or encouraging women to enter into male professions (including the army, the police), or including women at the highest level in all key decision-making posts in the government and the State? Should it be towards getting men into the female professions (nursing, clerical work, primary education), and reducing sex segregation at work? Should the focus rather be on changing existing interpersonal relations, promoting male responsibility for home and childcare, or on the way young boys and girls are socialised and educated? Or should greater soci.l value and rewards be given to the work women do at present — housework and childcare, servicing and caring? In other words, should strategies concentrate on structures, behaviour, or ideology?

Obviously, strategies have to be devised in relation to the actual situation faced by women in different social settings, and the identification of culturally specific gender interests. They will also be shaped by the configuration of forces that can be mustered in support of change. An initial appraisal would seem to suggest that women themselves must be readily mobilised to support changes which will enhance their position in society. But in reality the situation is more complex. Although what can be defined as strategic gender interests have been the focus of struggle in some countries unity has been elusive. Campaigns for women's right to abortion, or against the leniency in sentencing of rapists, or against the lack of police and judicial concern over dowry burnings, or in favour of older women's right to maintenance after divorce etc. have not been capable of uniting the majority of women behind them. A number of explanations for this lack of unity can be found in the literature. The commonest is that women are blinded by an ideological veil or are the victims of false consciousness.

Clearly problems of ideological barriers, lack of self-esteem, high levels of passive acceptance and resignation exist (see the paper on Egypt p. 111f.), but these are probably of less importance than the perceived lack of acceptable alternatives which do not entail intolerably high costs. In other words, while women may suffer a common history of oppression and subordination, this experience is mediated by other experiences which may lead many of them to conclude either that they cannot change their situation or that attempting to do so will only worsen their present position which they have at least learned to cope with. Thus their lived experience of oppression is not translated into any action to change their situation or even to support others wishing to do so. It may even lead to certain categories of women supporting the structures and institutions of male dominance[6] and seeing other women as 'the main enemy'. Firstly, in this situation, creating a climate of opinion which allows discussion at the national level of the negative effects of the current situation and possible alternatives to it can be a useful strategy.

Secondly, it is doubtful whether all women either recognise their gender interests or, more critically, regard them as primary. Most women's experiences as members of an oppressed group or class, for example, give rise to group-focused loyalties, which repress or underplay gender oppression. Many women may come to believe that changes in other oppressive conditions are necessary preconditions for change in gender relations.

Thirdly, cross-group alliances are inherently unstable: differences of class, caste, race, or religion can be deeply corrosive, as recent events in many countries have shown. Thus while all women may support the demand for better public health provision for children, wealthier women may withdraw their support if privileges hitherto

6. See Deniz Kandiyoti, 1988.

held are threatened and this is construed to be detrimental to their children's interests. This is as much a problem of 'primordial loyalties' as of the way in which a mother's responsibilities are structured socially. Strategic alliances are also difficult to maintain in situations where a series of changes are sought, any one of which may appear to threaten the practical interests of certain sectors of the alliance or may leave them feeling more vulnerable. An example here is the response to more liberal divorce laws by older women with no workplace experience who fear their husbands' ability to jettison them in favour of younger women. Their economic vulnerability as much as the double standard of physical desirability make their fears all too realistic. Unless this is recognised and provision made in the divorce reform package, their support is inevitably doubtful.

It is of course not impossible to forge alliances across class and other divides and in many situations women appear to be able to manage this better than men (the class position of great numbers of women being inherently fragile). However such alliances have to be continually maintained and reinforced. In this process two strategies should be emphasised: firstly, the current situation and its negative consequences for women and men alike (in other words for the society as a whole) must be continuously brought to public attention so as to create a climate of opinion which lessens fear of radical change (and may avoid the dangers of the backlash as described in the paper on Egypt p. 114). And here the question of the role that men may be expected to play becomes quite salient.

Whether male dominance can be dismantled in the long run without giving rise to negative short-term effects at least in those areas where it is supported with greater ideological elaboration (in political philosophy, culture, religion) is a point of concern. Furthermore there is little consensus amongst scholars as to whether men are unwitting victims of the structures of male dominance or active promoters of them. Certain men do indeed suffer from particular forms of male stereotyping as the literature on men and masculinity shows,[7] but it is not immediately evident that the majority of men, whatever their class, would welcome change in the socially constituted relations between the sexes, in the sexual division of labour, or in the construction and ordering of sexuality. And yet without

7. There are a number of useful readers on masculinity e.g. A. Tolson (1977), R.W. Connell (1983), J. Weeks (1981), M. Kaufman (1987).

incorporating at least some of them into the struggle a successful outcome must be unlikely. This point is of special relevance when we come to discuss the role of planners and planning in promoting women's needs (practical needs perhaps but strategic gender interests?), and that of the State in facilitating the incorporation of women into the development leadership.

While any strategy must recognise the differences between women and the difficulties that this presents for long-term collaboration, it is also important to look beyond oppositional interests to those which potentially can unite. Successful political struggles involve defining areas/issues on which common cause can be made. In this regard, the principle of looking for affinities in position rather than identity of position may be useful. For example, a strategy to meet the practical need of women factory workers to be involved at all levels in their trade union should wherever possible be transformed into the longer-term goal of getting women into other arenas of power where decisions affecting society as a whole are taken. This must at least initially involve contesting deeply-held notions of women's incapacity for management and power, as much as challenging the notion that women's right to paid work is secondary to that of men's. Going beyond factory-based struggles and challenging much wider structures of gender discrimination will inevitably involve women workers making alliances with women from other sectors and possibly even of different class origins. But such broadening of the struggle is essential if present societies divided by numerous forms of discrimination are to be changed to a more egalitarian form.

The Identification of Women's Needs

In the previous discussion it was noted that women's practical gender needs are empirically verifiable. This should in theory be relatively straightforward — just ask the women — but in practice the matter is more complex. The papers in this collection illustrate a number of ways in which women's views can be solicited — through sample surveys, informal interviews, seminars or other formal meetings — and some of the difficulties each method involves.

The Togolese team, for example, interviewed women individually, but found respondents reticent and distrustful of questions about their incomes (a common research problem) despite the fact that lack of money or access to it is said to lie at the heart of Togolese women's difficulties (p. 195). The Chinese paper describes a number of ways in which the Women's Federation consulted women about proposed government policies as well as the impact of existing policies (pp. 156–63). It does not, however, address the possibility that an institution so closely connected to the policy promoters may be unable to collect a wide range of views.

The difficulties inherent in the relationship between 'powerful outsiders' and those they are working for is also addressed in the paper on Ecuador (p. 46). It questions the methodology of 'participatory research' which has been widely promoted as a means of involving a group or community in the identification of its own problems and needs, and the solutions to them. But as has become increasingly clear, peasants, like other oppressed groups, develop sensitive antennae attuned to the wishes of those working 'in their benefit' and often reproduce such wishes as their own. A somewhat similar problem often faces feminist activists who are neither associated nor identified with government nor with particular political parties. Women will often discuss openly, even with great vehemence, their sufferings at the hands of men; these may appear to be more central to their experience of oppressive living conditions than class or other forms of exploitation. They may even agree upon a series of activities to be undertaken to relieve or at least publicise the situation. But despite this explicit recognition of male dominance and its negative impact on women's life chances, and even expressed determination to contest it, in a more public arena such defiance may not be acted upon. The telling of the suffering may in itself be the defiant act.

Another variation on this particular theme is well illustrated by the Ecuadorian account of seminars organised by trade unions at which working women discussed their situation. In many respects their analysis is deeply familiar, yet there are curious omissions: there is for example no reference to sexual harassment at work, or to the difficulties women experience in getting elected to important trade-union positions. Yet these are to the forefront in studies of difficulties working women face in the workplace in Britain, Peru, Brasil, Malaysia. The forum at which 'women's problems' are aired obviously dictates what women consider a permissible agenda.

Even where a more conducive environment is provided which enables women to explore amongst themselves what their needs are without fearing to offend or contradict outsiders, further problems still remain. Firstly, the injunction — just ask the women — appears to assume that all women know what is required to ameliorate their living conditions or, more critically, improve their social position. But the assumption that all women have a clear analytical understanding of the structures underlying their position underestimates the power of ideology, and also the reality of many women's circumscribed lives. Furthermore it appears to assume that women have already worked out a viable alternative.

Secondly, there is a problem of prioritising and ordering needs in such a way that the effect of meeting them will be cumulative rather than mere aggregation. What is meant here is similar to the concept of 'generative actions' discussed in the Ecuador paper. These are actions which have the capacity 'to act as multipliers of further actions in a dynamic and permanent process in which the community is gradually and increasingly involved' (p. 47). In prioritising needs and selecting them to meet those which have the capacity to form the base upon which other actions can be based, one has moved from aggregation to a cumulative process.

Lastly there is the problem of short- and long-term needs, and those which address women's position rather than condition. Most women of course can and do identify their immediate practical needs, but moving from these to the identification of longer-term interests, ones, however, not so general as to be of little value, is a much more complex proposition. The immediacy of most women's praxis, its constricted and individuating character, as well as the inevitability, and repetitive, never-ending quality of domestic tasks and familial responsibilities constitute considerable limitations on many women's ability to envisage long-term goals.

To facilitate longer-term strategic thinking two things are generally considered necessary: *consciousness-raising* and *raising social awareness*. Usually consciousness-raising refers to the process of socialising women's individual experiences of oppressive personal relations, enabling women to locate them within a wider context. This allows them to begin to identify the societal structures which underlie their subordinate position. Consciousness-raising may also give rise to discussion of the wider system of discrimination and differences based on age, class, religious belief or even ethnicity and race. In the process women often acquire a clearer sense of the long-term social changes that will be necessary if equality is ever to be won. This in turn points to the necessity for alliance building.

Social awareness in contrast refers more to raising public concern as to women's situation — often centring on their condition: their lack of education, their overwork, etc.

In most countries, primacy is given by governments or official women's groups (party arms, national groups) to raising social awareness: to investing energy and creativity in public education programmes or to devising special campaigns directed at women to raise their awareness of possible alternatives to their situation, and sometimes to men to elicit their support for change (see the paper from Togo). The dialogue established by such campaigns may provide the basis for women of all social classes and groups to articulate their own short- and long-term interests whether as women, or as mothers, wives, sisters, colleagues or friends. Not only can national resources be mobilised for such campaigns but also international resources including conventions and agreements such as the UN Convention on the Elimination of all Forms of Discrimination Against Women, and the UN Forward Looking Strategies. Raising public concern over what we call in shorthand 'women's issues' is the best guarantee that we have as yet that something will be done about them, because it tends to mobilise substantial numbers of women. But whether the means by which change and transformation is to be achieved involves active intervention by the State of course depends on the nature of the polity itself.

Strategic thinking is also facilitated by keeping the notion of transformation firmly in mind. A useful concept is that of *transformatory potential* which can be used to identify those practical needs which have a greater potential for engendering change. By this I mean that priority should be given to meeting those practical needs (possibly addressing women's condition) which can provide the enabling conditions for interventions directed to strategic interests (i.e. addressing women's position); or to meeting practical needs in such a way that the question of strategic gender issues arises almost spontaneously. For example, as the paper from Ecuador argues, most women identify a cash income as the most pressing of their needs, and many groups working with women are almost inevitably dragged into devising income-generating projects. Yet income-generating projects are unlikely to bear the seeds of transformation if they are based on women's traditional skills, produce goods for an unstable market, provide low returns to labour, and are politically invisible. Projects based on some form of collective organisation,

15

which demand learning higher levels of skill and an understanding not only of the productive process but the economic system are more likely to bear the seeds of change. Initially at least this is likely to place greater burdens on the women involved, both activists and workers, and the longer-term training element has of course cost and time implications for funders as much as those involved in the project. Yet if such elements are not built into projects, they risk serving neither to ameliorate women's condition nor to enhance their position.

Using the concept of transformatory potential also implies examining whether the strategy is likely to facilitate the building of coalitions or alliances with other groups with similar aims; and searching for areas where women can work together and even devising projects which attempt to connect groups of women who are otherwise in structural opposition.[8] Again this is very time-consuming work but the coalescing of women into a mass force is clearly a necessary step in any strategy which aims to break down the centuries-old legacy of gender discrimination and masginalisation.

Planners and the Plan

Planning is seen as a critical area for intervention by many working in the women and development field. It is seen as the mechanism by which the State orders the economy, allocates resources and creates employment. This is in part an effect of the role that States in developing countries have been expected to play in supporting and encouraging economic growth ('development'), but also in part results from the demand made by many women that childbearing and care should be seen as a social responsibility not merely an individual one. However, reliance on planning is complicated by several factors: types of planning vary widely, as do the agencies of planning; the relation between planners and politicians varies as does that between planners and those who have to implement their decisions.

As for the first, a useful distinction has been made between *parametric* and *pervasive planning* (White, 1984). In many countries the State merely indicates or encourages certain types of economic

8. Magdalena Leon in Colombia has designed such a project: it involves both domestic servants and their employers.

developments by means of regulative processes of macro-economic management; the establishment of a favourable institutional environment (i.e. responsive financial system, a legal framework); and the provision of necessary infrastructure (i.e. road, telecommunication, educational and health systems). This form of planning tends to be associated with States in which the market mechanism plays an important role in allocation but where the government decides upon the longer term strategic interests of the nation, which are then promoted through State intervention in allocation of resources towards sectors identified as strategic (see White and Wade, 1985). Pervasive forms of planning involve use of much tighter instruments of direction and control, which are both administrative and political. '[I]n a capitalist context the State may strive to establish a "social structure of accumulation" by nurturing the emergence of financial and industrial bourgeoisie' (White, 1985, p. 100). In the socialist context the State may inhibit all forms of individual initiative, or permit some degree of operational independence (for example to the parastatals).

Whatever the type of overall planning, a second area of difficulty is that in many developing countries the primary allocation of resources (which is often the main concern of women and development practitioners) is not carried out by the central planning office: rather this occurs ever more often in the Finance Ministry or Treasury. Planners have then to make their plans within the context of pre-set parameters. Even in those countries where there is a central planning unit, planning is not confined therein. Rather the unit may itself draw up parametric measures which have then to be fleshed out at the sectoral level, in a variety of ministries and units within ministries. If women and development concerns are to be integrated in the planning process, it is clear that this involves a very complex relationship between promoters of women's needs and a whole panoply of planning agents and agencies.

Much of the current crisis in planning and the disillusion with planning as a development instrument derives from the fact that the plans that have been drawn up with such care work indifferently if at all (is this particularly the case of pervasive planning?). One explanation for this is that as economic life becomes more complex it is 'increasingly difficult for plans to fit into the concrete realities of economic and social life and, still more, to have any effect on them, or to transform them' (Comeliau, 1986). Another is the complexity of coordinating all the various instances of planning activity, particularly given the marked tendency of many ministers to treat their ministries as fiefdoms.

It is perhaps ironic that women and development advocates and practitioners are turning their attention to planning just when planning and indeed State management of the economy is coming under sustained attack. Current orthodoxy favours jettisoning pervasive forms of planning and 'rolling back the State' so as to let the market act as the principal dynamo of economic growth and allocator of resources.

Some women and development scholars would argue that in part failures in planning have come about because of planners' poor understanding of how the economy really works, and what development itself should entail. Firstly, planners, they say, need to embrace a less restrictive concept of development: they must go beyond the focus on economic growth to concern for the betterment of the quality of life for all. This necessarily involves a wide range of social and cultural dimensions. Secondly they must also widen their conceptual grasp of the economic dimension. Some of the papers in this volume follow this line of argument.

What many WID practitioners argue for is, firstly, the recognition that the economy is not comprised only of formally constituted work units — factories, universities, regulated workshops, offices — nor only of activities that can be valorised through the market mechanism.[9] Secondly, that those activities which are informal and domestic are absolutely essential for the reproduction of family units, communities and by extension and in aggregate for the maintenance and reproduction of society itself. Lastly, that informal and domestic tasks are allocated to women in almost all known societies through social processes and not because of women's genetic endowment, or their mental, emotional or physical weakness or inferiority. Thirdly, attempting to tackle women's concerns through a sectoral approach is inadequate. Precisely because of women's involvement in domestic as well as extra-domestic activities, their responsibility for children, basic provision of family welfare and so on, requires an aproach that focuses on the ways in which sectors are interrelated and articulated within a given socioeconomic structure. A critical aspect here is the way women's activities are represented ideologically as being sectorally confined

---

9. I deal with this at greater length in my paper: 'Benefits and Barriers', written for the Commonwealth Secretariat (Young, 1987).

— i.e. to the domestic sphere. A corollary of this is that macro-economic planning itself is not gender neutral and needs careful attention to uncover the structures of discrimination embedded therein.[10]

What then do the writers urge planners to do? The first step they should take is that of *recognition*. Planners, as most of the papers acknowledge, plan in theory for the entire population, but most planning deals with rather abstract categories: labour, capital, man-power, human capital, the household. Built into these abstract categories are however assumptions which largely derive from a male-centred view of the universe. So the assumptions lying behind the categories must be questioned and the differential experience of men and women within social processes acknowledged. This may mean that new working categories will have to be developed which are possibly less abstract than the old ones pretended to be. Planners will then have to supplement these new purified categories with others which are more concrete and recognise the heterogeneity of the social universe. Amongst others would be those categories deriving from so-called informal and domestic activities.

The second step that planners must take is that of giving some economic value to these activities, that is the step of *valorisation*. It would not be impossible to devise shadow prices or some form of economic measurement to indicate the value of production within the home, or the informal sector. The planners' third step will be to look at the needs of informal and domestic producers for education, on and off the job training, technical upgrading of their instruments of production, i.e. the step of *technification* and *modernisation*.

Initially, the step of *recognition* would have to include: (1) a radical examination of the assumptions which underlie the categories used in data collection[11]; (2) where appropriate, the disaggregation of all data collected by sex[12]; (3) collection of data on the

---

10. See paper by Diane Elson (1987).
11. A useful discussion of this issue is found in A. Evans 1987.
12. The Unesco Secretariat paper makes the timely observation that solving the problem of inadequate data is a highly complex matter. 'Establishing statistics will take time (a century is an optimistic prediction) and cost money, and they will not be entirely satisfactory. For statistics do not make it possible to bring out what women's problems and priorities consist of: statistics make it possible, instead, to monitor a given phenomenon over a period of time and to verify the impact of policies and socio-cultural changes' (Unesco DEV-87/CONF.801-2, 1987). To draw up development plans which correspond more closely to actual needs, planners need also to have good qualitative data.

informal sector and on activities necessary for the maintenance of the household unit and the (re)production of human capital; (4) expansion of indicators so a more realistic assessment of development can be made.

These recommendations may appear to assume that planners are waiting to be told how to incorporate women's issues into their plans. But in reality most planners have failed to be roused by the criticism that planning is male biased. Why should this be? We have already referred to a number of factors which may contribute to this, but the relation between planners, politicians and the political process may be more critical.

One view of planners is that they are technical experts (a little ignorant on gender matters but none the less trained professionals who will take up gender issues if it is shown to be 'relevant' and as long as reliable, quantifiable data on them are readily available). An alternative view holds that planners are the front-line agents of State intervention in the economy; they are thus not merely technical experts but also political actors. Planning in turn is not merely a technical exercise but a process in which choices have to be made between economic options with different social, political and even cultural outcomes. These choices are in most cases profoundly political because

> the repercussions of those choices extend well beyond economic techniques; they involve ultimate goals, they project a type of society and of social relationships, as well as cultural ambitions; they are political because they are linked to collective value judgements, and in the last analysis those judgements stem from a social consensus or a given ideology, or from the encounter of several ideologies. (Comeliau, 1986)

As part of the administrative apparatus of government, planners have not only to meet the short-term goals imposed on them by governments which may change (and often with them the economic, social and political complexion of the society which is envisaged), but also to work within the constraints imposed by planning decisions made in the past and by the structure of the national economy, itself embedded in a global economic system.

If we accept this alternative view of planners, what implications does this have? As part of the State apparatus, planners are responsive to directives and pressures from a variety of political actors of varying degrees of power and persuasiveness probably to much the same extent that the political system itself is. Thus in many cases to get planners to recognise an obligation to do something about even the more immediate practical needs of women, such needs have to be expressed in such a way as to become a pressing political problem which requires a planning solution. For this reason it is frequently argued[13] that women must constitute themselves as a pressure group so as to be able to operate within the political game of getting one's interests accepted as socially relevant and thus built into State policy. This view of course embodies certain conceptions as to the nature of the State, how the political process operates and indeed how civil society is constituted. How do they match up to the realities of developing societies?

The State as a Mechanism for Meeting Women's Needs

It has been assumed even in the West that for large-scale and long-term change in the condition or the position of women to be possible, the powers of the State have to be mobilised, through planning and expenditure of social capital on necessary welfare provisions, through drawing up laws and regulations, and through the use of State agents to enforce anti-discriminatory measures etc. In developing countries the state has played a much more central role in the direction and even running of the economy than in most of the advanced capitalist countries of the West. Thus most WID activists take it for granted that the State or one of its organs is the most apt mechanism for meeting women's needs. Two papers in this volume present a somewhat different view.

The paper on China (pp. 135f.) argues against State provision of all women's needs, such as their need for employment or an income of their own, and thus for childcare facilities, in favour of women themselves taking the initiative and being rewarded accordingly. This view appears to derive from two factors: the cost to the State of such provision, and the inability of State functionaries to run enterprises efficiently and effectively.

The rationale for such caution is by now quite well known in development circles. In the case of providing the enabling condition for women's emancipation, the argument centres less on whether the State is able to generate the funds to cover the cost of such

---

13. As I do myself in the paper for the Commonwealth Meeting of Ministers of Women's Affairs, mimeo 1987.

provision than on whether alternative uses for State revenues would not produce a better outcome more rapidly. In other words that investment in industry, manufacture, and/or agriculture, by raising levels of production, productivity, employment, even wages, would create the conditions which would generate greater wealth for individuals, enterprises and the State and allow many needs to be met through the normal processes of economic modernisation. Since by definition most countries in transition have to struggle to increase their productive capacity and to retain the wealth they have created, the crucial question that needs to be addressed is which interventions have the greatest 'spread effects' and should therefore be given priority.

The issue of organisational and managerial capacity of bureaucrats is possibly more contentious — little comparative research appears to have been undertaken in LDCs to assess whether the State as entrepreneur is equally, less or more efficient than the alternative. None the less there appears to be a growing consensus that the State as entrepreneur (as opposed to it as provider of basic services) leaves much to be desired. Criticism of State incapacity is widespread, as are accounts of prolific corruption, nepotism and ineptitude within State enterprises. Furthermore in many developing countries the State's ability to reach the bulk of the population (usually in rural areas) is slight (China is a shining exception here). To overcome these barriers to rapid economic development the new orthodoxy argues that the State should dissociate itself from managing the economy, and that every encouragement should be given to private enterprise and expansion of the market. Arguments favouring 'rolling back the frontiers of the State' and the privatisation of many of the present functions of the State command considerable ideological support both within LDCs and ADCs (Advanced Developed Countries), and of course within the multilateral financial agencies. What is much less obvious is whether the conditions for such withdrawal really exist.[14] For women and development practitioners this turn to the market is even more problematic. There is considerable evidence to show (indeed some from China itself) that women lose out in terms of employment (particularly in access to career posts or management positions), income and access to valued resources without some intervention on the part of the State (whether by legislation, monitoring of legislation, or special

14. For those interested in this topic see IDS Bulletin, October 1987.

provisions).

But what are the alternatives to State provision? Obviously the market is one, community is another much invoked in these times of State retreat, and voluntary associations another. There is little direct investigation in the women and development literature on the relative merits of these alternatives. However, the pervasive sexual division of labour in the (formal) labour market, women's consistently lower relative wages, and often extremely low wages in absolute terms, poor working conditions and insecurity of employment, do not auger well for the provision of women's economic or employment needs via private enterprise or the market. Many do of course argue the case for the benefits to women of self-employment, despite the evidence that the vast majority of women involved in such activity get miserably small returns for their labour and effort. The wider and more vexed question of whether the wholesale encouragement of self-employment leads to increased competition and thus greater risks, or to the release of initiative and creativity in fitting in multiple roles, is much less discussed.

As for community based forms of welfare support, this is very largely dependent on the unpaid and voluntary labour of women. For those who have some resources, involvement in community based services can help to stretch resources and in some ways redistribute them within a relatively bounded group. For those who are very poor, community based activities demand the gift of time and energy which they cannot afford, so unless radical changes can be introduced into this sphere there is little ground for optimism here either. Furthermore, the evidence from community based schemes appears to suggest that parochial, narrow and conservative attitudes tend to prevail which are themselves inimical to women's struggle to change their social position.[15]

Voluntary associations might well be a mechanism which could operate to provide many of women's basic needs, and might even be able to campaign for some strategic interests as well. But the development of a wide range of such associations requires a certain political and institutional framework which in many LDCs is clearly lacking. In other words it requires a type of State and a political environment which permits the formation of special interest groups (whether based on class, occupation, religion, gender, etc.), political groupings or parties, trade unions; allows lobbying

15. See on this point G. Dalley, 1988.

and other such advocacy activities; and has a legal system which protects the rights of citizens against the power of the State and ideally provides protection for the weak (economically, socially or politically) against the powerful.

Political cultures are very varied, political systems likewise. In some countries the form of political process may be such that there is space for the political activity of interest groups to compete against each other to influence State decisions, or indeed to mobilise public support against certain government decisions. And it may well be in such countries that power is widely spread throughout the populace and the political process is much less corrupt and ineffective precisely because of the strength of civil society itself to act as watchdog over State activities. But in others, political power is the purview of a very small coterie of people, the main pressures that may be exerted on them being mediated through kinship or locality (i.e. primordial loyalties), and civil society itself is weakly developed. In such countries, it is not immediately apparent how women could organise to promote their own interests nor if they are able to do so whether it would in any way affect government policy.

Lastly there are numbers of developing countries where civilian government is weak as are the institutions of civil society and in the wings the military waits to capitalise on any mistakes made. Given the nature of gender relations any attempt to ameliorate even women's condition may give rise to a specific type of social unrest the military or authoritarian parties or groups can utilise to their advantage (as the paper on Egypt shows (p. 111f.)). The assumption that the State will respond positively to the pressure that organised social groups can bring is brought into question by the experience of attempts to widen (or strengthen) basic democratic structures in a number of countries: an equally likely outcome appears to be that such pressure is interpreted as hostile and undermining of State authority, and that it leads to curtailment of basic civil liberties.

There is an urgent need for more work to be done on the nature of political cultures, political processes, the degree of development of civil society and the nature of the relation between State and civil society in developing countries (it may not be found important to make distinctions between civil and military regimes), and the place and form of women's political activities in such situations. Until this work is done it is really very difficult to engage in informed discussion of possible and necessary strategies involving the intervention of the State for the advancement of the cause of women.

Research is also needed which examines the way in which various governments have brought in new and often progressive legislation that either directly or indirectly addresses women's concerns. It should also examine the degree to which this legislation gets implemented, and the impediments to its full acceptance. The Ecuador paper for example describes a situation where a government passed very progressive measures which were however not implemented because bureaucrats dragged their feet. It raises interesting questions as to the mechanisms by which progressive legislation can be passed without apparently there being any constituency for it. In this case the government was looking to the international community for approbation rather than a domestic constituency. In a number of other countries much progressive legislation for women is on the statute books but never implemented. Why should this be so? One possible explanation is that the State just has not got the administrative capacity to deliver policy promises. Another is that unless there is an incentive, or a cost, for bureaucrats to take what may be personally difficult and even unpopular steps with certain sectors of the public, they will procrastinate. As we have seen in the so-called developed countries the judiciary, employers, even trade unions can remain stubbornly androcentric despite legislation and public opinion. Unless women can constitute their interests as being coterminous with the public interest, much progressive legislation will either not get on to the statute books, or even when on, will never be implemented. This may be particularly pertinent just now when few States in developing countries appear to be capable of delivering even minimalist measures in this period of financial stringency and structural adjustment. What political conditions would favour women being able to persuade the State to take up their cause now?

Meeting Women's Needs at the Local, Regional and National Levels

Despite the complexities outlined above, there is little doubt that if women are ever to become the equal partners of men in society, the State must include in its political and social project an expressed commitment to the equality of all members of society, equality before the law being one essential prerequisite of true democracy.

But what form should State support for women's equality take? The paper from Ecuador recommends that:

> The State should not attempt to solve all the problems identified by women, but should limit itself to those that have the greatest impact on a number of other aspects of social and economic life. The need to define priorities carefully arises from the fact that the State has limited resources . . . State paternalism should also be avoided . . . The State should in many areas be responsible only for providing enabling conditions . . . (see p. 70)

As an example of such enabling measures the paper cites the national planning unit's strategy for development which makes a strong recommendation for the promotion and the organisation of women in all walks of life: 'The State must . . . create the legal and institutional framework for the development of women's organisations, which must result from women's own interests and initiatives. Non-formal educational activities promoting awareness of women's rights and their exercise must be undertaken' (see p. 64).

To facilitate women's participation, the strategy argues that a number of basic conditions have to be met:

> women's integration into the labour market without discrimination must be encouraged; aid must be provided to (specially designed) non-formal educational programmes; discriminatory legislation must be corrected; children's centres, nurseries, and infants' and mothers' centres must be provided in rural areas as well as in the cities; actions and programmes must be undertaken that dignify women, to offset the commercial exploitation of women's image. (ibid)[16]

From our point of view what is interesting about this list of enabling conditions is that it addresses women's strategic interests rather than their practical needs. What is not exactly clear however is which of these conditions has necessarily to be provided by the State, apart from the legal and institutional framework allowing interest groups to be set up and undertake political activism, and the repeal or reform of discriminatory legislation. Financial support for non-formal education programmes, setting up women's and children's centres, etc. could derive from the State or the private or charitable sector; ending labour market discrimination presumably

16. The strategy for women appears not to have been implemented because the setting up of the specialised unit to carry it out was blocked by key bureaucrats.

would have to be the work of both individuals, employers' and workers' organisations, and the State. Actions designed to combat the exploitation of women's image by the media, commercial interests, etc. would be best promoted by the State but one can also imagine women's organisations themselves undertaking this. The critical question to ask is not, who would execute the activities, but, who would fund them? And certainly this is where arguments must be made in favour of State commitment; the State's (lack of) administrative capacity to implement policies then becomes less critical.

Whatever provisions are made whether in national plans or in the plans of ministries or other government entities, they must be backed up by a means by which planners/bureaucrats can get continuous feedback from those involved and those who benefit, so as to readjust their strategy if necessary. Continuous micro-level needs and resources assessment surveys can feed planners with up-to-date data (Heyzer, 1985). Data can be fed from the local level to the district and from the district to the region and so on up the line.[17] But how can an overall planning framework be designed into which a vast number of local and localised needs can be articulated?

We have already made the point that the parametric type of planning provides a framework which allows a mixture of State and market interventions, in other words it is a complex but not insuperable technical problem given the political will. The feasibility of this strategy may be questioned by those who see planning as an inherently inflexible instrument, however, rather than planning itself, it is particular modes of planning and particular structures of bureaucracy within which planning units are located which make for inflexibility. What is essential is some definition of priorities and a strategy by which local needs can be met over the short and longer term. Clearly some mechanism must be devised by which resources are allocated to the various intermediate levels and more especially to the local level. While this must imply some redistributive mechanism there must also be some way by which planners at the local level can count on locally raised resources whether in the form of labour or money.

A more radical step than relying on a process of feedback would be to decentralise the planning process itself to the local level. Local

---

17. See WAND/Population Council (nd) for an example of this planning methodology.

planning advisory groups can be set up comprising people from a wide range of sectors who will identify areas where policy development work is needed. The decentralisation of planning should entail a far greater degree of democratisation of the planning process than is customary, and this itself can be a strategy to involve women more closely. Democratisation is of course not an easy process: authoritarian social systems breed conformity, compliance and fear which means that the needs identified at the local level may well only be those of certain powerful groups. Powerful persons or groups (e.g. chiefs, party cadres, landowners) may subvert the system; women may be systematically excluded, or only women who can be trusted to represent the interests of men included. Women's busy schedules and self-perceptions as much as their illiteracy, lack of experience and knowledge of wider political issues, may inhibit them from taking part.

In undemocratic systems decentralisation may only enhance social inequalities and even in relatively democratic systems, unless there is a commitment from the State (and others) to subvert local power holders, it may well not benefit the less socially visible/powerful groups. While such support is present, the process of involving people in discussing their needs is in the long run likely to result in ever wider sectors of the population being drawn into the dialogue and may result in strengthening the institutions of civil society. But it is still necessary to recognise the fact that men do not necessarily adequately represent women's concerns. The lessons learnt from the WID experience to date could all be said to point to a similar conclusion: women need to represent their own needs and interests; they need to do this politically. Without greater involvement of women in political processes at all levels and thus their participation in decisions as to society's economic, social and political project, greater democratisation of society cannot take place; without greater democratisation of society women's strategic interests cannot be met.

Identification of needs at the local level, constant feedback of data to strengthen policy effectiveness, and the enhancement of the institutions of civil society are the potential benefits of decentralisation and democratisation of planning. What has to be ensured is that women are central actors in the structures set up to enable identification of local needs, to permit consultation prior to policy design, during implementation and throughout the evaluation procedures. But this will almost inevitably involve providing the means by which women, both as individuals and representatives of groups, are enabled to participate actively. Enabling conditions may include giving specialised training to certain categories of women to overcome their present disadvantages and to ensure that they take part actively in these processes. But more than this, women themselves must begin to organise autonomously around these new opportunities for them to get their voices heard.

It means that the mobilisation of women as women, as most of the papers in this book underline, is a foremost priority, both for the identification of women's practical needs and their strategic gender interests. Women's organisations will have to accept the challenge that they must play a critical role in the design of strategies to ensure women's successful participation in the future as political actors of equal importance and dignity as men. This means that women's organisations themselves will have to be clear about the strategies they will have to adopt if the State is to be compelled to provide the conditions which will promote women's strategic gender interests. They will also have to be clear about priorities. 'We are weak', the saying goes, 'but we are many'; the latter is an advantage only if we are also united in pursuit of our aims.

Bibliography

Comeliau, C., 1986, *Questions aux Planificateurs*, DEV/EPD/44. 1986 Unesco

Connell, R.W., 1983, *Which Way Is Up?*, Allen & Unwin, Sydney

Dalley, G., 1988, *Ideologies of Caring*, Macmillan Education

Elson, D., 1987, *The Impact of Structural Adjustments on Women: Concepts & Issues*, DSA mimeo

Evans, A., 1987, *Enhancing Gender Awareness: Socio-Economic Statistics*, IDS mimeo

Heyzer, N., 1985, *Missing Women*, Asian and Pacific Development Centre

IDS Bulletin, 1987, *Politics in Command*, vol. 18, no 4

Kandiyoti, D., 1988, 'Bargaining with Patriarchy', in *Gender & Society*, September 1988

Kaufman, M., (ed.), 1987, *Beyond Patriarchy*, Oxford University Press, Toronto

Metcalf, A., and M. Humphries, 1985, *The Sexuality of Men*, Pluto

Molyneux, M., 1985, 'Mobilisation without Emancipation', in *Feminist Studies*, 11, no. 2

Moser, C., 1985, *Gender and Planning*, DPU Working Paper no. 11, Development Planning Unit, London

Tolson, A., 1977, *The Limits of Masculinity*, Tavistock, London

WAND/Population Council (nd): *Planning for Women in Rural Development: A Source Book for the Caribbean*, Population Council

Weeks, J., 1981, *Sex, Politics and Society*, Longman, London

White, G., 1984, 'Developmental States and Socialist Industrialisation in the Third World', in *Journal of Development Studies*, Vol. 21, no. 1

White, G., and R. Wade, 1985, *Developmental States in East Asia*, IDS Research Reports 16

Young, K., 1987, 'Benefits & Barriers', mimeo.

1

Problems that Concern Women and their Incorporation in Development: The Case of Ecuador[1]

Centro Ecuatoriano de Investigaciones Sociales

Ecuadorean history contains a significant number of women who, because of their intelligence, courage, or leadership, left their imprint on society and are today celebrated by the women's movement. None the less women's struggle for their rights through organised participation in Ecuadorean political life is a recent phenomenon. Its beginnings stem from the period 1975 to 1978, when widespread discontent with the military regime led to an increased mass mobilisation against it. Throughout this process, which led to free elections on the basis of a new Constitution, and the election of a democratic government in 1979, the spontaneous participation of women in various protests was a noticeable feature. As a consequence, women's fronts were set up within trade unions, peasant federations, neighbourhood organisations, and some political parties.

The rise of a women's movement within a generalised national struggle, undoubtedly led to a lack of specificity as regards what may be considered normal women's demands. This is gradually being overcome as the women's movement matures and consolidates, but the lack of clear-cut objectives and strategies still constitutes one of its characteristics. As part of the process of consolidation and in order to reach a finer understanding of the varied situations of women of different social and economic strata, a

1. The article was written by Francisco Pareja of CEIS in collaboration with Ruth Moya. The information for Section 1 was compiled by Lilia Rodríguez, President of CEPAM.

number of symposia, conventions, seminars and courses have been organised over the past two years by women's organisations of various types. In this paper we will review some of these meetings (Section 1) for which there is written information, as well as analyse a number of projects managed both by the State and private entities (Section 2 and 3). We will also briefly review some of the most salient features of State activity in the area of women's concerns (Section 4). Lastly (Section 5) we summarise what we consider the major steps planners need to take to incorporate women's concerns into their practice and identify a number of areas in which research is still needed.

Section 1: Recent Symposia and Seminars with Working-class and Peasant Women

Meetings Held by Female Urban Workers

The first of the two meetings reviewed took place in November 1980. It was the second such national meeting of women workers, and was organised by the Confederation of Ecuadorian Workers (Confederación de Trabajadores del Ecuador — CTE), 1 of the 3 national trade unions. The second was a Seminar organised by the Ecuadorian Centre for the Promotion and Action of Women (Centro Ecuatoriano para la Promoción y Acción de la Mujer — CEPAM)[2] in June 1984 to discuss the problems related to the occupational health hazards of female workers. It was attended by representatives of the women's fronts of the 3 major trade unions: CTE, Central Ecuatoriana de Organizaciones Sindicales Libres (CEOSL), and Central Ecuatoriana de Organizaciones Clasistas (CEDOC). Thus, while the first meeting was more general as regards the subjects discussed, though more restricted in its representativeness, the second was organised around a single topic but had a broader representation.

At the CTE meeting a series of resolutions (17 in all) were adopted after 2 days of discussion (CTE, undated). We have classified them under what inevitably must be somewhat arbitrary headings:

2. CEPAM is a private, non-profit organisation which was set up in 1983 to work with women of the rural and urban sectors.

(a) *Legal rights:*
This was the most important set of demands presented by the meeting and included the demands shown:

— Special insurance for women working in contaminated or dangerous environments should be set up. A similar demand, plus the payment of higher salary, was made for women who work in sorting shell-fish inside cold- storage plants.

— All women should be able to affiliate on a voluntary basis to the Ecuadorian Social Security Institute (Instituto Ecuatoriano de Seguridad Social — IESS) and receive social security.

— Family and maternity benefits should be increased.

— Retirement should be optional and pensions should be equivalent to a full salary and periodically readjusted to the cost of living. The time off legally allowed for childcare should not be taken into account when computing retirement rights. The law granting women the option to retire after 25 years of work, without age limit, should be applied and Congress should find and allocate the necessary financial resources.

— The length of maternity leave should be increased.

— Legal provisions to cover support for children of dissolved marriages, or born outside marriage, should be increased.

— Women should be represented in various organs of the State.

(b) *Specific social services:*
This refers to 2 broad concerns: children and health.

— Nurseries, free of charge, should be set up at workplaces and a doctor should be present. Pediatric centres should be set up in all cities and the services should be free of charge.

— Health centres should be set up, especially in rural areas, and training courses on health, hygiene, and first aid organised.

(c) *Other issues:*
Two of these refer to what can be termed 'general quality of life issues', and one each to 'training' and 'organisational issues':

— The State should establish a system of price control for basic staples.

— Health care should be socialised.

— The State agency responsible for training the labour force should expand its facilities, so as to provide more services to women.

— The three major national trade unions should appoint a permanent commission to deal with the problems faced by female workers.

At the June 1984 meeting, women representatives of the 3 major national trade unions met for 3 full days of discussions, in a non-partisan and informal milieu, where they could express themselves without reserve. Basically, 4 areas were touched upon: general diagnosis and recommendations; legal issues; social services; and organisational issues. For each of these topics, the Seminar contributed not only to the inventory of demands specific to women, but also added to the understanding of the problems faced by women in their work and in society.

(a) General diagnosis.   Although women's incorporation into the country's development and the productive process is important and contributes significantly to the generation of national wealth, it is neither fully *recognised* nor *valued*. Wages for female workers are considered by employers to be complementary rather than essential to family income, which is one reason why they are kept unjustifiably low — lower than men's wages for similar work. Furthermore, women are mainly employed in jobs (considered to be feminine) with low skill requirements, which also keeps women's wages low.

The working woman performs a double function: as mother-–housewife, and as worker. As such, she runs the risk of overwork and subsequent exhaustion. A woman's double set of duties reduces her hours of rest and negatively affects her health, and can lead to accidents at the place of work, as well as to tension at home. It may not only lead to an excess of tension, but often worse consequences as well: alterations of the nervous system, character mutations, headaches and fatigue, ulcers, hypertension, etc.

Recommendations.   The rich and informative diagnosis was not matched by an equally prolific ability to imagine ways and means to face and solve the problems identified. This is not surprising, since many of the problems are contextual or are perceived as such; they constitute inseparable elements of a socio-economic context whose global improvement or transformation is perceived as a task beyond the powers of any single social agent of change.

Seminar participants suggested the following necessary elements for an improvement in the living conditions of women:

— The principle of 'equal pay for equal work' should be complied with and all cases of discrimination denounced.
— Women should struggle to obtain guaranteed job stability.
— A permanent consciousness-raising campaign among women should be carried out to obtain a change of attitude that must lead to a revalorisation of womanhood.
— Trade unions in their collective bargaining strategies should include the provision of financial resources for social services such as nurseries, eating facilities, transportation and medical service as a basic demand. These services should, however, be administered by the workers themselves in order to guarantee their effectiveness.
— Solidarity among female workers should be increased and concrete means implemented to prevent the sexual abuse to which women workers are subject, especially the younger and more inexperienced ones.

(b) Legal issues. With respect to provisions forms, participants recognised that they are 'advanced' in Ecuador; lack of implementation is the basic problem. Concrete instances of this are non-observance of women's rights to maternity and breastfeeding leave, unwarranted differences in the rights of female workers in industrial establishments, in public service, and in domestic service; failure to observe the prohibition on night work for women, etc.

The participants did not propose any new legal reforms, but insisted on finding ways to ensure the application of existing legislation.

(c) Social services. In this area, a more detailed analysis was made. The specific topics were:

Health — female workers frequently suffer from health problems. Among the causes cited are: inadequate premises (lack of ventilation, insufficient light, lack of adequate toilet facilities, absence of drinkable water); insufficient food rations and refreshments; lack of compliance with the legal prohibition on night-shifts for women. All

35

All these factors make women particularly prone to accidents on the job. Pregnant women are especially vulnerable and miscarriages are not infrequent. The provision of medical services in factories is totally inadequate.

Suggestions and recommendations to improve the situation were as follows:

— Periodical medical examinations should be made. These should not be mere general, routine inspections, but specifically geared to prevention of occupational ill-health.

— Industrial hygiene and health committees should be set up and run by workers. Their tasks should include: ensuring periodic inspections by the Health Department of the Social Security Institute (IESS); providing information on particular health hazards, and displaying it in visible places; training workers in health and hygiene skills.

— Trade unions should be provided with permanent health advice.

Childcare — the legal provisions that require the establishment of nurseries in workplaces with a minimum of 50 female workers are not complied with. This anomalous but generalised situation should be the object of special attention on the part of the State and trade unions.

Food — both quality and quantity of food and refreshments available in the workplace are inadequate. Participants recommended that collective bargaining should include the quality of the food that employers must provide in accordance with the law.

Quality of life — the trade union movement in general should transcend narrow economism, and concern itself with quality of life issues.

(d) Organisational issues. The participants took stock of the low proportion of women among organised workers. Those women who are unionised also have very low levels of participation in their organisations in part due to the difficulties and limitations arising from women's double burden. Attitudes of male superiority are as prevalent within trade unions as they are in society at large, and help to make it almost impossible for women to hold positions of responsibility in the unions. Ties of friendship and solidarity among women are weak, facilitating the introduction of divisions and competition among female workers by employers.

Recommendations included setting up and carrying out organisational and consciousness raising campaigns among women, as well as greater emphasis on political and trade union education.

Meeting of Women Who Belong to Neighbourhood Organisations

In March 1984, CEPAM organised an informal meeting of leaders of various neighbourhood based organisations in Quito. Seventy delegates met for 2 days and discussed topics of particular interest and concern to women, in their lives as members of local communities.

(a) General problems. The neighbourhoods that these female leaders represented lack basic services: light, drinking water, piped water, health centres, markets, schools, etc. The lack of water is a particularly acute problem: it must be carried with great difficulty from distant centres of supply. The absence of markets is responsible for the high prices of staples sold at small neighbourhood stores which can stock little of what is needed.

Another serious problem is inadequate transportation. Living in neighbourhoods far from the city's commercial and administrative centre means that access to any service not available in the neighbourhood or carrying out any necessary formality involves great expense, discomfort and loss of time. What is worse, children who daily travel long distances to school are in constant danger of their lives because of the disastrous state of public transportation and the lack of security.

Another very serious problem is the inadequate number of health or medical centres. In the centres that do exist there are either too few personnel or personnel are poorly trained. There are long queues and medicines are too expensive and can seldom be purchased. Many children die as a consequence.

The existence of all these problems has led women to organise themselves. Frequent meetings are held in the popular neighbourhoods at which information about different experiences is exchanged. This has resulted in the identification of some common objectives, making unity more feasible. As a result a number of gains have been obtained: authorities at the national and the city level have been confronted and the provision of services to poor neighbourhoods demanded; in some areas things have improved.

At the individual level the women's main problem is that they have not received adequate education or training. This means that they cannot obtain well paid jobs, their only choice being either to stay at home 'doing nothing', or 'going out to sell something' — i.e. becoming involved in the petty trade that constitutes a marginal means of survival for a considerable section of the urban population.

(b) Family problems. It is common knowledge that working-class women are the victims of double exploitation: in society as members of a particular socio-economic class; in the family as members of a sex which is oppressed by a harsh and unjust sexual division of labour; and the weight of ideological prejudices about women and their roles.

Problems within the family are very common: women have difficulties with their husbands, their children and their children's education, etc. Many worries and concerns are not discussed within the family because of fear or embarrassment: health and sexual problems, as well as the controversial topic of family planning, fall within this category. The organisation of women's discussion groups provide the opportunity to examine these problems, and share each other's experience in dealing with them.

Family life is difficult for women because of the enormous responsibilities they must bear, especially when children are growing. There are too many bars and billiard parlours in the neighbourhoods and in them drugs and alcohol abound. Mothers consider this problem practically unsolvable since there are no alternative amusements for the young. Relations with husbands are also difficult. Women are sometimes physically abused and there is no one to turn to for help. Even though many women are victims of these situations, they must bear it in silence.

(c) Organisational experience. Perhaps one of the most interesting and important features of this meeting was the discussion held on the topic of organisation as a means to face together and attempt to solve the problems previously discussed. We will present a brief summary of the rich discussion that took place. In order to convey more directly the gist of the discussion, we shall make use of the first person plural, even though what we present is not a textual transcription but rather a free account.

We have organised in order to project ourselves as persons with rights and obligations of our own; to prove that we are as capable as any other human being; that we possess abilities that so far have not been employed to the full. We have also organised in order to solve some concrete problems of our neighbourhoods, since we suffer more directly than men from the lack of public services. In addition, we have organised in order to share different experiences and search for alternatives: to support the work and effort shown by other organisations, such as trade unions, neighbourhood committees, parents' committees, etc., so that one day this situation of social injustice, discrimination, and oppression may change; so that we women may contribute our effort to the birth of a new society.

The individual experiences that we have shared show that we must work harder and develop a higher consciousness about our objectives. We must not dissolve once we have obtained our immediate aims, because our vision must embrace the longer term. This is why our permanent task must be to reflect on our long-term aim, which is the construction of a new society, a new Ecuador, where all may enjoy employment, health, adequate nourishment, recreation, housing, education; where privilege and exploitation will be ended; where men and women may share life in plenitude, without feeling diminished in our personalities, without oppression, without subordination.

The transformation we seek will not come about overnight or automatically. We must work hard for it, beginning with ourselves, conquering fear, shyness, and mutual distrust, and leaving behind the four walls of our homes so as to organise. We must also begin with our children, educating them differently from the way we were educated: teaching them solidarity and fraternity, so that our boys will not become 'machos' and our girls submissive and obedient, women without personality. We are responsible for shaping the new generations and the future. When we decide to participate in organisations, we face many problems with our families. When our husbands and children do not understand our motives, there is even the danger of the family breaking up. This is why we must try to incorporate them, too. At first it is not easy, but gradually men also come to accept women's participation in organisations.

For the fulfilment of our objectives we must make common cause with other organisations: workers', peasants', settlers'. We must also seek unity among women's organisations.

Meeting of Peasant Women

The last meeting to be reviewed here was organised by the National Federation of Peasant Organisations (Federación Nacional de Organizaciones Campesinas — FENOC) and took place in March 1984. Women, leaders of their rural communities, the majority of them from the Highlands, participated.

The role of women in the organisation and the difficulties they face within it were discussed and analysed in terms very similar to those of the neighbourhood leaders' meeting. It was specifically pointed out that women's lack of training and formal education, men's discriminatory and prejudiced attitudes and the very heavy work burden that peasant women must bear constitute particularly difficult obstacles that must be overcome.

Participants identified extreme poverty as the dominant characteristic of their situation, and restricted access to the land as the fundamental cause of that extreme poverty: 'Human beings need means of survival. For us peasants, our means of survival is the land; without land we have nothing' (FENOC, 1984). Among other problems which participants considered of prime importance, although not specific to women, were the lack of basic services (particularly acute in the rural areas): there are very few schools for children, they are normally very distant, and their quality is deplorable (one of the problems most often cited was the absenteeism of teachers).[3] The scarcity and low quality of health centres was another acute problem.

Participants agreed that changing their situation meant that society as a whole had to undergo a process of transformation. Nevertheless, some small advances and improvements could be accomplished in the meantime, and for this, women's participation is essential. Furthermore, active involvement with their community could help achieve women's desire to be considered 'complete persons, with the capacity to think, to work, to create, to struggle, and to make decisions' (ibid.).

Among the recommendations adopted, the following were the most significant:

— Women must continue to organise in order to participate in

3. These conclusions are tentative. The fundamental problems are the disfunctional type of education imparted, which does not provide the skills and knowledge that the rural population needs (hence the high rate of absenteeism), and linguistic and cultural difficulties of a bilingual population.

everything with men.
— Women must educate themselves in order to better understand the country's problems, and to prepare themselves better for work and decision- making.
— Men must also make an effort to understand and respect women's rights.
— The problems with children should not be treated as each individual family's problem. They should be tackled by everyone, within the organisation.
— The organisation is not just an instrument in the struggle for land and work. It is also a means to develop solidarity and sisterhood among women.

In summing up the experiences gained in the meetings we have reviewed, it should be noted that working-class and peasant women whether on factories or on the land, whether slum-dwellers or residents of working-class neighbourhoods, coincide in their conviction that problems specifically pertaining to their condition will only be truly and completely overcome as part of an overall process of socio-economic change. Nevertheless, they consider it possible and pertinent to link their long-range objectives and aspirations to some immediate demands which serve to bind women together. These more immediate demands, already reviewed in the preceding pages, can be classified under social security and legislation; health and hygiene; social welfare, infra- structure, and services; non-formal education and organisation.

Women's Perception of their Problems

In spite of the different experiences of women from dissimilar socio-economic backgrounds, there are some common elements in the perception that working-class and peasant women have of the problems they face.

A first point that stands out is that, in contrast to what perhaps characterises the middle-class feminist ideology in Ecuador and other parts of the world, working-class and peasant women do not counterpose their problems as women to those they face as members of a particular social class. Class and women's problems are not seen as separate: sexual oppression and subordination are not perceived unilaterally, as independent of the social context. Rather, it is often said that men should enter into the discussion and the struggle, so that they may understand that 'women's problems' are part of a group of social ills which are the result of concrete forms of social organisation. In this respect, working-class and peasant women show a truly surprising degree of awareness. This contextual view of the problems that women of the popular sectors identify as the most important is also made clear by the nature of those problems. Betterment in salaries and wages, housing, employment, health, education, social security, access to the land, etc., constitute the concrete demands that women are making; none of them are strictly 'women only demands'.

The relatively weak perception of the problems of sexual oppression may be a consequence of the pervasiveness of an ideological veil that prevents or makes difficult the development of a clearer consciousness. It could be suggested that there is in fact an immediate perception of the problems derived from women's situation, to the extent that they form a part of daily experience. However, their causes seem to remain incomprehensible. These problems are seen as 'natural', perhaps as a consequence of an age-old ideology sanctioned by powerful and influential institutions, such as the Church, the family, the educational system, the press, etc.

Many deficiencies and weaknesses undoubtedly still plague the women's movement in Ecuador. Much of this is a result of the relative youth of the movement and will be overcome as it gains in experience and maturity. Among those weaknesses and limitations, the following stand out: in the formulation of specific demands (health, housing, employment, education, etc.), a lack of clearly defined aims and strategies can be sometimes observed, so that the listing of demands often acquires the characteristics of a rhetorical and ritual litany, rather than those of a programme for action. This impression is reinforced by the fact that demands are made almost exclusively to the State, about whose responsiveness there is considerable scepticism. This almost exclusive presentation of demands to the State also implies an undervaluation of the organisation of women as an adequate, even if complementary, means for the advancement of women's cause.

These limitations are related to the lack of systematic knowledge about the nature of the problems that women face. This, in turn, has to do with the virtual absence of scientific research undertaken by or linked to women's popular organisations. Lastly, the present stage of development of the organised women's movement has not yet given rise to the structuring of general leadership and coordinating instances. Different organisations put forward packages of demands but in isolation from authors, which often reflects mutual distrust and competition.

Section 2: Development Policy and Peasant Women

This section and the following one are largely based on materials presented at a Seminar co-organised by the Ecuadorian Centre for Social Research (Centro Ecuatoriano de Investigaciones Sociales — CEIS) and the CEPAM and subsequent discussion of the papers. Given that they varied as to quality and richness of information, the present account will reflect this fact. They were, however, representative of important recent experiences in the definition and execution of rural development programmes in which peasant women have been involved. Two of the experiences presented at the Seminar were carried out by the State, the third by a private entity that works with peasant women's organisations.

The first two experiences to be reviewed were carried out by FODERUMA (Fondo de Desarrollo Rural Marginal — Fund for Marginal Rural Development), and SEDRI (Secretaría de Desarrollo Rural Integral — Secretariat for Integrated Rural Development). FODERUMA, founded in 1978, is a programme designed and carried out by the Central Bank of Ecuador and consists of a credit and technical support programme directed towards the poorest sectors of the peasantry, who have never had access to private or public credit. SEDRI was created in 1980, as a coordinating body directly dependent on the Presidency of the Republic, with responsibilities which included: selecting areas or regions for Integrated Rural Development Projects (IRDP), making diagnoses, formulating the projects, coordinating their implementation, and evaluating them. The Programme constituted one of the cornerstones of the new government's development policy. The private experience to be reviewed is of the Andean Centre for Popular Action (Centro Andino de Acción Popular — CAAP), a private entity that runs non-formal educational programmes in peasant communities of the Sierra region.

FODERUMA's Programme for Peasant Women

FODERUMA founded its Programme for Peasant Women in May 1981 with financial and technical assistance from UNDP (United Nations Development Programme), UNICEF, and UNFPA (United Nations Fund for Population Activities). It has been implemented in only 4 small geographical areas, with different social, economic and cultural characteristics, and basically constitutes an experimental programme whose main objective is to identify criteria for projects for peasant women. FODERUMA began by recognising the fact that very little is known about rural women and that this posed both theoretical and operational difficulties and challenges. It did, however, make an initial diagnosis which served as initial guidelines for the Programme. These are summarised below:

(1)   Peasant women perform specific roles within the family and the community, which are defined by ethnically and regionally specific cultural values and behavioral patterns. Taking these specificities into account is therefore vital for an adequate treatment of the situation of rural women and for the success of any programme.

(2)   There is a clearly defined sexual division of labour within rural societies which encompasses familial as well as communal space and includes income-generating activities as well as those relating to other forms of social interaction. None the less, factors such as massive cyclical male out-migration force women to assume functions they would not normally perform. This double determination must be carefully assessed by FODERUMA in the formulation of its projects.

(3)   The incorporation of women into the decisions, actions, and benefits of development is fundamental for their own advance and for the country's general development process. Any actions undertaken should therefore secure sustained achievements for women at the level of family and community (FODERUMA, 1981, pp. 3–6).

These general guidelines allowed more specific recommendations to be drawn up for FODERUMA's extension workers, who were given the responsibility of introducing and coordinating the Programme's actions within selected communities. The following is a succinct version of these recommendations:

—   Cultural determinants, as well as social, economic and political factors, must be taken into account.

— An integrated approach to development actions is needed and inter-institutional coordination at the local level must be secured.

— The organisational process of the community itself must be supported by incorporating the community's own aspirations into the project's definition.

— A strategy for the gradual handing over of responsibilities to the community must be established.

— The community, and especially women, must be trained to take part in the development of the project (ibid., pp. 10–20).

FODERUMA's general aims (further defined in more concrete terms in each specific project) were: to increase the participation of women within the productive process; to increase the income of both the family and the community; to obtain greater participation of women in existing popular organisations. This last objective responded to the need not to supplant existing organisations by new ones brought into the community by outside agents.

Two subprogrammes within the Programme for Peasant Women, which were made specific projects within each community, involved provision of non-formal education, and technical and financial assistance. The first comprises actions such as community organisation; health and infant care; domestic economy. The second includes: environmental sanitation; housing improvement; food and nourishment; improvement of income levels.

General Appraisal of the FODERUMA's Programme

Although no specific evaluation of the Peasant Women Programme has as yet been made by FODERUMA itself, the general impression obtained from reading official documents and interviewing its staff is that the Programme is still considered to be experimental. Similarly, no methodological effort has been made to systematise the experience gained. This is a result of the priority FODERUMA gives to action, and of its lack of emphasis on the need to evaluate. The emphasis on the urgent need for action has meant that it has been impossible to evaluate the Programme or to decide whether it should be continued along the same lines or modified. The discussion that took place at the CEIS–CEPAM Seminar allows us to present a few tentative general conclusions. FODERUMA's procedure in planning its actions is based on the premise that they must be based on the community's own priorities. To establish the latter, a process of participatory research is used. It was recognised, however, that despite the worthiness of the intentions, grave doubts arise as to the efficacy and appropriateness of the method in practice. Do promoters, even without intending to, impose their priorities and particular vision of reality, thus replacing or deforming the community's own perception? If that is the case, then the value of the information obtained and the criteria apparently expressed by the members of the community through the process of participatory research, must be treated with a good deal of caution and even scepticism. This problem appears to be particularly acute when identifying women's view of their problems and their vision and experience to an outside agent. Often, extension workers are told what the community believes they wish to hear.

As for promoting women's participation in the community's own organisations: it was observed that women frequently do participate in peasant organisations even though they may only be a minority of the women within the community. This participation can be broadened only if FODERUMA and similar programmes promote a greater recognition of women's role within the peasant economy[4] through providing better educational and employment opportunities for women, and training in several productive activities, multiplying skills, improving on indigenous techniques, and promoting a higher degree of consciousness. For all these actions to be effective, it is essential that the community's own initiatives should be respected and supported and the imposition of criteria from outside avoided, independently of how valid they may appear to the promoter's eyes.

The Experience of the Secretariat of Integrated Rural Development

One of the main aims of the democratic government that took office in August, 1979, was to achieve a modern rural economy and society through the improvement of production and productivity and the integration of the impoverished peasantry into the rural modernisation process. For this purpose, Integrated Rural Develop-

4. The peasant economy is based on small plots of land: production is fundamentally for family consumption, the only labour force employed is the family's and traditional technologies are utilised.

ment Projects (IRDP) were defined, and SEDRI was created to coordinate and supervise their execution. More specifically, the IRDP's objectives were defined as follows:

(1) To increase agrarian production and productivity and improve rural incomes through encouragement of production of food staples and export crops, along with inputs for industry.

(2) To improve and rationalise the distribution of resources and incomes among the rural population, including the redistribution of productive land and other resources, with the purpose of bettering the quality of life of the rural population.

(3) To increase the capacity of the agrarian sector to absorb labour by modifying technological patterns, through programmes to upgrade the skills of the labour force, and through a better knowledge of actual and potential resources available as well as of the possibilities for their utilisation.

(4) To implement inter-institutional coordination through SEDRI to carry out IDRP's objectives (Ministerio de Agricultura . . ., 1984).

Seventeen IRDP's were agreed for the 1980–84 period: 16 are today being implemented, and 1 has been interrupted due to the opposition of the intended beneficiaries. The 17 projects cover nearly 25 per cent of the total productive land and affect directly or indirectly about 671,000 persons, mainly poor peasants who represent roughly 8 per cent of the total rural population of Ecuador. The estimated total investment is of US$ 720 million (SEDRI-1984).

The IRDPs aim to help small producers by raising their productivity, thereby increasing their income levels, and also the production of foodstuffs for the market.

Methodologically, the IRDPs use operational plans consisting of a group of 'generative actions', whose basic characteristic is their capacity to act as multipliers of further actions in a dynamic and permanent process in which the community is gradually and increasingly involved. The idea is essentially simple and is similar to the concept of inter-industrial relations, which allows the identification of potential multiplier effects which one particular productive decision may have on a multitude of other productive sectors. Furthermore, for the identification of these 'generative actions', more than technical criteria are taken into account: participation of peasant organisations through the formulation of their own diagnosis of their problems, as well as their own priorities, is considered essential (at least in words) for the success of the project.

The IRDP methodology does not include projects specifically directed towards women. The particular characteristics of many peasant communities, as well as the projects' own dynamic, however, have led to the generation of actions in which mainly women participate. In fact, in many peasant communities, factors such as the lack of access to productive land, surplus labour and the absence of alternative employment in the immediate region generate a dynamic process of temporary and cyclical male outmigration in which the family plot continues to constitute the basis of the family's survival and reproduction. Massive adult male outmigration leads to women, children and the old, being the only population living permanently in the community. Women are thus forced to take on additional roles, among which is that of relating to IRDP personnel. Since women become the head of the family for part of the year, actions involving women are inevitably identified and implemented, even if such actions were not originally contemplated. In spite of the fact that programmes for women have in fact been carried out, this development has never been systematically discussed within the IRDP Executive Unit responsible for carrying out projects.

Among the actions carried out with the participation of women were: small-scale guinea-pig breeding,[5] dressmaking, blackberry growing, training courses on textile craftmanship, etc. Judgements differ about the significance and impact of these projects. Some people maintain they have had little social or economic impact and continue to be implemented only because of intertia and the mechanical adoption by SEDRI's staff of criteria put forward by international development agencies. According to others, these experiences have had positive results, among which is the strengthening of the peasants' communal organisation. Two such projects are described below:

The Quimiag–Penipe Project. This Project is located in Chimborazo province, where Indian peasant communities live in extreme poverty. The Project covers an area of 29.5 thousand hectares, at between 2,280 and 3,200 metres above sea level. Only 11,000 hectares — 60 per cent acutely affected by erosion — are under

5. Guinea pigs provide practically the only meat consumed by the Indian peasantry. Their growing scarcity, and the recent demand for them in the cities, make it increasingly difficult for the peasantry to use them as a staple of their own diet.

cultivation. Activities specifically directed to or carried out by women include:

(1) Credit was granted to the Mothers' Committee of the Community of Puculpala for the cultivation of blackberries (100,000 sucres, approximately US$ 3,000 at the time); and the Mothers' Committee of the Communities of Ayanquil, Azacucho and Utuñag, for breeding guinea pigs (73,000 sucres each, approximately US$ 2,400).

(2) Women were used in the construction of the Project's infrastructure (irrigation canals, communal house, etc.).

(3) Women were drawn into the management of 28 community centres for the provision of social services, organised by the Peasants' Union of Quimiag–Penipe, with the Project's assistance and collaboration.

(4) Women were encouraged to participate in various phases of the commercialisation of marketable products.

At the moment a number of actions are at the planning stage: training in health and nutrition; participation in a traditional crops project; cultivation of medicinal herbs.

The Salcedo Project. This project is located in the central inter-Andean region, in Cotopaxi province. It covers an area of 53,870 hectares, of which about 63 per cent are under cultivation. Small producers predominate and the main crops are potatoes, maize and barley. Women have participated in the following activities:

(1) a programme designed to test and disseminate different and more productive varieties of barley and maize;

(2) a pilot programme for the adoption of new technologies for the control of pests;

(3) guinea pig breeding, through the Mothers' Centre; the families involved contributed financially to the project.

The Experience of a Private Organisation

The Andean Centre for Popular Action (CAAP) is a non-profit private organisation, which works with the peasant communities of the Sierra. CAAP provides technical assistance in specific areas, from political and organisational education to the development of specific skills. It emphasises the recovery and reintroduction of traditional cultivation and other practices, which are disappearing as a result of the advance of modern capitalist agriculture. CAAP also conducts action-oriented research to provide criteria and information for the practical activity to be undertaken.

CAAP recognises a process of acute differentiation within the peasantry, ranging from their full integration into the capitalist productive process as wage-earners to their increased marginalisation from access to productive resources. To this must be added a cultural and ethnic dimension in the case of the Highlands, where the peasantry recognises itself as the only rightful heir to a rich pre-Columbian Indian cultural tradition. The superposition of these two determinations — that of class and culture — leads the peasantry of the Highlands to defend staunchly its cultural and ethnic cohesion, which is besieged by capitalist rural development. CAAP considers that to ignore these special determinants and conditions is tantamount to aiding the destruction of a proud community.

Women's main concerns are identified as focusing on health and nourishment. Their concern for health is seen as a manifestation of their responsibility as guarantors of the biological survival of the family unit. As a result of a woman's concern for nourishment, which is obviously closely linked to problems of health and the fact that the male peasant's income is inadequate, a peasant woman often transcends what is normally considered to be her 'natural' role and 'invades' the area of the male. She tries to increase family income by taking on wage work and producing agricultural and handicraft goods.

On the basis of this framework, CAAP's projects for peasant women aim to:

(1) Help in the exchange and diffusion of traditional healing practices and of medicinal herbs.

(2) Offer advice and training on the use of pharmaceutical products, especially those most commonly prescribed by doctors, or most commonly bought.

(3) Support the reintroduction of traditional crops, which improve and supplement the peasant diet.[6]

(4) Introduce small-scale land-intensive cultivation of vegetables, so as to add vitamins to the peasant family's diet and to improve organic techniques of soil conservation.

---

6. Rural modernisation has brought with it a deterioration of the peasant diet, as dishes made with subsistence crops of high nutritional value are now being replaced by low-quality, but cheaper processed food.

Some General Methodological Conclusions

Since development policies and programmes directed towards peasant women, whether carried out by public or private agencies, are still rare and of recent date, no definitive lessons can be deduced at this stage. Nevertheless, some rather tentative methodological considerations can be put forward:

The first point that should be made is that the definition of a single national policy towards the peasantry in Ecuador and towards the feminine component of that population, is problematic. Ethnic and cultural specificities and different processes of dissolution and/or strategies of survival of the peasant economies have to be taken into account.

With regard to women, the problem seems to be even more complex. Peasant women of the Ecuadorian Sierra are the victims of triple exploitation: as peasants (class-determined relations of exploitation), as members of a cultural/ethnic minority (racial and cultural prejudice as elements of a relation of submissiveness and estrangement with respect to the rest of society), and as women (sexual oppression and subordination, within the family and in society). The difficulty increases if we add that class related processes vary in accordance with different historical backgrounds and socio-economic environments; the cultural/ethnic determination has regional and subregional specificities, which sometimes generate significant differences with respect to the ideological perception of reality; the characteristics of the sexual dimension of oppression also vary in accordance with different socio-economic processes (i.e. male migration) and cultural conditionings (i.e. different cultural/ethnic subgroups).

How policies and programmes should take the sexual division of labour within peasant communities into account, provides a pertinent example of how rural communities pose particularly difficult problems. In the first place, in contrast to the formal urban economy and modern agriculture, the economic unit of labour is not the individual wage-earner, but the family as a whole. This tends to obsure the existence of different sex roles and often implies that decisions are jointly taken within the peasant family unit. This ambiguity is increased with male cyclical migration which drastically disrupts 'normal' allocation of roles between male and female.

Should policy attempt to support a particular sexual division of labour, or should it aid in its disruption? The provision of technical and other skills through non-formal educational programmes ceases then to be a neutral proposal: it can help the consolidation of either of these two processes. How should those responsible for designing policy proceed? An apparent answer would seem to be: ask the community. But difficulties abound here too. To what extent does the community express what it really feels and needs? All the programmes reviewed in this paper include in their basic premises respecting a community's own criteria and its own organisation. None the less, well-founded reservations persist as to the extent to which the community's criteria are really being correctly conveyed and interpreted. So-called 'participatory research' techniques do not yet appear to provide a fully satisfactory solution to this problem.

On the positive side, some preliminary conclusions can be drawn. On the one hand, it is relatively clear that peasant women are mainly concerned with what we could call 'quality of life' issues, or satisfaction of basic needs, particularly in relation to health and nourishment. This provides a better basis for the design of prog-rammes and policies for rural women than the sort of activities which are so often considered 'appropriate' for women, such as dressmaking. Non-formal educational programmes for women must however respond to the particular characteristics of the com-munity and of the processes it is undergoing. Migration and the need that women have to acquire 'male' skills, is an example. Another general recommendation is that the outside development agency, be it public or private, must avoid making the community more dependent: its urgent need for resources and services and the agency's real or apparent ability to provide them, may lead to the community giving up its own perspectives and wishes.

Whatever the case, what is clearly needed is research into the situation of rural women and more rigorous evaluation of practical experiences in the design and execution of programmes and projects with the peasant population. Hasty and unreflective action is both counterproductive and unwarranted.

Section 3: Programmes with Low-income Women of the Urban Sector

In this section, we will review a number of programmes undertaken by public and private agencies on behalf of urban women (Farrell, 1984; Freire, 1984). The most significant is the Mother and Infant

Food Supplement Programme (MIFCP), conceived initially as an answer to the problems of malnutrition. We will also review a number of projects which seem to provide employment and a source of income to women of the poorer or marginal neighbourhoods and to promote their organisation and greater political awareness.

It should be declared at the outset that none of the people with whom we have discussed the question of what sort of policies and programmes should be adopted believe it possible at this stage to develop a single methodology for the design of policies for low-income urban women. Our quite widespread consultations lead us to suggest that the experience accumulated by the women's movement (including the various entities, public and private, that carry out programmes with women) has reached an intermediate stage, in which the drawing of clear-cut conclusions is not yet possible.

The Mother and Infant Food Supplement Programme

The diet of a high proportion of Ecuadoreans lacks basic nutrients and, although there is as yet no reliable quantification of the prevalence of malnutrition at the national level, it can be inferred that the urban poor are among those most badly affected, not only by deficiencies in calories and proteins, but also by anaemia caused by iron deficiency. The problem becomes particularly acute among women, whether rural or urban, because of their double workload.

The poverty of large sectors of the population and the high levels of malnutrition led the Ecuadorean State to set up a Mother and Infant Food Supplement Programme (MIFCP) administered through the Ministry of Public Health. The Programme was started in 1975 as a temporary measure. Its basic objective was to prevent protein-calorie malnutrition among pregnant women, breastfeeding mothers and infants under 2 years of age, and to reduce malnutrition among children under 6 years of age. A specially prescribed mixture of oats, soy milk and rice was distributed among the target population. Although the Programme was not designed exclusively for the urban population, distribution difficulties in the countryside has in practice limited its range to the urban areas. The proposed coverage for 1984 was 300,000 persons growing to 450,000 persons by 1988. The estimated cost in 1984 for administration and distribution was 72 million sucres (approximately US$ 1.2 million).

In evaluating the MIFCP it has to be pointed out that in so far as it seeks to relieve the effects rather than tackle the causes of extreme poverty, the programme is basically distorted. If it had been conceived as a temporary, emergency action, this might be acceptable, but it has in fact been in existence for 9 years, during which time the State has consistently failed to address the underlying socio-economic causes of extreme poverty and malnutrition.[7] The MIFCP can therefore be seen as a substitute for needed reform.

With respect to the actual results of the Programme, the following comments can be made:

(1) Given that there are no precise criteria for determining the population to be benefited, those who receive the rations are not always those at higher health risk. There is simply no way to correct this.

(2) The Programme does not aim at preventing potential new malnutrition cases; it only covers the population already affected. The continuous provision of rations to the same recipients is not guaranteed.

(3) Logistical difficulties (storage, transportation, distribution, etc.) have not been adequately studied nor treated, which leads to very inefficient distribution of the rations, at a few overcrowded outlets.

(4) Rations are normally shared among all members of the family, thereby negating the objectives for which the Programme was designed.

The MIFCP in no way involves participation of the community nor the women within it. It is clearly a welfare programme, designed as a palliative to a problem with deep structural roots.

Productive Projects with Women

Setting up income-generating projects has become a common practice among organisations working with poor urban women and it has also become a common aspiration of women's groups. Such projects are normally seen as an answer to two different problems:

---

7. The inadequate production of foodstuffs, as well as their unequal distribution, has its origin in various complex determinants, such as the concentration of property and control of productive resources, the use of productive land, and its increasing orientation towards the production of goods for selective rather than mass consumption and agro-industry, the rural distribution of social wealth, lack of employment.

providing employment and income for women of low-income neighbourhoods, and maintaining group cohesion through the generation of interests beyond those of an organisational or political nature.

The widespread attempt by most urban women's organisations to set up small-scale profit-making communal enterprises represents an attempt to valorise economically those abilities considered to be innate to women (such as dressmaking, sewing, making paper flowers, etc.) and usually exercised within the confines of the home. The choice of these traditionally 'feminine' activities as appropriate for community income-generating enterprises, corresponds to the image that low-income urban women have of themselves rather than to women's true capabilities or know-how. This is one reason why these projects are seldom successful.

It has to be asked whether these actions or projects are appropriate, and to do this from two viewpoints:

(1) Overcoming traditional patterns of subordination and role allocation are usually considered the best way to achieve women's dynamic and egalitarian participation in society thus the main aim of women's organisations.

(2) Any action undertaken with women's groups should lead to increasing their awareness of the social, economic and political organisation of society, so as to permit them to appreciate women's place within it. This increased awareness should discriminate between the sexual and the class determinants of women's position.

A recent study of micro-enterprises in the popular or marginal neighbourhoods of Quito and Guayaquil[8] is helpful in addressing these questions, two of its general conclusions being particularly significant for our purposes. Firstly, within popular neighbourhoods there is a marked tendency towards overwhelming numbers of micro-productive units. This is not a surprising finding. Since the so-called 'modern' sector of the economy in developing countries typically absorbs only a fraction of the country's active population, the excluded population has adopted a survival strategy based on setting up small economic activities (the so-called informal sector).

8. A study conducted by the Instituto de Investigaciones Económicas of the Catholic University of Ecuador. The sample included 123 micro-enterprises in Quito; 53 in the centre of Guayaquil; and 62 in its outskirts. Cited in Farrell, 1984, p. 3.

Secondly, small units suffer from a number of market-related difficulties — having to compete with more sophisticated industrial products by charging lower prices; encountering great difficulties in procuring needed inputs — which inevitably lead them to eliminate various costs of production from their economic calculations and to drastic constriction of their profits. For these reasons the family labour force is not remunerated, the electricity employed is charged to 'household expenses' when, as is commonly the case, the workshop is located within or beside the home, etc.

Micro-enterprises face an additional limitation in that they cannot respond swiftly to technological innovation. On the one hand, the level of skills of their labour force is generally low, learned in the family environment or through temporary employment in the modern sector. On the other hand, small enterprises have very low start-up costs and are often started thanks to the family's savings.

The study found that very few small enterprises were owned or managed by women and that those few were involved in traditional women's activities such as dressmaking and food processing. Moreover, few of those employed in these small enterprises were women — around 25 per cent (Farrell, 1984, p. 7). Women of the domestic unit who work in the family workshop are not normally recognised as workers: their activity is considered as a simple extension of their domestic chores, and no recognition, monetary or otherwise, is accorded to it.

Returning to the question of the appropriateness of income-generating projects within the context of the aims of the women's movement, we will begin with the provocative statement that there is a basic contradiction in such a policy. Women have been technologically segregated by the web of social and familial relations that also determine their subordination. That is to say, there are well-defined skills and know-how considered appropriate for women, while the rest are supposedly reserved for men. When a women's organisation decides to embark upon an income-generating project, it does so only in part to provide an additional source of money, but chiefly to cement the group's cohesion for what is generally considered to be the organisation's main objective: the overthrow of sexually-determined relations of discrimination and subordination. But — and here lies the contradiction — the most immediately obvious know-how and skills to be utilised within the income-generating project are precisely those derived from women's traditional roles. Thus the productive project, intended to help achieve the organisation's main objective, ends by negating it.

This situation is made even worse by the fact that micro-enterprises have little chance of success, and due to their size are also unlikely to provide employment to more than 6 or 7 members of the organisation, thus discriminating against the rest. The few women privileged by their employment in the project lack the time to participate in the organisation's other activities. They thus become doubly estranged.

To these basic problems must be added others, less important, but which nevertheless have contributed to the failure of many of these projects. In most cases, income-generating projects are started without any preliminary feasibility studies, due to the naïve conviction that the market has unlimited absorptive capacity. Equally naïve is the belief that people of the immediate community will purchase the products simply as a gesture of solidarity, and that the micro-enterprise will have a sort of 'captive market' whatever the quality of the product. Thus little effort is made to ensure excellence. An additional problem of a different order is that these small enterprises usually depend on recurrent financial inputs from an external agent, be it an international organisation or a non-profit private entity. This in-built dependence often spells the breakdown of the project when the donor abandons it.

No clear conclusions can yet be deduced from the experience with such projects, but a few questions can be spelled out. Does a woman's partial insertion in paid work contribute significantly to family income? Does involvement in income-generating projects really help to develop women's greater awareness of the problems of sexual subordination and discrimination, and therefore lead to destroying the ideological veil? Are the organisational and administrative efforts of setting up a productive project really justified in view of the difficulties involved? Does the emphasis on economic objectives not devalue other more important aims of the organisation?

There are no clear answers to these questions, and they are at the moment being discussed by women's organisations and within the women's movement itself in Ecuador. However, we can draw a few general conclusions from the discussion that took place at the CEIS–CEPAM Seminar, which may serve as general guidelines for the formulation of policy directed towards low-income urban women.

Some General Conclusions and Recommendations

The experience with income-generating projects within the context of women's organisations seems to show that they do not provide an answer either to women's need for paid employment and income or to the long-range organisational aims of the women's movement. Furthermore the use of traditional female skills is self-defeating. On the other hand, the idea of 'alternative projects' for women that adequately respond to their economic needs and aspirations, and also lead to a more dynamic and non-traditional women's participation in society is for the time being somewhat theoretical. The need to find clear and concrete responses to the problems presented above by means of detailed research into the issue must be the first priority of the women's movement of Ecuador.

In general terms, the following conclusions can be drawn from project experience to date:

(a) Women's grass-roots organisations and the external agents working with them need to obtain more complete and qualitatively richer information about market conditions for 'alternative products', and to make this information available to the women's movement.

(b) Women need to be taught new, non-traditional skills (the State can help here), and to obtain access to technological alternatives, enabling them to produce products of better quality and greater marketability.

(c) Technical training programmes must carefully take into account the limitations faced by low-income women, among them illiteracy, and difficulty in handling abstract concepts such as are implied in elementary mathematics, etc.

(d) Women's grass-roots organisations need to discuss thoroughly the appropriateness of income-generating projects and their relation to the other more important objectives of the organisation.

(e) The results of income-generating projects whether negative or positive, need to be continuously publicised.

Section 4: The State, Development Planning and Women

The Ecuadorean State's preoccupation with women's issues is quite recent; practically nothing before the late 1970s could be construed as denoting some degree of awareness or interest in the subject. Furthermore, neither the women's movement nor the academic community's interest in the theme had made its presence felt before the late 1970s. The State's indifference must therefore be understood, at least in part, as a result of this lack of interest by society, clearly manifested by the absence of organised pressure groups, the lack of informed public opinion, and the virtual non-existence of research and publications on the subject.

The National Development Plan of 1980–84

Moreover, as the following account will show, the Ecuadorean State's policies with respect to women's issues have not been the product of a national practice, and a concomitant theoretical reflection on that practice. That is to say, the State did not gather from a pre-existing experience the appropriate lessons for ensuring the definition of a successful and meaningful policy. The weakness, inadequacy and the practical irrelevance of the State's pronouncements and actions in this sphere, about which we shall have more to say, are partially derived from this lack of correspondence between national practice and national policies. However, as the Ecuadorean women's movement gains momentum and experience, the State's position is undergoing a positive change, defining policies and implementing programmes more in accordance with the true characteristics and needs of Ecuadorean working-class and peasant women.

Some Antecedents to the State's Involvement with Women's Issues

A number of actions or events can be seen, in the light of later developments, as antecedents, and have now become part of the historical background of the women's movement, whether as appropriate antecedents or as examples of what should not be done. The State in Ecuador has for some time implemented programmes whose principal beneficiaries are working-class and peasant women. These comprise the distribution of basic staples to groups in extreme poverty, such as the mother and infant 'food supplement' programme of the Ministry of Public Health; school breakfasts; and the organisation of training courses for women to acquire skills such as dressmaking, beauty care and hairdressing, secretarial skills, accounting, toy-making, trade and various services. These State programmes are criticised by representatives of the women's movement as being at best ineffectual, consisting as they do of isolated actions which are not integrated into the productive sector and therefore bring no permanent positive effects, or at worst, undesirable because they reinforce women's traditional roles. They are conspicuous examples of a 'welfarist' ideology which must be superseded and, in that sense, they are taken as examples of what should not be done.

Their importance for us, however, goes further than the doubtless useful role of serving as negative cases. In spite of bitter criticism, the fact is that similar programmes are still being promoted and not only by State agencies. Even popular women's organisations themselves feel obliged to implement 'traditional' programmes, probably because 'traditional' patterns of behaviour and ideology are more difficult to transform than was initially thought.

It must be recognised, at least formally, that the State's involvement predates the growth of a women's movement. The reason for this is quite clear: the pressure of international opinion as expressed through international agencies. In fact, as early as 1970, the Interamerican Women's Commission of the Organisation of American States (OAS) requested the Ecuadorean government to create a bureau or department within the State's administrative structure which would define and implement policies and strategies directed towards women, taking due account of Ecuador's social, political, economic and cultural characteristics. In response to this formal request, the government of Ecuador created the Departamento Nacional de la Mujer (the National Women's Department — DNM) February 1970, as a dependency of the then Ministry of Labour and Social Welfare. The Department had in fact no life beyond its formal existence, but was the direct antecedent of the National Office of Women (Oficina Nacional de la Mujer) now in existence.

In 1975, Ecuador officially participated in the World Conference for the International Year of Women. As a result the government approved the World Plan of Action, which contained specific recommendations on legislation, administrative mechanisms, employment, education, health, political participation, the struggle against prostitution, the media's commercial utilisation of women, etc. The 1975 International Declaration was also useful to the then infant women's movement of Ecuador enabling it to exert pressure on the government to re-activate the DNM, although to no immediate avail.

The combined pressure of the international community and the nascent women's movement on the Ecuadorean State took a new turn in 1978. In that year, the High Level Governmental Experts Committee on Women's Integration into Social and Economic Development in Latin America of the Economic Commission for Latin America and the Caribbean (ECLA) met in Quito to evaluate the Regional Plan of Action as defined in 1975. In that same year the State's National Planning Board (NPB — later to become the National Development Council — CONADE) was preparing a technical document with preliminary proposals for the National Development Plan to be drawn up during the following year. A number of organisations, largely of middle-class professional women, and many of them largely inactive until the ECLA meeting, approached the NPB to impress upon it the importance of defining a policy for the integration of women into the development process. In response, the NPB conducted a series of inquiries and discussion meetings with numerous women's organisations, which resulted in clarification of the basic premises that would serve to define the pertinent programme in the National Development Plan for 1980–84.

The National Development Plan 1980–84, drawn up during the second semester of 1979. This Plan, the first ever to be adopted by a democratically elected government in Ecuador, purported to be an effective instrument for socio-economic change, as well as for strengthening and advancing democracy. In fact, the Plan defined as its 3 objectives: strengthening the democratic system, ensuring economic development, and securing social justice. To achieve this, structural reforms were proposed in taxation, administration, agrarian sector, education and political process. With respect to the latter, the Plan stated that its objective was to lessen the concentration of political power through the increased franchise of the population and the promotion of an active and conscious mobilisation of the people and of popular organisations at the local level (*Plan Nacional 1980–4*, p. 24). This objective was closely linked to the aim of guaranteeing the popular classes' active participation in the social and economic benefits that the expansion of production and the growth of wealth and social services were meant to bring about (ibid.).

It is as part of this policy of social mobilisation for political and socio-economic change, that the Programme of Popular Promotion and, within it, the Subprogramme for Women and the Young, were defined. This point is significant in that it reveals a conscious attempt to reach beyond the paternalistic and welfarist conception of social policy which had for so long permeated the Ecuadorean State. Linking the provision of social services to the promotion of popular organisations, whose ultimate *raison d'être* is the overall transformation of society, gives a new dimension to the concept of social policy itself (at least in words). In fact, when listing the objectives sought by the subprogramme, the first aim proposed was to 'obtain the creative, critical and conscious participation of the young and of women in the life of the nation, as well as their integration into the social, economic and political development of the country' (*Plan Nac.*, vol. II, p. 30). Likewise, another aim was to 'organise eighty non-formal education courses of basic, middle and higher levels to form leaders so that they may promote popular organisation . . .' (ibid.). The general objectives of this sub-programme, as defined in the Plan, were thus directed towards the promotion of women's participation in the social, economic, and political life of the country, and sought also to generate new opportunities in education and employment, through non-formal educational programmes and the organisation of self-managed community productive enterprises (ibid.).

It is true that the women's programme was initially harnessed to a programme for the young, although the 2 sectors of the population are quantitatively and qualitatively different. Nevertheless, it must be emphasised that this was the first attempt by the State to define a programme for women within an overall development policy. This contrasts with much of the State's practice in this area, which continues largely to consist of isolated and incoherent actions. In fact, the next official National Development Council document, the *1984 Outline of a Strategy for Development* (CONADE, 1984) shows greater clarity with respect to the nature of the problems faced by peasant and working-class women.

The 1984 Strategy

In the first place, and in marked contrast to the 1980–4 Development Plan, the Strategy recognises the specificity of women's issues, and separates them from those of other social groups. In fact, it states that the call to society to participate in the implementation of the proposed Strategy, ' . . . presupposes the recognition of interests and participatory opportunities that exist within society' (ibid., p.

270). Like the earlier Plan, the Strategy locates its suggestions for a policy towards women within the more general policy framework of social participation. Although there is a subtle but important difference between the concepts of popular promotion and social participation, in that the former bears paternalistic overtones, the basic proposal is similar in both instances: the transformation of a socio-economic and political structure that is seen as unjust and as the main obstacle to development.

More specifically, social participation is seen as conducive to a double democratisation: of society and of the State. With respect to the first, ' . . . it will advance to the extent that the marginality that affects a great number of Ecuadoreans is reduced . . . to the extent that the opportunities for a real practice of civil, economic, social, cultural and political rights, are extended' (ibid.). With respect to the parallel democratisation of the State, it must imply ' . . . in addition to the setting up of an adequate (institutional) framework for social participation, the strengthening of the (State's) capacity to receive, process, and attend to the demands of all basically popular social sectors, and of all socio-economic regions of the country' (ibid.).

It is within this context then, that the participation of women is conceived. As a general statement, the Strategy's basic postulates present a definite improvement on previous official pronouncements, and it is therefore of sufficient interest to quote it in full:

As worker, peasant, teacher, professional, employee and mother, women's role in the economic and social development of the country is fundamental; nevertheless, it is a role that does not receive due recognition. This lack of recognition betrays the existence of a problematic whose principal features are subordination and discrimination; this affects mainly women of the popular sectors, and, by minimising their active and creative contribution, reduces the nation's development potential. This is why it is absolutely necessary to ensure women's integration into a full social life, which demands the exercise of their rights and the use of all the potentials of the role women can play in the construction of a more just and humane society. It must be recognised that, even within the situations shared by working-class and peasant women, differences exist that must be taken into account in the formulation and implementation of policy; one is the situation of urban women, and another is that of rural women. Again within each of these further specific problems exist.

If women's integration is to take place, it is necessary to promote the

63

organisation of women in all confines of life. The State must . . . create the legal and institutional framework for the development of women's organisations, which must result from women's own interests and initiatives. Non-formal educational activities promoting awareness of women's rights and their exercise must be undertaken. . . . The Oficina Nacional de la Mujer has an important responsibility in this matter.

Women of the popular sectors are called upon to participate actively in the execution of this Strategy, particularly in the priority policies of food and nutrition; housing; health education; and cultural policy; as well as in other social policies.

For women's participation to be feasible and fruitful, the necessary conditions must be provided. Thus, women's integration into the labour market without discrimination must be encouraged; aid must be provided to (specially designed) non-formal educational programmes; discriminatory legislation must be corrected; children's centres, nurseries, and infants' and mothers' centres must be provided, in rural areas as well as in the cities; actions and programmes must be undertaken that dignify women, especially to offset the commercial exploitation of women's image (ibid., pp. 273–4).

These paragraphs show a significant advance on the part of the State as regards its understanding of women's issues. It shows an undeniable sympathy with the points of view expressed by lower-income women's organisations, and even some incorporation in policy recommendations of demands expressed by the women's movement. The tone is not paternalistic; the text recognises instead that women's organisations must, of their own initiative and from their own perspective, define their full integration into society. The State's role is limited to the provision of the conditions enabling this. If the policy proposals put forward by CONADE were truly decisive as regards the actual implementation of policy and actions by the State as a whole, then it would be possible to believe that the Ecuadorean women's movement has already gained the ear and the will of the State, and that the two will now set forth together to bring about the desired transformations. That, however, would be an illusory and false conclusion. To what degree do actual programmes carried out by the Ecuadorean State reflect the views expressed by the National Development Council? We will now turn to this important question, by examining the work of the National Women's Office, the organism charged with the responsibility of putting into practice State policies.

The National Women's Office

Although the National Women's Office (OFNAMU) was formally created as early as 1970, it was only with the advent of a democratically elected government in 1979, that it acquired any real existence. In May 1980, OFNAMU was officially designated as a department within the National Directorate of Popular Promotion, of the also newly created Ministry of Social Welfare. Placing OFNAMU within the Ministry was considered to be a temporary solution, since the real intention was to give it the character of an advisory entity within the Presidency of the Republic itself, pending the necessary legal and administrative formalities. This decision clearly conveys the weight ascribed to the OFNAMU and its intended activities by the new government. Bureaucratic opposition, as well as the premature and tragic death of the President and his wife, brought that particular initiative to a standstill.[9]

The first two tasks faced by OFNAMU were its institutional consolidation, and designing a plan of action. As for the first, the main problems facing OFNAMU (which have not yet been solved) were its lack of autonomy, the scarcity of qualified personnel, and the inadequacy of its budget. These led, in the first place, to a lack of action for a considerable period and consequent frustration, and secondly, to the irrelevance and minor impact of the actions later implemented. In addition, bureaucratic, administrative structures, managed to impede the State's own initiative. As for the second task: the OFNAMU proceeded to develop the general policy definition put forward in the 1980–4 National Development Plan. Its main sources were the Development Plan itself, the UN's Decennial Plan for Women, and the Regional Plan of Action for Latin America and the Caribbean. A complementary Five-year Plan was drawn up, a summary of which is given below:

Structural Aspects
— To formulate women's components of Integrated Rural Development projects.
— To secure measures for the redistribution of income.
— To coordinate the active participation of organised women.

9. It was the strong personality and the personal interest of the new President's wife, a women's leader in her own right, that made it possible to carry out some of the actions envisaged in the 1980–84 Development Plan.

Legislative Aspects
— To revise legislation and obtain the enactment of laws that guarantee women's equality.
— To oversee the enforcement of the laws.
— To adopt the recommendations and put into practice the commitments made in international agreements.

Administrative Aspects
— To obtain the financial and administrative autonomy of OF-NAMU.
— To set up and strengthen an inter-institutional committee.

Employment
— To obtain equal employment opportunities for women.
— To formulate a national policy and draw up plans for the provision of non-formal education for women.
— To promote the formation of self-managed women's productive enterprises.

Education
— To formulate formal and non-formal educational policies for women.
— To create a non-formal career centre.
— To promote the incorporation of women into secondary and higher education.
— To coordinate actions for the implementation of massive educational programmes on radio and television.

Housing
— To coordinate the construction of urban subcentres with all basic services

Health
— To draw up and implement programmes of education in health, hygiene, care of infants, and nutrition
— To extend provision of social security services to the affiliate's family, and increase peasants' social insurance
— To improve the State's health services
— To coordinate efforts for the training of human resources for health services

Political Participation
— To promote women's political participation at every level
— To promote political education
— To ensure compliance with United Nations resolutions pertaining to women

Other Aspects
— To carry out research on the women's condition in the various sectors of society
— To carry out education campaigns directed towards the revalorisation of women's image
— To eliminate the use of women as sexual symbols in the mass media
— To design programmes for women in special situations: prostitutes, drug addicts, prison inmates, etc. (Rocío, 1984).

As can be seen, this was an excessively ambitious plan of action for a newly created small dependency within a Ministry, and for a period of only 5 years. It is an indication both of the enthusiasm and of the naïvety with which OFNAMU's creation was received by those initially responsible for it. However, OFNAMU was not meant to carry out alone all the actions listed above; it was intended to coordinate carefully inter-institutional programmes of various government agencies. But even this was made impossible because of its modest place within the bureaucratic structure.

What evaluation can be made of OFNAMU at this point? It would be unfair to attempt to contrast its aims with what it has been able to achieve. In the first place, the plan is too ambitious and many of the proposed actions lack precision and concreteness. Secondly, OFNAMU has been in existence too short a time to have been able to tackle the long standing problems affecting most of the female population. Thirdly, OFNAMU has had to face intransigence, lack of sympathy and understanding and sometimes a virtual boycott of key segments of the State's bureaucracy: it has been financially choked; its requests for technical personnel have been largely refused; and the jealousy and distrust of government agencies and institutions whose activities OFNAMU was meant to coordinate, has forced it to rely almost exclusively on its own meagre resources. This has resulted in it carrying out a few small actions, whose impact on the problems faced by women of the popular sectors has been negligible.

As regards the correspondence between a critical conceptualisation of women's issues, and the practice of OFNAMU, the record so far appears mixed. On the positive side, OFNAMU has demonstrated great respect for women's organisations and their views; it has not attempted to set up government-sponsored parallel organisations. On the contrary, OFNAMU works with already existing associations, supporting them through its programmes and actions, such as running training courses on organisational techniques. On the negative side, to some extent precisely because of its respect for those organisation's own criteria, OFNAMU has continued to carry out courses and seminars along traditional lines, such as dressmaking. OFNAMU has not been able to correct this distortion in the non-formal educational system, which reinforces traditional roles for women and directs their efforts towards products already in superabundant supply.

Summing up, the few actions the State has explicitly undertaken for low-income women of the popular sectors have been organised by OFNAMU. It has basically promoted organisation and training among women in the urban and rural areas, through mothers' centres, women's associations of various types, etc.; the establishment of a few self-managed productive enterprises, although along traditional lines, such as making dresses and toys. It has carried out a significant number of training courses, many of them directed to the personnel of self-managed enterprises, on subjects such as nourishment and nutrition, care of infants, etc. On the other hand, OFNAMU has contributed to the diffusion of a new attitude towards women, through the organisation of national seminars on subjects such as legislation, on work methodology with women's popular organisations, women's political participation, etc.; and also through broadcasting short consciousness-raising programmes on television (13 in all). The main limitations and obstacles encountered have been the lack of human and financial resources and the bureaucracy's distrust. To these must be added the uncertainty with respect to the new government which took office in August 1984. As it subscribes to a conservative ideology, it is probable that OFNAMU's work, if the organisation itself survives, will undergo some change in its orientation. In summary, it is still too early to make a judgement on this matter; furthermore the women's movement of Ecuador has already attained a level of maturity that ensures its continuance and growth, independent of State policy.

Section 5: Methodological Recommendations for Planners and Researchers

The study carried out and summarised in this report involved basically consulting official documents, interviewing government officials and women's leaders, direct observations of rural development projects considered significant from a women's perspective and, above all, taking part in the very rich discussions that took place at the Seminar organised by CEIS and CEPAM. Throughout this report, we have consistently drawn conclusions and made recommendations and reflected on the information and experiences reviewed. In so doing, we have attempted to extract lessons of general as well as specific value and pertinency.

Reality is complex and often contradictory and does not always permit the simple, clear-cut conclusions planners demand. Thus they face a dilemma: on the one hand, planning requires general principles of universal validity, but these may turn out to be too abstract to be of operational value. On the other hand, a planner may have so much specific and concrete information that it may be impossible to use it to formulate policy proposals of sufficient generality to make national or regional planning possible. Between these two extremes, the planner must somehow find the terrain where policy definition and programme formulation are both general enough to avoid casuistry and concrete enough to be pertinent and applicable. We have attempted to facilitate this endeavour when evaluating various Ecuadorean experiences and extracting appropriate lessons from them.

What we have done is to isolate a few basic ideas of particular importance and relevance which should be taken into account by planners and policy makers, whether they belong to public or private entities. They have been grouped into two categories. The first are directly relevant to planners and policy makers; the second are relevant research needs and problems. We consider research to be essential if planning is to respond to the needs of women and not merely to reflect prejudiced and subjective beliefs.

Planning Policies and Programmes

(1) In order to incorporate women's demands into the formulation of State policies, it is not enough to obtain and compile criteria from women's organisations. The extent to which

those expressed demands may have been induced by the State itself, or by private development agencies, and may not therefore truly reflect the women's true aspirations, must be evaluated.

(2)   The State should not attempt to solve all the problems indentified by women, but should limit itself to those that have the greatest impact on a number of other aspects of social and economic life. The need to define priorities carefully arises from the fact that the State has limited resources which should not be dissipated in numerous ineffectual actions. State paternalism should also be avoided. Women's organisations must search for their own solutions, on the basis of their own alternatives and initiatives. The State should in many areas be responsible only for providing enabling conditions, of which the most important is respect for grass-roots initiatives.

(3)   It is easier to identify the problems low-income women face than to find adequate solutions, because particular social and economic problems are part of a general socio-economic structure and cannot therefore be solved by isolated actions. Planners must visualise particular problems within their global context, and avoid the sectoralisation of policy; their proposals should be integrated into a general development strategy.

(4)   Careful thought should be given to the appropriateness of defining policies specifically for women as if they constituted a particular sector within social planning. An alternative is to promote women's active and even privileged participation in policies within integrated development planning, particularly those which have to do with the satisfaction of basic needs and with overcoming structural obstacles to development.

(5)   Women of the popular sectors, be they urban or rural, give priority to the satisfaction of basic needs, particularly those relating to health and nutrition. To the extent that a 'basic needs' development strategy necessarily probes into the causes of poverty and marginalisation, women's participation in this area makes them strategic agents in the process of society-wide social transformation.

(6)   the design of policy, the question is not how women's integration in the formal sector can be increased, but what the modalities of their actual incorporation are. Statistics do not adequately reflect women's very significant involvement in

the informal sector of the economy. Planners should carefully examine the stages and sectors of the formal and informal production process in which women are actually incorporated, as well as their conditions of work, in order to formulate policies and programmes that truly respond to women's needs.

(7) The State must recognise that women in the informal sector are less organised than those in the formal sector. The former therefore have less opportunity to express their demands to the State. Ignoring this may lead to defining policies mainly relevant to formal sector workers and may not reflect the needs and expectations of the majority of women who are in the informal sector.

(8) Non-formal educational programmes directed towards women should not only contemplate training in various skills; they should also help dispel the ideological and cultural veil that sanctions traditional roles for women and that justifies forms of oppression, subordination and exploitation.

(9) Women's identification of traditional activities, such as dressmaking, like others for which they demand the State's assistance in the form of training, credit, etc., responds to their daily experience, but also denotes difficulty in overcoming traditional norms and roles. The planner and policy maker should not take these expressed demands at face value, but understand instead that they reveal a desire for change and improvement. The development of a more critical attitude and the search for true alternatives should be supported to probe below the surface of spontaneously expressed demands.

(10) In defining non-formal educational programmes linked to income-generating projects, due account should be taken of women's ability to learn new technical skills and knowledge, given their low educational level. Consideration should also be given to the conflicts that may develop between the requirements of a market-oriented productive activity and the other functions which women are inevitably called upon to perform and which relate to the family's reproduction and cohesion. Otherwise, it is possible that training and income-generating projects may intensify rather than reduce women's oppression and two-fold exploitation.

(11) In the design of income-generating projects, the following points should be considered:

— Find products which face less competitive or saturated markets than those based on women's traditional skills.

— Emphasise ways to improve product quality and thereby enhance potential for market acceptability and means by which the female workers involved can be given appropriate training.

— Ensure that the demands of the project do not drastically reduce the time available for women's participation in their community. Mechanisms such as double and triple shifts would allow the benefits for an income-generating project to be shared among a greater number of women within the community.

— Ensure that through women's involvement in the project, the ideology that sanctions women's traditional roles in the productive sphere, along with the corresponding technological segregation to which they are subjected, are overcome.

— Do not pretend that community income-generating projects will solve women's employment and income needs for more than a very small minority of women. They are only justified to the extent that they are part of an overall programme with women.

Research Needs

(1) Data and other knowledge about women's problems, indispensable for the definition of policy, are still lacking. The rapid development of serious research is thus an urgent need, deserving stimulation and support.

(2) Research on women has to a considerable extent employed methodological instruments such as interviews and life histories, which are of unquestionable value and interest. Nevertheless, a more systematic and critical analysis is necessary. The domestic unit should be analysed as a production unit in the poorer sectors of Ecuadorean society, and women's roles identified within this context. This contextual analysis of roles should also allow the social and economic causes that determine the feminine condition to be identified and described in detail. The relationship between the roles women perform within the family and society and socio-economic structures should be revealed and analysed.

(3) Given the fact that Ecuador is a multi-cultural country with regional and sub-regional specificities that render gross generalisations impossible, research is urgently required on a number of groups, for example peasant women of the Lowlands.

(4) Census as well as other data-collecting procedures should be refined to collect information on the women's patterns of work, focusing particularly on the mobility of the female labour force within the informal sector, its versatility, work performed within the home, etc.

(5) Statistics and other knowledge acquired through research should be made available to women's organisations in order to support their own process of awareness. Likewise, discussion of and reaction to research results should help the research process, in so far as hypotheses can be set against women's own perception of reality.

Bibliography

CONADE, 1984, *Ecuador, Lineamientos de una Estrategia para el Desarrollo*, Secretaría General de Planificación

CTE, undated, *La mujer trabajadora ecuatoriana: sus luchas y objectivos de hoy*, Folleto N°2, Departamento Nacional de la Mujer Trabajadora

Farrell, Gilda, 1984, 'Algunos aspectos sobre la implementación de proyectos productivos con mujeres en las áreas urbanas' (paper prepared for and presented at the CEIS – CEPAM Seminar)

FENOC, March–April 1984, *Lucha Campesina*

FODERUMA, 1981, 'Programa de la Mujer Campesina; antecedentes, bases operativas, programación: Segundo semestre 1981' (mimeographed)

Freire, Wilma, 1984, 'Análisis crítico al Programa de Contemplación Alimentaria Materno-Infantil' (paper prepared for and presented at the CEIS–CEPAM Seminar)

Ministerio de Agricultura y Ganadería, *Informe de la Gestión minsterial 1983–1984*

Plan Nacional de Desarrollo del Gobierno Democrático 1980–1984, Primera Parte: Los Grandes objetivos Nacionales

Rocío, Rosero, 1984, 'Las políticas nacionales de integración de la mujer al desarrollo' (paper prepared for and presented at the CEIS–CEPAM Seminar)

SEDRI, 1984, 'Situación de los Proyectos de Desarrollo Rural Integral' (mimeographed)

2

THE RESPONSE OF PUBLIC AUTHORITIES IN ITALY TO THE NEEDS EXPRESSED BY WOMEN

Daniela Colombo (Italian Association for Women in Development)
Luigi Frey and Renata Livraghi (Parma University)

Introduction

Since the end of World War II, one of the most important social changes in Italy has undoubtedly been the increasingly widespread trend among women toward individual autonomy and social impact. Analysing the key elements of this tendency — its range and pattern of development over time — is no easy task. However, two principal aspects emerge from the Italian experience over the last 30 years: women have sought autonomy through paid employment outside the home; women have aspired to have greater active participation in, and influence on, the socio-economic system through career preparation, including education and job training.

This study seeks to identify the chief characteristics of these two phenomena, and asks to what extent has the availability of employment and higher levels of career preparation allowed women to fulfil their needs. Statistical data show that the socio-economic system has not met women's needs. In fact this unsatisfactory situation has spurred women to call upon government, both local and central, to take action on a wide range of issues which affect their status. In some areas women have called upon local governments to promote programmes to improve the socio-economic system's answer to women's efforts to upgrade their position. This study focuses on two regions: Emilia-Romagna and Lombardy, with a view to giving concrete examples of how women's activism has affected government measures and to examining the diverse programmes and results obtained.

Section 1: The Female Labour Force, Job Training and Education in Italy

The Central Institute of Statistics (ISTAT) studies of the work-force from 1959 to 1966 show that though the female population rose considerably (by nearly 1.4 million) in this period, the female labour supply decreased. The female labour force activity rate (the ratio between the work-force and the general population) dropped from 28 per cent to 22 per cent, apparently indicating a trend away from labour force participation.

This situation was erroneously interpreted[1] to mean that fewer women needed a job in view of the 'positive' effects on available family income of economic development during the so-called 'Italian economic miracle'. In reality, the apparent reduction in the female work-force was the statistical outcome of profound social transformations.[2] The female supply of paid labour actually increased due to these changes. During the 1960s there was massive emigration from the South toward the central and northern regions, from the countryside to the cities; this general exodus from rural areas was linked to intensive industrialisation and urbanisation.

Within this framework women evidently ceased to work in the agricultural sector (primarily as family helpers) without, however, shifting to off-farm activities. In reality, many women would willingly have gone to work in the city, home of their newly-immigrated families. However, the 'official' labour market did not accommodate this new influx. The fact that the female unemployment rate in the mid 1960s remained roughly at the same levels as the late 1950s shows that the labour market did not adapt to women's increased participation. The clearest evidence that women were seeking paid employment outside of the family has emerged from research both on work in the home, put out by manufacturers, and on the cottage industry. These studies show that during the latter

1. G. de Meo, President of ISTAT (Central Institute of Statistics), interpreted the situation in this way: his argument was later restated and expanded in *Evoluzione e prospettive delle forze di laboro in Italia*, ISTAT, Rome, 1970.
2. See, for example, 'Occupazione e sottocuppazione femminile in Italia', *Quaderni di Economia del lavoro*, no. 3, 1975 (F. Angeli, Milan).

half of the 1960s 'unofficial' female underemployment increased tremendously in non-farming activities, especially in the major urban areas.[3]

Female labour force activity rates prior to the end of the 1960s are not a useful data source for understanding the trend toward greater economic and social autonomy; if anything, it is the other way around: the unemployment rate indicates a growing unmet need to participate. Given the mass migration of the 1960s, it is probably better to use the female employment rate in non-agricultural activities (women working in industry and the services compared to the current female population) as an indicator of increasing female labour force participation during these years, rather than general labour force activity rates.

After 1972, female labour force participation markedly increased, returning to the levels of the early 1960s. Female unemployment also rose as did 'unofficial' female underemployment. In the 1970s and the beginning of the 1980s women's labour status emerged as an increasingly important aspect of the overall employment situation in Italy; that is to say the socio-economic system's failure to meet the demand for paid employment without resorting to *ad hoc* strategies, in particular with regard to young and mature women.[4] The crisis in production following the second 'oil crisis', from 1979 onward, as well as unemployment/underemployment in industry and part of the services sector due to new technology, have widened the gap between the growing number of women looking for work and the number of women 'officially' absorbed by the labour market. Unemployed and underemployed women have been plagued by a series of problems deriving from this gap: spurred by these difficulties, they have mobilised and pressured government and the trade unions to take measures to improve the status of women in general.

3. See L. Frey, *Il Lavoro a Domicilio in Lombardia*, Giunta Regionale Lombardia, Assessorato al Lavoro e ai Movimenti Demografici, Milan, 1972, for surprising findings on this subject. A broader critical review of research on female underemployment is contained in *Quaderni di Economia del Lavoro*, no. 3, 1975. *L'Inchiesta*, an Italian journal, also offers interesting articles on this subject in various issues from 1975 onward.
4. See *Quaderni di Economia del Lavoro*, no. 3, 1977, which focuses on 'Nuovi sviluppi delle ricerche sul lavoro femminile' (New Developments in Research on Female Employment); with regard to female youth employment, see L. Frey, *La problematica del' lavoro giovanile e le sue prospettive negli anni '80*, F. Angeli, Milan, 1980.

Changes in Women's Access to Education

The rapid rise in the supply of teenage and young female wage labour during the 1970s derived in part from a veritable 'revolution' which occurred over the previous two decades. This was a giant leap forward in the participation of young Italian women in the upper levels of compulsory education (see Table 2.1), which is a fundamental aspect of the qualitative transformation of the Italian population since World War II. It has radically changed the average female educational levels; furthermore, the concentration of women in those segments of the labour supply with higher educational backgrounds has increased (resulting in a significant impact on employment patterns).

The percentage of girls in lower middle school (*scuola media inferiore*) rose from 39 per cent in 1951 to 47 per cent in 1971, finally levelling off at 48 per cent, a figure only slightly lower than their proportion in the relative age group. This gap is largely due to continuing sex discrimination in the southern regions and inner rural areas. Female participation in secondary schools (*scuola secondaria superiore*) and universities increased most dramatically during the 1960s and early 1970s. In the early 1980s, the proportion of girls in secondary schools (47 per cent) was similar to that in lower middle schools, while the figure for university attendance was only slightly less than in secondary schools (compared to 26 per cent in 1951).

As early as the mid-1970s the educational level of female youth between 6 and 14 was almost identical to that of male youth, and the level of education of young women aged 24 and under was roughly equivalent to their male counterparts, even though the female influx into the universities was smaller (see Table 2.2).

The rapid improvement in female educational levels over the last 30 years has left a series of unresolved problems:

(1) The increase in the level of schooling principally affects the younger generations; mature and older women are only marginally involved. In general, the disparity in women's educational levels has heightened the differences in their needs.

(2) Socio-cultural factors have led to the concentration of girls in certain types of education programmes rather than others.

(3) Partly due to this 'ghettoisation' in education, but above all due to an inadequate link between level of schooling and employment, women's growing expectation of greater participation in the socio-economic system has remained unsatisfied.

Table 2.1. Students and teachers in lower secondary schools, high schools, and university in Italy from 1951/52 to 1978/79

		1951–52	1961–62	1971–72	1975–76	1978–79	1980–81
Lower secondary schools	MF	795.720	1.539.026	2.286.850	2.778.597	2.923.074	2.884.779
— pupils	F	312.766	650.860	1.071.589	1.321.447	1.395.772	1.375.370
	% F	39.3	42.3	46.9	47.6	47.8	47.7
high schools	MF	416.348	839.995	1.732.178	2.096.582	2.347.224	2.433.230
— students	F	156.060	311.478	727.460	929.813	1.100.911	1.174.807
	% F	37.5	37.1	42.0	44.3	46.9	48.3
of which: vocational schools	MF	36.072	123.586	275.458	347.593	419.922	448.119
— students	F	9.966	41.698	117.647	157.203	192.585	206.891
	% F	27.6	33.7	42.7	45.2	45.9	46.2
Technical colleges	MF	133.064	359.757	720.326	932.003	1.057.938	1.081.014
— students	F	26.555	80.320	183.043	290.361	374.031	402.620
	% F	20.0	22.3	25.4	31.2	35.4	37.2
Commercial technical colleges	MF	64.388	159.273	254.216	391.897	504.204	533.344
— students	F	19.111	59.507	134.666	217.546	284.853	302.180
	% F	29.7	37.4	53.0	55.5	56.5	56.7
of which: teacher training schools	MF	2.203	6.137	22.330	27.330	30.404	30.794
— students	F	2.203	6.137	22.330	27.330	30.404	30.794
	% F	100.0	100.0	100.0	100.0	100.0	100.0
Teacher training colleges	MF	79.467	113.872	184.847	171.096	189.504	206.677
— students	F	65.805	99.832	163.356	155.831	176.107	192.514
	% F	82.8	87.7	88.4	91.1	92.9	93.1

Lycees for science							
— students	MF	39.746	67.955	280.293	360.090	265.251	353.224
	F	7.042	13.361	106.785	149.235	155.274	151.798
	% F	17.7	19.7	38.1	41.4	42.5	43.0
Lycees for the humanities							
— students	MF	120.067	150.171	203.950	190.874	196.942	205.943
	F	42.998	61.583	107.522	104.798	109.800	117.903
	% F	35.8	41.0	52.7	54.9	55.8	57.3
Lycees for the arts							
— students	MF	1.689	4.324	21.367	25.083	22.837	21.304
	F	907	2.954	13.635	16.164	14.873	14.098
	% F	53.7	68.3	63.8	64.4	65.1	66.2
University							
— enrolled students	MF	226.543	287.975	759.872	935.795	1.032.559	1.037.874
	F	59.693	59.520	285.247	367.780	431.963	452.825
	% F	26.3	27.6	37.5	39.3	41.8	43.6

Source: ISTAT, *Annuario statistico dell' istruzione, 1982,* tomo I, Roma, 1984. Our Calculations

Table 2.2. Level of schooling by categories of age and sex — situation on 1 January 1976

	male	female	male and female
	School population		
6 – 10 years	2.297.704	2.219.932	4.517.836
6 – 13 years	3.706.315	3.525.403	7.231.718
6 – 18 years	4.939.475	4.557.671	9.497.146
6 – 24 years	5.512.971	4.881.513	10.394.484
14 – 18 years	1.233.160	1.032.268	2.265.428
14 – 24 years	1.806.656	1.356.110	3.162.766
19 – 24 years	573.496	323.842	897.338
	Total population		
6 – 10 years	2.354.820	2.241.005	4.595.825
6 – 13 years	3.771.165	3.589.426	7.360.591
6 – 18 years	5.490.710	5.658.459	11.599.169
6 – 24 years	8.311.669	7.950.861	16.262.530
14 – 18 years	2.169.545	2.069.033	4.238.578
14 – 24 years	4.540.504	4.361.435	8.901.939
19 – 24 years	2.370.959	2.292.402	4.663.361
	Schooling levels		
6 – 10 years	97.6	99.1	98.3
6 – 13 years	98.3	98.2	98.2
6 – 18 years	83.1	80.5	81.9
6 – 24 years	66.3	61.4	63.9
14 – 18 years	56.8	49.9	53.4
14 – 24 years	39.8	31.1	35.5
19 – 24 years	24.2	14.1	19.2

N.B. The schooling levels (percentage ratio between school population and total population) have been calculated for the most important age groups: 6–10 (Elementary School), 6–14 (compulsory school), 14–18 (High School), 19 –24 (mainly university attendance), 6–18 (Primary and Secondary School), 6–24 (general levels). To this end, the school population in the different classes recorded at the beginning of the 1975–76 school year was divided by age according to the situation specified in the source.

Source: ISTAT, "Eistribuzione per età della popolazione scolastica", Note e Relazione, n. 54, Rome, August 1976.

Table 2.3. Population — 14 years and over — by level of education, age and sex

	thousands of units					% of comparison				
	14 – 19 years	20 – 24 years	25 – 29 years	30 – 59 years	60 and over	14 – 19 years	20 – 24 years	25 – 29 years	30 – 59 years	60 and over
Men Total	2.758	2.021	1.809	10.979	4.668	100.0	100.0	100.0	100.0	100.0
No diploma or elementary certificate	380	230	342	5.896	3.792	13.8	11.4	18.9	53.7	81.4
Middle School certificate	2.220	951	774	2.836	471	80.5	47.1	42.8	25.8	10.8
High School certificate	158	830	584	1.606	249	7.7	41.1	32.3	14.6	5.3
Degree		10	110	641	156		0.4	6.1	5.8	3.7
Women Total	2.701	2.068	1.905	11.361	5.823	100.0	100.0	100.0	100.0	100.0
No diploma or elementary certificate	329	287	477	7.333	5.169	12.2	13.9	25.2	64.5	88.5
Middle School certificate	2.147	899	773	2.384	410	79.5	43.5	40.8	21.0	7.6
High School certificate	225	868	554	1.261	200	8.3	42.0	29.2	41.1	3.4
Degree		14	101	383	44		0.6	5.3	3.4	0/8

Source: ISTAT, 'Rilevazione delle forze di lavoro — medie 1983', Supplemento del *Bolletino mensile di Statistica*, 1984, n. 3.

As to the first point: as late as 1983, a high percentage of persons over the age of 30 had not even finished elementary school (i.e., the minimum level of compulsory education established some years ago).

With regard to the second: an analysis of data on girls' participation in secondary education provides interesting findings. Between the 1950s and the 1970s the concentration of female students in vocational secondary schools (*istituti professionali e tecnici commerciali*) as well as in classical and scientific preparatory schools (*licei classici* and *scientifici*) has considerably increased; in fact, during this period, sizeable variations are noticeable in the distribution of the general student population in such schools. The overall student population in the public vocational schools (*istituti professionali*) roughly doubled between 1950 and 1970; at the same time the growth in the female student population more than covered this overall increase, particularly in the business schools (*istituto commerciali*): in the school year 1971/72 16 per cent of girls enrolled in upper secondary schools were attending business school. A similar trend occurred in the scientific preparatory schools: while the overall student population in these schools more than doubled between the early 1960s and the early 1970s, the female student population rose from roughly 4 per cent to 15–16 per cent, a startling increase. In the technical business schools (*istituti tecnici commerciali*) since the late 1960s, girls have comprised more than 50 per cent of enrolment. In fact, even though male enrolment has declined, the total number of students among the secondary schools has not due to the increased number of girls. However, with regard to the classical preparatory schools (*licei classici*) the appreciable rise in the female student population, from 36 per cent in 1951 to over 55 per cent in the 1970s, has not been sufficient to offset the decline in male student enrolment; indeed, the proportion of students in these schools with respect to the overall student population has fallen from 29 per cent in 1951 to 12 per cent in 1971. This downward trend has continued.

Considerable shifts in overall proportions have occurred since 1950, especially in the proportion of female students. The highest concentration of female students is to be found in the elementary teacher-training schools (*istituti magistrali*). The concentration of female students in the art schools (*istituti e licei artistici*) has also increased; female students have even made inroads with the traditional male citadels — technical and engineering schools. On the whole, female enrolment in secondary schools has increased, including those schools with a traditionally high male enrolment. Nowadays almost 50 per cent of all high-school graduates are female; the percentages are even greater not only in schools with traditionally high female enrolment — girls' technical institutes, elementary teachers' training schools, linguistic *lycées* (*istituti tecnici femminili, scuole ed istituti magistrali,* and *licei linguistici*) — but also in technical institutes, tourism schools, classical preparatory schools and artistic institutes/*lycées* (*istituti tecnici commerciali, istituti per il turismo, licei classici* and *istituti/licei artistici*). This has had an important impact on the labour market for high-school graduates.

On the one hand, there is a tendency for young women almost immediately after graduation to enter segments of the white-collar labour market which are already full to capacity, e.g. elementary- and middle-school humanities teachers; on the other, there is a tendency to compete with male high-school graduates in fields where technical, business-school graduates are preferred by employers (for example, as bank clerks and in services for firms), as until recently there was a fair labour demand in these areas. A slight decrease is now visible due to new technologies. This second trend has contributed greatly to making some of the contradictions of the Italian labour market visible, in particular with regard to sex discrimination and relations between women with different levels of education.

There is also a growing number of female high-school graduates who go on to university, postponing their entrance into the labour market, as compared with young men, who have always opted to a greater degree simultaneously to work and study. Up until the early 1970s the increase in female university students was mainly concentrated in 4 departments: the Humanities and Education Departments (*Facoltà di Lettere/Filosofia* and *Magistero*), where high-school graduates predominantly from classic *lycées* and teaching schools/institutes (*licei classici* and *scuole/istituti magistrali*) tended to enrol, and the Sciences and Pharmaceutical Sciences Departments, where graduates of scientific college preparatory schools (*licei scientifici*) tended to enrol. In Sciences they opted in particular for biological sciences, mathematics, physics and natural sciences. Furthermore, a fair number of female high-school graduates entered the Departments of Law, Political Science, Medicine and Surgery, Economics and Business Administration; finally, increasing numbers of students of both sexes entered other departments.

During the 1970s, due both to the easing of university entrance requirements at the end of the 1960s and to the gradual pressure exerted by employment constraints, there was a considerable drop-off in enrolment in some departments. Indeed a strong trend away from certain majors was evident, the behaviour of female students being an important determinant. Enrolment fell off most sharply in the Education Department (*Magistero* — which offers majors in the humanities and in pedagogy); this department was already over-crowded in the 1960s, being the natural choice for female students graduating from teachers' schools (*istituti magistrali*). The second largest decline occurred in the Humanities Department (*Lettere e Filosofia*), followed by several majors offered under the Sciences Department, which experienced a relative slump during the 1970s. Thanks to the new regulations easing entrance requirements, gradu-ates of both sexes from technical high schools (*istituti tecnici*) now had access to departments previously open only to students with classical preparatory-school diplomas (for example, the Department of Law), or to those with a diploma from scientific *lycées* (*licei scientifici*), (e.g., the Departments of Medicine and Engineering). In short, high-school graduates coming out of a variety of institutes were able to choose from a much wider range of university depart-ments.

None the less, by the close of the 1970s a considerable proportion of the female university population was still opting for typical female dominated degrees: in fields mainly leading to careers in teaching at the junior- and high-school level (*scuola media e secon-daria superiore*). In the academic year 1979/80 approximately 38 per cent of female students (see Table 2.4) were enrolled in the Human-ities, Education and Foreign Language Departments (*Lettere/ Magistero/Lingue*), while only 13 per cent were enrolled in the Department of Sciences (*Scienze*). Female enrolment in Medicine, Economics, Business Administration, Political Sciences and Law is gradually increasing; in fact the concentration of female students in these disciplines is now equal to, or greater than, one-third of the total female university population. The shift towards engineering, industrial chemistry, agrarian sciences and veterinary sciences is occurring at a slower pace. Engineering is a particularly significant example: at the end of the 1970s only 3 per cent of the students enrolled in this department were women. Nevertheless, given the increased enrolment of girls in industrial technical high schools (*istituti tecnici industriali*), and scientific preparatory schools (*licei scientifici*), and given the new job opportunities opened up by new technologies, there is bound to be a rise in female enrolment in

Table 2.4 University students during academic year 1979–80[a]

	Total		Those who have failed to graduate				Composition %	
	F	MF	% F/MF	F	MF	% F/MF	M	F
Mathematics, Physics, Natural, Sciences	56.528	106.851	52.9	16.368	30.372	53.9	8.5	12.8
Navigations	25	273	9.2	4	42	9.5	0.0	0.0
Industrial Chemistry	81	381	21.3	17	13	15.0	0.1	0.0
Pharmaceutics	17.245	29.834	57.8	4.349	8.232	52.8	2.1	3.9
Medicine and Surgery	60.702	179.929	33.7	10.303	39.883	25.8	20.1	13.7
Engineering	3.282	88.125	3.7	530	25.357	2.1	14.3	0.7
Architecture	16.427	59.996	28.8	2.969	11.600	25.6	6.8	3.7
Agricultural sciences	5.403	26.462	20.4	825	6.090	13.6	3.6	1.2
Veterinary medicine	3.035	13.839	21.9	214	1.859	11.5	1.8	0.7
Economics and commerce	30.064	96.362	31.2	4.168	19.144	21.8	11.2	6.8
Economical sciences and banking	782	3.396	23.0	86	613	14.0	0.4	0.2
Economical and social sciences	346	908	38.1	53	144	36.8	0.1	0.1
Maritime economics	131	595	22.0	22	127	17.3	0.1	0.0
Statistics, Demography	901	2.583	34.9	241	884	27.3	0.3	0.2
Sociology	724	1.759	41.2	228	703	27.3	0.2	0.2
Political Science	11.848	35.269	33.6	3.063	10.718	28.6	4.0	2.7
Law	58.691	148.236	39.6	12.812	40.536	31.6	15.1	13.3
Letters	72.776	105.670	68.9	20.947	30.484	68.7	5.5	16.4
Literature	83.153	105.358	78.9	26.989	34.433	78.4	3.7	18.8
Languages and foreign literature	12.539	16.172	77.5	3.311	4.326	76.5	0.6	2.8
Physical education	7.930	16.878	47.0	955	2.497	38.2	1.5	1.8
Total	442.613	1.035.876	43.0	108.454	268.157	40.4	100.0	100.0

[a] foreign students included

Source: See Table 2.1, our calculations

traditionally male departments. Italy should soon begin to reach the average levels of female enrolment in these disciplines encountered in other industrialised countries both inside and outside of Europe.

These changes in university studies have already had an impact on the flow of graduates. In 1952 there was a total of 20,606 students, 6,483 of whom were women; by 1979 the total number had climbed to 76,061 of which over 43 per cent were women.

A substantial increase in the job market in teaching and other tertiary sector activities (such as health professions, banking, and other private and public services) prevented a rise in unemployment and underemployment among university graduates as early as the 1970s, similar to the situation of Italian high-school graduates and of university graduates in other industrialised countries (such as Great Britain, despite the rigorous entrance requirements and specific student quotas in force). Unemployment rates of university graduates grew at a slower pace than had been predicted in the early 1970s, which was due to the fact that the flow of graduates did not increase as much as expected (for various reasons, partly connected to the new phenomenon of the student/worker).

At any rate, the high schools and university degrees mainly chosen by female students have certainly been responsible for deluding women's hopes for more active participation which motivated them (and their families) to seek higher education in the first place.

The 1981 population census registered 433,000 women with high-school diplomas and 65,000 female university graduates looking for jobs. These figures are equivalent to 59 per cent of all unemployed holders of diplomas and 61 per cent of all unemployed graduates. The number of unemployed women with high levels of education has risen since, and the general short-term trend is upward. Together with other unemployed women with lower educational levels, these women are an important 'structural' aspect of the unemployment problem in Italy, and are even more important when considering sexual equality. However, this does not alter the fact[5] that the quest for higher education on the part of women is an important step forward towards a greater potential participation in the socio-economic system. Due to this, many women have become more competitive on the labour market, with respect to female, as well as to male workers.

The repercussions of the past difficulties regarding female unem-

5. See R. Livraghi's article 'Formazione e parità tra i sessi', *Notiziario CERES di Economia del Lavoro*, no. 4, 2 April 1984.

ployment occupations (and unsatisfied expectations) could probably have been reduced if there had been some sort of general strategy, involving the direct participation of women, aimed at linking the new transformations in education to the structural evolution of the productive system.

The Contribution of Teachers and Families Towards the 'Feminisation' of the Quest for Education

Education policies in Italy during the last 30 years have aimed at providing compulsory education up to 14 years for all (leading, wherever possible, to the lower-middle-school certificate, *licenza media inferiore*), as well as at increasing the availability of high-school and university education. However, no specific differentiation between the sexes was made. The teaching staff, particularly in high schools and universities, have played a fundamental role in implementing these policies. Without doubt, they played an important part in encouraging young women to go onto higher education and in not obstructing the influx of female students into the higher realms of education in any way. Evidence of this is given by the data on the percentage of girls passing their secondary-school exams (*scuola secondaria superiore*), which on average was higher than the percentage of boys. Probably influential is the generally high proportion of women teachers in secondary schools despite the relatively low proportion of headmistresses with respect to headmasters. At the beginning of 1980, the proportion was 18.9 per cent in the State vocational schools (*Istituti professionali di Stato*), 14.1 per cent in scientifically based *lycées* (*licei scientifici*), and in teacher-training schools (*scuole magistrali*), 11.8 per cent in technical business schools (*istituti tecnici commerciali*), and only 6.6 per cent in technical industrial-training schools (*istituti tecnici industriali*). In Italian schools, the headteacher has much influence.

In most regions parents have exhorted their daughters to go into higher education in order to improve their general culture, even though the professional or job prospects were not particularly encouraging. However, the influence of family members still dominated by old prejudices, has led to an excessive 'specialisation' of the subjects studied by girls,[6] and has thus increased the gap between the expectations of young, highly educated women and their effec-

6. See Livraghi in *Quaderni di Economia del Lavoro*, no. 23, 1984.

tive job prospects.

Some teachers, aware of the increasing gap between expectations and the real prospects of their female students[7] have attempted to counteract this in two ways (despite the opposition of public officials and headteachers):

— experimenting with new forms of educative techniques, regarding both structure and content;
— introducing initiatives aimed at guiding the scholastic and professional formation of the pupils.

Interesting experiments have been carried out (especially over the last 15 years) both in secondary schools and universities. In the secondary schools, there is generally a conventional distinction between 'maxi-experiments' (involving the entire structure and content of a whole year's course) and 'mini-experiments' (limited to teaching methods used for one or other of the subjects included in the traditional curriculum). During the 1982/3 academic year, 487 experiments (of which 222 were 'maxi' and 265 'mini') were accepted by the Ministry of Public Instruction, i.e. 6.5 per cent of all the scholastic units included in secondary education. These experiments have a three-fold purpose: to form the basis of general secondary-school reform, under discussion for many years; to provide a closer link between the school and the labour market; and, to take account of the specific problems of female students.

The lack of a clear strategy is also seen on examining teachers' initiatives regarding scholastic and professional guidance. However, the regional or local authorities have already indicated their aim of producing coordinated strategies for programming schooling, and of organising talks about jobs and professions. In order to demonstrate the utility, and the limitations, of this type of project, we will examine 2 regional experiments which have achieved notable results in this field over the last few years. The experiments were carried out in Lombardy and in Emilia-Romagna, 2 regions which:

(a) have experienced problems of female employment during the 1970s and early 1980s, especially of women holding diplomas or degrees;
(b) have attempted under pressure from women's organisations and associations (linked to political parties and social movements) to help present and future female workers;

7. In the less privileged classes, this is the case for both boys and girls.

(c) have attempted to put into practice a system of scholastic and professional guidance.

As well as these regional projects, other useful examples are to be found in the initiatives of the provinces and municipalities around Milan (a typical example of a 'metropolitan' city) in Lombardy, as well as the experience of Parma (in Emilia-Romagna), an urban centre of much smaller proportions.

Section 2: Women and Educational and Vocational Guidance Programmes in Lombardy and Emilia-Romagna

In Italy, the responsibility for vocational guidance has been gradually transferred from the State to the regions during the 1970s. Each region has formulated its own regulations for, and definition of, vocational guidance. In the province of Parma, for example, guidance is aimed at providing information, and keeping the teachers up to date. Greatest attention is given to the lower middle schools because it is here that pupils must decide on their educational and professional future. The organisation of vocational guidance services is the most confused and weakest sector in the field of education. Analysis of regional laws shows a lack of coherence at the national level.

(a) In many cases legislation is insufficient: many regional laws only mention guidance, without covering the actual organisation of the service.

(b) Several regions prefer to use proposals, regulations, official statements to regulate initiatives rather than legislation.

(c) Regions employ a great variety of operative solutions: regional and provincial centres, delegation to intermediate local authorities pilot experiments, which make comparison difficult.

(d) Regional legislation does not permit delegation to private agencies, which, on a local level, have been very active in providing vocational guidance.

(e) There is a sharp distinction between the ordinary and the special statute regions. In the latter there is a more active State presence (Ministry for Labour, Enpi), in the organisation of vocational guidance.

(f) Vocational guidance is organised by region, yet schools are grouped into 'districts', creating problems in coordination.

For these reasons there is an urgent need for a national legislative framework, capable of coordinating the activities and the various responsibilities of the regions, defining their responsibilities, and establishing links between national, regional, and local organisations.

Until now, only a few regions have attempted to define the professional qualifications of vocational guidance officers. In Tuscany, the main body of vocational guidance services, run by the Provincial Councils consists of teams of 6 officers including: pedagogues and experts in teaching methods; sociologists; economists/statisticians; secretary and public relations expert in the use of graphics and audio-visuals, plus office staff. Use will also be made of external consultants. In Lombardy, vocational guidance is entrusted to the Centres for Technical and Educational Innovation (CITE). CITE personnel also provide many other educative and technical services. The teams include 'social and educational operators', corresponding to the professions of social workers, experts in educational and vocational guidance, researchers, pedagogues and audio-visual experts.

In virtually no case is there any specific reference to vocational guidance for women.[8] This is due to the lack of the concept of effective sexual equality in Italy.

Section 3: National Machinery for Equality

The National Committee for Equal Employment Opportunities (NCEEO) was formed by the Ministry for Labour and Social Security only in December 1983. To date the Committee's activities have consisted of: analysis (and consequent disapproval) of the current situation of work for women; furthering the application of the law on equality; favouring the introduction of Equality Advisors into regional Commissions, as described in Law No. 862, passed in December 1984.

In Italy, the respective treatment of men and women is fairly satisfactory, if compared to many other countries. However, there are still differences between the gross earnings of the two sexes, and between the various sectors of economic activity and professional

---

8. The only region to specifically mention vocational guidance for women in their definition of vocational guidance is the region of Piedmont.

qualification (see Table 2.5 and 2.6). Furthermore, legislation on women's conditions (especially regarding employment) is still inadequate, and is still less adequately applied. Low penalties are imposed upon violators of this law, and court interventions in this field have been unsatisfactory, control or prevention of discrimination has been lacking, and information and assistance necessary for women to be able to accede to their right to equality, as defined by the law,[9] has been lacking. In Italian legislation there is no section aimed at putting 'equal opportunities' into practice nor any administrative procedure — positive actions — designed to help bring this about. However, during the last few years, there have been attempts to formulate real solutions to this problem.

The Equality Advisor

The Equality Advisor, a newly created post at a regional level, is entrusted with the task of coordinating the activities of the NCEEO and local authorities. In comparing the experiences of other countries, the NCEEO noted that even at the EEC level, information on Advisors and their activities is incomplete and confused. Given the interest in the potential of Equality Advisors, the European Commission is currently organising a detailed evaluation of Equality Advisors in different countries.

A preliminary study showed that: (a) Equality Advisors only exist as such in Denmark, though in France a similar function, operating on a regional basis, has recently been established; (b) in many countries, though Equality Advisors do not exist as such, government institutions doing much the same job do already exist; (c) in several countries, there have been private initiatives in this field. In Europe, the most significant activity of this type is to be observed in Holland. The United States and Canada also have similar institutions.

From this the NCEEO has drawn several conclusions: (1) in France, personnel who are to fill this function will preferably have a background of involvement in the 'problem of equality' between the sexes: furthermore, people without experience of public administration are preferred to those directly involved with generalised policies on labour. The advisors depend directly on the Ministry for

9. See M.V. Ballestreto, 'Legge di parita e discriminazione del lavoro femminile', in M.V. Ballestreto, L. Frey, R. Livraghi, G.C. Mariani, *Lavoro femminile, formazione e parita uomo/donna*, F. Angeli, Milan, 1983.

Table 2.5 Indices of yearly gross renumeration of women according to the branch of economic activity and qualification (men's renumeration = 100,000)

Class of economic activity	Manage-ment	clerical workers					blue-collar workers		
		1st class	2nd class	3rd 4th 5th levels	Intermediate	High level	Intermediate	low	Average
Energy water gas									
— men	100.0	100.0	100.0	100.0	100.0	100.0	100.0	100.0	100.0
— women	74.4	92.6	89.9	82.9	80.2	101.4	96.5	90.1	93.9
transformation industry									
— men	100.0	100.0	100.0	100.0	100.0	100.0	100.0	100.0	100.0
— women	80.7	86.5	87.5	87.0	79.5	76.9	80.6	80.4	71.9
Mineral industry									
— men	100.0	100.0	100.0	100.0	100.0	100.0	100.0	100.0	100.0
— women	82.1	84.4	89.2	87.1	78.7	81.2	86.1	84.1	86.0
Metallurgic industry and transports									
— men	100.0	100.0	100.0	100.0	100.0	100.0	100.0	100.0	100.0
— women	82.1	89.1	89.5	89.9	80.6	83.7	87.4	95.3	92.9
Chemical industry									
— men	100.0	100.0	100.0	100.0	100.0	100.0	100.0	100.0	100.0
— women	81.5	87.4	90.6	81.6	83.9	81.3	83.7	87.8	87.5
Clothes leathers industry									
— men	100.0	100.0	100.0	100.0	100.0	100.0	100.0	100.0	100.0
— women	72.6	79.5	85.9	91.4	85.9	83.0	83.2	81.8	71.3
Food industry									
— men	100.0	100.0	100.0	100.0	100.0	100.0	100.0	100.0	100.0

— women	89.4	88.9	85.5	89.7	81.9	82.8	81.6	80.1	79.1
Others									
— men	100.0	100.0	100.0	100.0	100.0	100.0	100.0	100.0	100.0
— women	101.9	83.2	80.0	82.3	91.4	81.7	86.8	87.7	74.1
Construction industry									
— men	100.0	100.0	100.0	100.0	100.0	100.0	100.0	100.0	100.0
— women	73.8	90.0	92.3	93.4	83.8	95.7	92.6	73.1	86.9
Industry									
— men	100.0	100.0	100.0	100.0	100.0	100.0	100.0	100.0	100.0
— women	79.6	85.5	87.0	85.9	79.2	75.6	79.1	81.9	71.1

Source: Annuario di Statistiche del Lavoro — 1983, Bonn, 1984

Women's Rights, and, on a local level, work together with the decentralised Ministry of Labour structures. In Denmark, a central feature of the activity of the Advisors is their attention to positive policies aimed at eliminating sexual discrimination within the work-force. Emphasis is given to professional training and employment of women in traditionally male dominated jobs. (2) A detailed comparative study is needed of the relations between functions and institutions in other countries. According to the suggestions of the NCEEO, Equality Advisors could well carry out some of the functions, that in other countries are controlled by a complex system of equal opportunities organisations. (3) The private management activity of Equality Advisors, observed mainly in those countries with a long history of equality legislation and culture, was judged to be particularly interesting. It is possible to learn much from this type of experience, in order to incorporate the more interesting features into future public intervention. This type of 'copying' is typical of 'late starter' countries, and follows the classic model of the relation between private initiative and public intervention in the field of economic development.

The NCEEO has defined the responsibilities of Equality Advisors working with the Regional Commissions for Employment in furtherance of the rights, in cooperation with the aforementioned commissions and the NCEEO. These responsibilities may be defined as follows:

(1) Information
— Equality Advisors may request information from the Regional Employment Commissions (CRI), and from the regional offices of the Ministry for Labour, in the following subjects:
   — available data on employment;
   — vocational training programmes and current activity;
   — job training programmes.
— Equality Advisors, in conjunction with Regional Labour Market Observers, the Ministry for Labour, and the NCEEO will prepare data specifically regarding female employment;
— Equality Advisors may request information from the various Unions on contracts, even at company level, wherever problems regarding equality may be occurring.

(2) Inspection
Equality Advisors may, together with the CRI, and using informa-

Table 2.6 Annual gross earnings indices for women according to class of economic activity and qualification (Men's earnings = 100)

Class of economic activity	Management			Blue– and white–collar workers			Average
sex	Level A	Level B	1st Level	2nd Level	3rd and 4th Levels	6th and 7th Levels	
Wholesale commerce							
Men	100.0	100.0	100.0	100.0	100.0	100.0	100.0
Women	75.5	72.5	80.0	79.3	84.8	69.2	68.8
Retail commerce							
Men	100.0	100.0	100.0	100.0	100.0	100.0	100.0
Women	84.0	81.3	83.4	86.3	81.6	83.0	74.2
Commerce							
Men	100.0	100.0	100.0	100.0	100.0	100.0	100.0
Women	74.6	74.9	79.8	80.7	80.1	72.5	59.4
Credit							
Men	100.0	100.0	100.0	100.0	100.0	100.0	100.0
Women	50.0	76.4	87.4	88.9	79.8	53.1	74.8
Insurance							
Men	100.0	100.0	100.0	100.0	100.0	100.0	100.0
Women	72.1	77.9	97.3	96.5	100.7	88.7	91.3

Source: ISTAT, *Annuario di Statistiche del Lavoro — 1983*

tion provided by the Council of Labour Market Observers, organise inspections on:
— the effective application of equality legislation;
— the effective application of the priority lists for giving jobs to the unemployed;
— the numbers of workers given jobs on an individual basis, comparing the ratio between the sexes of these new workers with the proportions existing within the entire labour market;
— on the job training contracts (ensuring a correct sex ratio, as above;
— vocational training, including that carried out on a company basis.
— in certain cases, inspections may be carried out on single companies, after consulting the NCEEO, and with the collaboration of the Labour Inspectorate.

(3) Evaluation
— Equality Advisors have the right to express their opinions and evaluations of all the cases mentioned in (2) above.
— The Equality Advisor will inform the CRI, which, in turn, will inform the Council of Labour Market Observers, in the case of any particular problems needing a more detailed analysis or direct inspection.

(4) Positive action
— Equality Advisors may make proposals for positive action in the fields of training, insertion into the labour market and women's careers, to the NCEEO.
— Together with the CRI and the Council of Labour Market Observers, Equality Advisors may propose specific projects to introduce women into traditionally male dominated jobs.

(5) Coordination
Equality Advisors are to inform the NCEEO of any regional initiatives, and are responsible for carrying out the initiatives of the NCEEO within the regions.

(6) Informing the public
— Equality Advisors are to inform women of their legal rights in the field of work, using written and audio-visual material, as well as mass-media campaigns (as in France). They should

work in close collaboration with the NCEEO;
— information on the women's rights and working prospects
should be specifically prepared for women of various different
age groups and social backgrounds.

Young girl students will be approached through schools and
vocational guidance organisations (as in Denmark); while 'hinge
courses' (such as those used in Canada) will be prepared for adult
women excluded from the labour market. The CRE and regional
offices of the Labour Ministry will publicise the admission standards for those wishing to participate in training courses for potential Equality Advisors. The commissions will submit a list of chosen
candidates to the NCEEO which will define the maximum and
minimum number of places available and their regional distribution
and organise a training course for the candidates. The general
administration of the course will be in the hands of a Labour
Ministry representative and one or more experts from the NCEEO.
At the end of the course, a list of successful candidates will be
communicated to the Ministry.

Section 4: Regional Machinery with Women: The Link between the 'Demand' Coming from Women and the 'Supply' Offered by the Institutions

Of the 2 regions covered by our study a Women's Regional Consultative Body (*Consulta Femminile Regionale*) (WRCB) exists only
in Lombardy, while it has recently been proposed to set up a
regional commission for equal opportunities in Emilia-Romagna. In
Lombardy, the WRCB was founded as an interparty group including members from political parties, trade unions, women's associations. It will advise on legislation and any initiatives regarding the
female condition, and ensure the effective application of the principle of social equality as stated in the Constitution of the Republic
and in the Regional Statute.

(a) Responsibilities
Its main responsibilities are:
— to make proposals for surveys and research on the conditions
of women in Lombardy, to be carried out by the competent
authorities; the organisation of meetings, conventions, semi-

nars, conferences and publications;
— to put forward proposals regarding new regional laws on women's condition, as well as evaluate proposals made by the Regional Council and Government;
— evaluate the level of application of laws on women's conditions;
— collaborate with similar regional organisations so as to coordinate activity;
— to collect and publicise all information on women's conditions and to ensure the best possible use of existing sources of information.

(b) New tasks

The Regional Law of 1984 includes one major principle, the result of years of political struggle for women's rights, which had been excluded from the first version of the law: 'The local Government and the Regional Council through their permanent consultative Commissions, must accept the views of the Consultative Body'.

This means that in Lombardy, the regional authorities, where women are in a minority (3 out of 80 members of the Regional Council) are obliged to accept all decisions made by the Consultative Body regarding any matter concerned with women's conditions. Women now have an institutionally recognised role in matters concerning them, where previously they had no say. The law also envisages a Women's Office, which is to provide organisational and logistical support to the initiatives and activity of the Consultative Body, which in the past was often unable to take any effective action.

Once more, despite the reigning climate of political apathy as regards women's rights, women have reacted, taking the ideal of the Consultative Body as a stimulus for a new wave of activity. This ideal is the capacity of women to organise themselves institutionally and, despite being dispersed throughout the country, to coordinate discussion and bring continual pressure to bear on all the formal institutional levels of patriarchal society. The women members of the *Consulta* often stress the difficulties they encounter as a result of typical male stubbornness, generally stemming from a complete ignorance of women's problems. Now officially recognised, the members of the Body have decided to widen their coverage and strengthen their presence, so as to promote further progress. This is increasingly necessary, due to the present crisis of the place of women in work, in public life and in society in general.

(c) Information
A survey has been made of all the women's associations in Lombardy, regardless of whether they were formed for cultural, social, or political purposes. Members of the Consultative Body have travelled throughout Lombardy, introducing women to its work, discussing their problems, and describing decisions made. It is through these meetings the Consultative Body intends to learn from the present situation, and from any new or positive aspect they may have missed. It is hoped that the Consultancy Body will be considered as a focal point by women who want to work.

(d) Networking
The Consultative Body aims at contacting the main social and political women's organisations in Lombardy to arrange a series of conferences in each province. This will permit the development and extension of a network of local organisations which will give Lombardy women a voice, and will help coordinate and aggregate the numerous local levels of political and social activity, which presents a variety and richness of experience not often recognised even by the women themselves.

(e) Policy directions
The Consultative Body will act as a link between the 'demand' coming from women and the 'supply' offered by the institutions. The Consultative Body intends to pay great attention to the social and health sectors, particularly at the degree of application of the regional plans for health and social assistance. The definitive version of the Regional Health Plan cannot be agreed without the approval of the Consultative Body. The fundamental aspects of the Plan are as follows:
— implementation of the hospital programme, especially concerning the reorganisation of the network of hospitals, evening out health standards; introducing day-hospitals;
— a project for maternity and infant care, assistance for children in hospital, etc.;
— health personnel policies;
— regional plan for emergencies and epidemics;
— finalised research projects;
— health education programmes;

— social and sanitary assistance for the mentally ill;
— assistance programmes for drug addicts.

An internal study group within the Consultative Body will examine the proposed 'Reorganisation of, and programmes for, social services in the Region of Lombardy'. The opinion of the Consultative Body will be of particular significance, as this law should respond to all the requirements that were at the centre of women's battles over the last few years, ranging from health advice centres to nurseries and child care centres.

Another priority sector will be commerce (the Plan for Commerce is currently under renewal). Women constitute the majority of employees in and users of this sector of the economy, and, as such, should be able to make proposals regarding the distribution of commerce, opening hours of shops, and, above all, on price control.

The Consultative Body will also be involved in drawing up the Plan for the Development of Tourism in Lombardy, and in the debate on the artisan sector. Furthermore, in the debate on territorial reorganisation women have a right to voice their opinions and play a role in decisions which affect urban policies and the future of the cities. At present, all territorial programmes are in crisis, due to the separation between institutional planning and real development processes.

The very characteristics of planning, its simplification of the problems, and its long-term nature, mean that it is unable to respond to individual situations or to grasp the interdependency between various aspects. Furthermore, it acts as a brake to progress: the ratio between inhabitants and services, between industrial destinations and employment, transport, etc.

If one starts from the assumption that the planning and programming capacity of the authorities is, by its very nature, inadequate, it is necessary to try to find more precise, but flexible methods of meeting the various expressed requirements and needs of all real situations in which women want to play a leading role.

(f) A Map of Requirements
The members of the Consultative Body agreed on the necessity of preparing a 'map' of requirements, containing the priority needs of particular communities (district, urban centre or province) in order to rationalise the use of resources, and to provide the best possible response to the requirements of the society, thus producing a

reorganisation of the whole region which gives the greatest possible benefits.

The activity of the Consultative Body will not, in future, be limited to control of current legislation, but will furnish concrete operational proposals on issues of interest to women. The Consultative Body is particularly interested in keeping up with what is happening within women's groups of various kinds. Within the trade unions, groups for coordinating the activity of various categories now exist; in the world of 'culture', there are women's bookshops, clubs with female or feminist based interests, as well as the associations which actually form part of the Consultative Body. Their objective is to give women the opportunity of voicing their opinions and problems, and to establish a common approach to the problem of women's condition. In this way, it is hoped that some progress may be made towards constructing what some call a 'women's own world', in which the Consultative Body plays a small, but significant, part.

Women have great ambitions, but limited means of achieving them. The small number of women in government institutions and indirectly elected bodies limits the use of alliances. Women still remain in the position of intermediaries between the world at large and public administration. For these reasons, the Consultative Body has always encouraged women to vote for women and organised a demonstration on this before the last European elections, which received heavy press and television coverage. This type of activity will certainly be renewed before the forthcoming administrative elections. Most of the women interviewed by the Consultative Body emphasise the difficulties of bringing women and politics together. Political activity has always been seen by women, as foreign to their nature and incompatible with their private and public lives. Rhythms of political life do not always coincide with those of women.

Education and Training: 'Further Education' Programmes

Local institutions as well as being responsible for educational and vocational guidance and training, also organise 'further education'. Two programmes, aimed specifically at women, are of particular interest. These are organised on the basis of the requirements of the women involved and cover different aspects of training, education and culture. The practical results of previous courses are also taken into account. These courses were held in the municipality of Milan (in further education centres) in Lombardy, and in the municipality of Bologna in Emilia-Romagna. Further education centres organise courses for women only after having investigated the requests of the students, and in agreement with the councils and the health advice centres in the zone.

These 2 municipalities have also organised 2 centres containing documentary information on various aspects of the female condition. Numerous initiatives have been organised by trade unions, political parties, and by the women themselves. The latter initiatives are particularly interesting as they reflect the real needs of women, as expressed at a local level. However, these initiatives usually involve only a limited number of women, are often of a temporary nature, and do not form part of any particular strategy aimed at improving the situation.

The Regional Labour Market Observers and the Problems of Women at Work

Neither the national or regional economic plans nor the educational and vocational guidance interventions explicitly take account of the problems of women at work. It is thus necessary to analyse the trends of local labour markets in order to satisfy the various different requirements of labour supply. This task is at present entrusted to the regional labour market observers, who due to their lack of awareness of the problem of sexual discrimination, have not so far paid much attention to this aspect. A few attempts at compensating for this have been made in the Emilia-Romagna region and the municipality of Bologna;[10] by the Provincial Administration of Parma,[11] and by the region of Lombardy.[12] The research carried out by these centres has shown that the exclusion of women from the labour market is due to a series of interdependent factors, which

10. See V. Capecchi, 'Nuove tecnologie in una societa che cambia', in *Notiziario d'informazione sul mercato del lavoro*, regione Emilia–Romagna, nos. 7–8, October 1984; V. Capecchi (ed.), *Prima e dopo il diploma: percorsi machili e femminili. Una ricerca del comune di Bologna*, Il Mulino, Bologna, 1983.
11. See L. Frey and R. Livraghi, 'Formazione e Lavoro femminile in provincia di Parma', in *Economia del Lavoro*, nos. 1–2, 1983 (Ceres, Rome).
12. See: G. Barile (ed.), *Le donne nell'economia lombarda. Documentazione*, Irer, Milan, 1979; Barile, *L'offerta di lavoro delle donne sposate*, Irer, Milan, 1983; *Lavoro femminile, sviluppo tecnologico, e segregazione occupazionale*, F. Angli, Milan, 1984.

together form a 'vicious circle'. It is thus necessary to know the trends of the various sectors of labour demand and labour supply in order to be able to prepare adequate measures aimed at stimulating structural changes which should guarantee equal opportunities for both sexes, and therefore, more efficient usage of available resources.

There is a relatively high proportion of women in the working population in Lombardy, and Emilia-Romagna (35 per cent and 37 per cent respectively) as compared to the national average (32 per cent in 1983). Female employment has increased in Italy over the last few years, although in Lombardy there was a slight decrease between 1982 and 1983 and between 1981 and 1982 in Emilia-Romagna. The increase of the tertiary sector lies behind the general increase, both at national and regional level.

In Lombardy, a particularly high proportion of women are employed in tertiary activities, especially in commerce, credit and insurance, and, above all, in public administration and the services. In Emilia-Romagna, too, many women are employed in the tertiary sector, especially in commerce, public administration and the services. On a national level, the female presence is also particularly relevant in the sectors of agriculture and industrial transformations. Both in agriculture and in industry, most women are employed as unskilled workers, and, in the tertiary sectors, in low-grade office jobs. In Italy, therefore, as in other industrialised countries, professional separation between the sexes is on the increase. Most women are employed in a small range of jobs which, on the whole, offer generally lower wages and worse career prospects than the jobs normally carried out by men. This situation has important implications on the transformation processes under way due to the introduction of new technologies, especially considering the fact that the jobs 'typically' carried out by women are already feeling the effects of new computer technology.[13]

The problem of labour supply should be the object of intensive study, in order to understand the reasons behind the professional decisions of the various categories of workers on the labour market. Women, however, form an extremely heterogeneous group, due to the great differences in the educational standards and working experiences of individual women. Any economic analysis of female

13. See D. Werneke, *Microelectronics and office jobs. The impact of the chip on women's employment*, ILO, Geneva, 1983.

employment must therefore take account of the different sectors of female labour supply in order to analyse them separately. It has been shown that traditional market mechanisms are incapable of bringing about a fairer distribution of the female work-force, thus reducing the various forms of professional separation and discrimination.[14] It is thus necessary, using appropriate methods, to encourage structural changes which take account of the various characteristics both of labour supply and demand. These policies should be aimed at reducing direct and indirect discrimination against some sectors of labour supply, and making human investments which effectively apply the concept of equal opportunities.

The National Committee for Equal Employment Opportunities, the Equality Advisors, and the various regional equality committees and consultancy bodies are not yet in a position to intervene actively. It is necessary first to activate a system of periodical surveys of the requirements of the various women's groups, and of the trends of labour supply in the various sectors of local labour markets. These surveys should be capable of evaluating the effects of different economic policies on different sectors of the population, taking account of both market activities and those not strictly connected to the market.

Section 5: Report on the Seminar Organised in Co-operation with the Women's Associations from Lombardy and Emilia-Romagna

The Seminar on 'the main requirements of Italian women and their participation in defining the response by public authorities' was held on 1 March 1985 in Parma at the Economic Science Institute of the State University. The representatives of 25 women's organisations in Lombardy and Emilia-Romagna participated in the Seminar. Invitations were sent to all the women's organisations in the 2 regions which had been identified in the first phase of the research. Given the specific theme of the meeting, the organisations which responded favourably were those more directly involved in labour, production and social security problems. All the participants were sent a copy of the paper on the research carried out by Prof. R.

14. See R. Livraghi, *Segmentazione dei mercati del lavoro e scelte professionali, con particolare riguardo al lavoro femminile*, F. Angeli, Milan, 1984.

Livraghi and Prof. L. Frey and an introductory paper on national and local programming and women's participation.

Forecasts of 17 per cent female unemployment in 1985 and above all the figure of 50 per cent for young women (between 14 and 19 years of age) reinforced the desire among the participants to do something and to fight against this situation even though they were well aware of their lack of decision-making powers.

After stressing the need to urge the political authorities to consider solving the employment problem as a prime objective, the participants showed great interest in the recent measures adopted in Italy to achieve real equality of opportunities, that is to say the Committees for Equal Employment Opportunities and the new post of Equality Advisor at a regional level. These new measures constituted a new direction for some of the women's organisations and aroused great interest and expectations as a possible means to link women's needs and public programmes.

Dependent Employment

The Seminar called upon regional administrations to make special efforts in the field of training and vocational guidance for women. Special emphasis was placed on a series of positive action projects in these fields which the regional authorities could set up with financial assistance from the European Social Fund of the European Economic Community. A working group was set up to study the subject of positive action and to examine the possibility of running some pilot projects.

Discussions indicated that women are well aware of the fact that employment is important because of the contractual power that a job and a salary gives them *vis-à-vis* the family and the community. But in order to be included in the labour market on an equal basis, is it essential that women have to adjust themselves to men and deny their diversity? The rhythm of women's activities is different from that of men: the lack of social services is a burden which women have always had to bear; and the time at work is lived by women in a completely different way from that of men. One problem then is how to define new roles for both men and women.

Whilst it was true that women employees in both regions had obtained the right to a period of time (150 hours) during working hours for their specific retraining, and paid leave was now to be granted to both parents in the case of sickness of children, this was not enough. The reduction of working hours to a 35-hour week and the trial use of new ways of organising working hours were viewed favourably, though some concern was expressed about cases in which the trade unions' bargaining power has proved weak and ineffective. Moreover, it was stressed that a reduction in working hours alone was not enough and local administrators must support the 35-hour week through a broad effort to improve and increase social services, as well as to control the reorganisation of employment.

Public territorial authorities should be urged to coordinate a series of activities on a local basis to meet the needs of the different groups of workers and their families. Families may now constitute productive units and therefore must no longer be considered as mere centres of decision making about consumer goods expenditure.

For these reasons, there was considerable interest in the extending of the powers of the Regional Women's Consultative Body in Lombardy and the women's organisations in Emilia-Romagna, reaffirmed their demand for the constitution of a regional Commission which could provide the link between the needs expressed by women and the public authorities.

Self-employment

A group of women attending the Seminar represented the Cooperative Movement. From their interventions it emerged that experiences of self-employment were concentrated in both regions at three levels:

— Production of services in the more advanced and modern tertiary sector. The socio-sanitary services cooperatives also include a large number of women.
— Cultural production: bookshops, research, training. This type of employment is linked with the very beginnings of feminist activities, both in its contents and by the method adopted.
— handicraft production and production in the manufacturing sector, recovery of work from previous factories or as an attempt to exclude moonlighting.

They highlighted the positive factor of greater entrepreneurship shown by the cooperatives, and want to concentrate greater efforts in the future on this factor. They also intend to work towards the creation of new and more favourable conditions for the development and strengthening of new areas of female employment and entrepreneurship both in cooperatives and otherwise. On this matter they intend to compare their situation with other women in economic, social and political sectors as well as with the institutions at various levels. They suggested that the search for valid solutions to the problems of female unemployment within the logic of development rather than welfare, should stress measures and policies to increase the active presence of women in the promotion of new and valid economic activities in the form of cooperatives, associations or autonomous work.

An appeal was addressed to local and national bodies and also to the European Economic Community to accept the idea that specific support should be given to those women (young or otherwise) who intend promoting new and qualified activities in cooperative form.

At the national level, they noted the importance of two recent bills: the new law on loans to cooperatives and the new law on youth employment. The Female Sector of the National League of Cooperatives and Mutual Societies support these laws in the expectation that this will enable the growth of women's self-employment in fields which will lead to the economic and social development of the country. The Female Sector of the National League of Cooperatives and Mutual Societies has called upon the parties involved in the application of such laws (trade unions, cooperatives, local bodies, public institutions, economic and financial bodies), when approving and allocating funds, to take due account of those projects which meet the objective of retraining women for their insertion in new areas of the market.

To attain such objectives, the Female Sector of the National League of Cooperatives and Mutual Societies is working on the creation of a Centre for the Promotion of the Entrepreneurship and Self-Employment of Women which would coordinate activities and promote interventions and projects in favour of women (at the level of economic and market research, of cooperative and managerial training, of elaboration and control of the promotion of women's cooperatives, of technical and legislative proposals).

They also aim at creating an Observatory on Female Employment in Cooperatives. In order to stimulate the development of widespread forms of female entrepreneurship, it was proposed that local bodies immediately study the possibilities of:
— promoting special credit lines for women's new economic

activities and entrepreneurship of following the examples of other countries;

— developing vocational training policies intended to promote women's economic management;

— creating centres to give guidance to youth and women on cooperation and advice to those intending to set up cooperatives. These should be established in close cooperation with bodies involved in employment policies and the Equality Commissions being set up or already active in many regions of the country.

Autonomous Employment

Autonomous employment in the strict sense is very different from cooperative-type association work. The discriminating factors are: the direct assumption of responsibility towards the outside world and the organisation of work (characterising autonomous employment), and the delegation of degrees of responsibility to representatives (characterising cooperatives). While the cooperative as a whole acts as a protective shield for the individual member against outsiders, the autonomous worker is alone and directly assumes by him/herself the responsibilities which his/her work entails. To filter the needs of female autonomous workers through to the public authorities seemed even more difficult than the other cases of dependent employment and self-employment in cooperatives. The need for training and retraining, opening up credit lines and centralised services, was stressed.

New Technologies

Great concern was expressed at the introduction of new technologies in production sectors where the number of women employed was quite high. Women experience difficulties in negotiating trade union agreements on the new technologies because of the low number of women at higher management levels in the trade unions and the lack of awareness of the problem. Information and research is needed to identify the most suitable strategies to protect the most vulnerable groups of women. It was asked that the Committee for Equal Employment Opportunities set up a working group on this problem; and it was hoped that the Committee would work in close cooperation with the Regional Commissions on Employment.

Public and/or Self-managed Services

In the North of Italy and in particular in the two regions involved in the research, a progressive increase in 'new families' (people living alone; families made up of one adult, mainly a woman, and one or more children; communal living) has been noted. This is linked to women's demands for autonomy even within the traditional family, their breaking out of the subordinate female role and coming out onto the labour market. Women then have particular demands to make of the social services: which of their requirements can be met by those services; what happens if the traditional family pattern is superseded?

One important aspect is that of housing. Various women stressed the importance of elaborating new housing programmes: houses for single people should be integrated with communal social spaces open to the outside; single rooms in buildings with centralised services, or others. However, attention was mostly focused on the aspects to do with housework and the education and care of the children. The solution proposed for the housework problem can be divided into two categories: one which propose independence; i.e.: rotation of chores (cleaning, cooking, care of children), which, whilst overcoming the sexual division of work and the role of housewife, perpetuates unpaid work; and one which solves the problem through provision of a series of public social services (canteen, laundry, nursery, etc.) which would be open at convenient hours, and staffed by paid workers.

The choice between public and self-managed independent services was a difficult one. Discussion suggested that the self-managed independent services had positive benefits since different services could be tried out. A request could then be made to the public authorities, for such services to be set up with collective-type management, as has been the case with women's health centres.

Services should however be adapted to meet specific needs for both women and working women; services should also be organised in such a way as to take into account the needs of both the user and the operators. Social services should be funded by the State, but their management should be delegated to self-managed independent groups. It was stressed that the self-managed independent service is not only run by those who work in it but also by those who use it. Users come in on an equal footing if they are willing to participate in activities and investigate whatever is needed.

In conclusion, the Seminar highlighted numerous problematic aspects of women's working life and of the female condition. It constituted an important moment for reflection and achieving a greater understanding of the problem and difficulties. What emerged clearly was the split between women's lack of decision making in economic and fiscal policies and their active participation in the economy.

3

WOMEN AND DEVELOPMENT PLANNING: THE CASE OF EGYPT

Sonia Abadir Ramzi and the Centre for Social Science Research and Documentation for the Arab Region

Section 1: The Egyptian National Plan

The national plan for economic and social development for the period 1982/3 to 1986/7 shows that only 31 per cent of the population is in the labour force and that the annual rate of population growth is 2.2 per cent. Although the rate of growth of the female labour force is greater than that of the male, none the less women's participation in economic activity is very limited, i.e. less than 10 per cent. Although any analysis of the national plan demonstrates this clearly, planners themselves have paid little attention to this fact. They have not made the promotion of women's participation in economic activity or their better integration in the processes of development an objective of national planning. The national plan aspires to the general development of the totality of society, that is of women as well as of men, but by disregarding the specificity of women's situation the progress of the entire country towards development may well be hampered.

One could ask why this absence of a strategy and of precise goals to further the participation of women in socio-economic development. It is clear that although underdevelopment not only harms women — men are also victims — none the less women are doubly disadvantaged because of their sex and their environment. They suffer more than men from the difficulties inherent in the conditions of underdevelopment and the low general standard of living. Statistical comparisons of the life chances of men and women show discrimination against women in a number of areas: education, paid work, politics, etc.

111

How can these inequalities be remedied? One of the responses must be a form of planning based on the premise of achieving equality and which would be able to provide the mechanisms by which women's potential for participation in social development could be released. It is clear that the economic, political, social and cultural structures of a country can favour either the liberation of women's capacities and their participation in development or their oppression.

The Participation of Women in Economic Activities

As is the case everywhere in the Third World, Egyptian women have never ceased to work, particularly those who belong to the popular classes. But the period since the 1952 revolution has been one in which among the upper and middle urban classes, i.e. the most educated, a new ideology has blossomed: the importance of work for women as for men. 'It is in assuring work for women and allowing them to cooperate with men that we will work toward their liberation', General Abdel Nasser declared in one of his speeches.[1] This was reinforced by the adoption of laws which guaranteed the equality of the sexes in access to employment and to wages. As far as salaries are concerned, Egypt is one of the countries where men and women do get equal pay but inequalities persist at the level of access to employment, to promotions, to choice of careers, etc. The economy in Egypt is however based mainly on male labour and employment is largely the domain of men. The majority of women are still marginalised from those productive activities recognised as such by society. A study made in 1974 showed that women represented only 2 per cent of the agricultural labour force, 6 per cent of the labour force in commerce and transport, and 17 per cent of that in the service sector.

In the course of the last three decades there has been an increase in the growth of women's activity rate. This growth is the result both of the higher educational levels of young girls, and of increased availability of employment in the public service sector, particularly in education, where occupations are more and more feminised. In the urban milieu, women are increasingly involved in different economic sectors. Paid work for women is now well established and even accepted by men. Women work to meet their own needs and

1. Made at Port Said, 21 December 1965

112

to contribute to their family's resources; they also work for personal satisfaction and to be economically independent.

The economy of the country, despite the great efforts made to stimulate industry, is in great measure dominated by the agricultural sector, a sector which suffers from pervasive economic, social and cultural underdevelopment. The Egyptian population is then largely rural despite the spectacular growth in the last few years of urban and industrial centres. Relatively few women are employed in the formal economy; of those who are the great majority are in agriculture. Studies show that the number of women in paid work at the national level is growing rapidly but that their 'productive' activities are mainly located in the informal and invisible sector, above all in the rural area.

Section 2: The Formal Economy

Women's Employment

In recent years there has been a change in women's behaviour and their aptitude for employment now tends to approach that of men's. The proportion of women who are economically active has greatly increased and their professional life is now more continuous: previously many women used to leave their profession when they married or had a baby. The 1976 population census showed that the active population — those aged 6 years or more[2] — represented approximately one-third of the population (31.5 per cent as against 30.1 per cent in 1960). Between 1960 and 1970 men's economic participation declined while that of women rose. This fall in male participation is explained by the expansion of educational opportunities and the out-migration of male labour, principally to other Arab states. The growth in women's participation is explained by the socialisation process which is increasingly pushing women into the labour market. For the decade 1961–71 the growth in the number of women in the labour force was about 36.7 per cent. At the same time the number of women employed in the agricultural sector declined from 43 per cent of the total paid female labour force (1961) to 25.1 per cent (1971). Women are rejecting agricultural

---

2. The economic needs of families obliged them to use children's labour. With the spread of education and economic changes, this age is now increasing.

work in favour of a longer period of education, or other more lucrative activities in recently established small agrobusiness, food or other industries. None the less the bulk of the female paid labour force is to be found in agriculture.

In the urban area more women are to be found in occupations and in areas of work until recently reserved only for men. Women's participation in the technical and scientific branches grew from 8.3 per cent to 19.3 per cent during the decade 1961–71. This phenomenon is even more evident in the transformation industries where the participation rate rose from 3.3 per cent to 11.7 per cent over the same period. This is the result of the extension of secondary education, in towns at least, and higher rates of attendance of young women in higher education. Higher levels of education help to explain the new aspirations of women of all social categories as far as work is concerned. On the other hand, the spread of education has also strongly influenced the average age of economically active women. A report to the International Labour Organization on the sex breakdown of the labour force showed that the rate of growth of the urban labour force has been more rapid than its rural counterpart (3.6 per cent and 1.3 per cent respectively); the rate of growth of women's activity has been 2.9 per cent per annum, that of men 2.1 per cent. The activity rate of the population in the urban areas is higher, in general, than that found in rural zones. This difference is more significant for women for whom the average registered in urban areas is 5.1 per cent against 0.2 per cent in rural zones.

This helps to explain why certain sectors in society oppose women's employment on the basis of an erroneous interpretation of religious texts. These views are promoted above all by educated men of the petty bourgeoisie who see women as their rivals in the labour market. The gravity of the problem is further accentuated by the fact that many women (more resigned than one would have imagined) also share this view, and do not realise how dangerous it is for their own situation. The notion of employment for women is thus brought into question. Only a small minority of university women have organised public protests to uncover and denounce the danger. They try to show through academic studies that employment for women was never forbidden by religious laws. It is regrettable that Egyptian women, who have always played a direct or indirect role in the development of society, are so threatened at the end of the twentieth century, that they have to fight to retain gains made as long ago as the beginning of the century. It is such a pity to see militants obliged to prove that they have the right to work instead of being allowed to channel their efforts in ways which would open new perspectives for society.

Impediments to Women's Access to Employment and their Development

The interrelationship between economic, social, legal, educational and cultural problems sadly set their mark on women's condition, and have had a profound impact on women's employment. Whether she works in the fields, in a factory or in management, whether she has little or considerable qualifications, the married woman who works must give equal attention to her family and her children. She confronts, as everywhere else in the world, problems stemming from her double burden. In addition to the work she has to suffer the excessive constraints of familial obligations. She has to cope with the difficulty of harmonising her active life outside the home with her responsibilities as 'mistress of the house' and mother of a family, responsibilities which she alone must assume. The father's contribution and that of the State in these areas is almost entirely non-existent.

The absence of creches, kindergartens or nursery schools force working women to make very difficult choices, between solutions that either do not benefit their own careers or do not foster the education of their children. Certain laws which attempt to favour working women have the same negative effects: for example, the law obliging enterprises employing 100 women to set up creches has all too often led entrepreneurs to reduce the number of their female personnel (Unesco, 1981, p. 37).

The absence of social services to lighten the domestic tasks of working women (provision of canteens, ready-made food at moderate prices) and inadequate transport are also factors which lengthen women's working day. A woman is the only person to pay for the deficiencies of the social system in her professional life, her health, and her hours of leisure or recreation. At present a proposal for a new law dealing with part time work for women is being discussed, but is this the solution? The availability of part-time work, the possibility of taking time off for family reasons directly concern women. However how can we avoid these modifications from reinforcing the idea that women's employment is secondary, that women cannot have a career, and should not be given too great responsibilities?

Another set of difficulties derive from women's low participation in trade unions. Trade unions have very few women members because having to divide their time between employment and domestic work women do not have enough time to be active in union affairs. Furthermore hours of meetings often do not suit them; this denies women the possibility of making collective demands in the privileged arena of political action. Greater numbers of women are found in secondary jobs than in well-paid ones because they are less qualified and less educated than men. Equality in education is officially recognised but there is still a long way to go: the theory of equality does not change actual practice. In fact there is considerable inequality between boys and girls in access to education. This inequality, initially not very marked, is more marked at each successive stage of education and reflects later on women's professional life. Inequality in the acquisition of technical knowledge and technical ability is also marked. Women usually turn towards so-called feminine careers. This state of things is further perpetuated by the disparity between study programmes offered to boys and to girls and by the stereotypical presentation made in school texts of the sexual division of labour. Educational planners and educators have not yet come to question their assumptions about the physiological and psychological differences between the sexes or to look at the real roles of men and women in the job market. This in turn prejudices its planning.

Section 3: The Informal Sector

An Overview of Women's Participation in this Sector

A whole informal, unofficial and invisible economy is in the hands of women in Egypt. Planners throw into the sphere of the non-economic or the social all those aspects of household life which do not have a market or monetary value and which cannot be statistically captured and recorded in the national accounts. None the less non-remunerated economic activities are very common and predominate in the lesser developed countries. This invisible economy for women, above all in rural areas, includes the non-monetary domestic economy to which is added fairly often cash earning and market activities. For rural women economic activity is not only composed of formal activities — organised production of commodities and the circulation of money. These unpaid activities are in great measure traditional: agriculture, trade and handicrafts. But this type of activity, even though it is not recorded in the national accounts, plays an important economic role. Women's traditional informal work remains neglected and underestimated by planners and statisticians and will continue to be so as long as it does not pass into the market sphere. Informal work is not evaluated in terms of productivity, and this despite studies which show that a majority of rural women in the poorest regions work at least 16–18 hours a day, without taking into account activities done simultaneously, for example feeding a baby and selling at the market. Women are involved in all the stages of agricultural production and whatever their age they continue to participate in different agricultural activities. These are made even more arduous given that they are carried out in the most difficult conditions, using antiquated technology. Neither mechanisation nor new technology is available to women.

As mothers they have to undertake numerous other activities (domestic work, bringing up children, etc.) which shows that marriage and family responsibilities are not an obstacle to women working although such multiple activities are undertaken at the expense of their leisure and their rest. Women who have to work to survive cannot leave the market for family reasons; their participation has no limit. This can serve as an indicator of the participation of women in development.

The rural family is a unit of production which utilises its capital according to its possibilities (plot of land, livestock, poultry) and its time to provide its own needs, and often those of others. These goods and services are not included in any budget nor in an overall evaluation of the economy.

In the unorganised urban sector the situation of women is not much better. The majority of workers in this sector belong to the poorer classes. They suffer from heavy and tiresome drudgery as well as very long hours of work and low income. In general the informal sector is characterised by a high degree of exploitation of female workers. This is a result of economic strategies built on non-equitable bases and a labour market which favours the minority (the exploiting classes) against the majority who are exploited. It has to be pointed out that the last decade has been marked by a reduction in traditional female domestic production due in great part to the outmigration of the head of the family to richer Arab countries. The increased wages of these men has led to an improvement in their families' standards of living and to women being encouraged to give up domestic production and to turn to consumption. This is one of the reasons for the extraordinary growth in the production of gold jewellery in the last few years. Women want it as much as a sign of wealth as an insurance against the vagaries of life. Given that the informal sector is generally tightly correlated to the degree of underdevelopment of a country, it is paradoxical that this sector can expand as a function of the growth in the income of certain social classes. This is the case of Egypt where today in the urban areas and above all among women of the better-off classes, a whole range of new informal activities have sprung up to meet the needs of a commercial class which has recently become enriched (kindergartens, provision of cooked dishes, the illicit sale of luxury objects, etc.). On the other hand the traditional system of rotating credit (based on the association of a number of women who contribute regularly to a fund which becomes the property of each one of them in turn) is becoming more and more developed. However this fund is generally used for purposes of consumption and will rarely be utilised as capital for productive activities. In the urban areas informal activities have been updated to correspond to new needs and possibilities. They have acquired an autonomy quite different from the older customs and habits, and their own dynamism which responds in part to the transformations of the market economy. If we are to understand women's work we have to analyse the complex relations between the formal and informal sectors, during a period of expansion of production or of consumption and equally during a period of an increase or a contraction in incomes. We must start from the principle that it is illusory to think that a household deprived of its necessary basic income will be able to make it up by turning to the informal economy. As a general rule women work in this sector to ensure provision of basic subsistence for their families.

The Characteristics of the Informal Sector

The more a woman finds herself in the lower echelons of the economic system, the more difficult her social situation and the greater her exploitation. A number of economic, social and cultural factors combine to constitute a major handicap to women's participation in development. Such participation is necessarily influenced by the dominant ideological representations of social life; thus the prevailing system of values and associated social practices can be cultural barriers to development.

Illiteracy

The ignorance of the popular classes is an evil which generates misery. Illiteracy and poverty are linked, each of these elements being at the same time cause and effect. The persistence of illiteracy on a large scale is a major obstacle to development: it condemns the battle against poverty to stalemate. Illiteracy is very high among women of the lower economic social group, which also suffers from an impoverished cultural environment. The rate of illiteracy is higher in rural than in urban areas, among women than men. The disparities between numbers of illiterates are therefore to be found at two levels: between town and country and men and women. Despite all the efforts undertaken, the percentage of illiterate women remains very high, about 71 per cent. Almost all women who work in the informal sector are illiterate and have no professional training, and even though women play an important role, particularly in agriculture, they receive no specialised training. Persistence of illiteracy is due to the following reasons:

(1)   rural women's heavy work burden which never leaves them time to become literate, even when the occasion is presented;
(2)   the lack of interest in being able to read and write which stems from the fact that in certain cases literacy has not in fact helped their economic condition;
(3)   negative attitudes on the part of men and even of women as to the usefulness of education for women.

High Fertility Rates

The inability to meet the goals set by family planning agencies has forced us to look into the area of socio-cultural factors for the reasons which have prevented us from reaching the anticipated results. These lessons equally permit us to point to ways of bettering the condition of women. The indicators of women's access to family planning services reveal their training. Integrating women into the process of development will allow a lessening of their procreative role, the only institutionalised social role given to them. Frequent and close pregnancies provoked by the refusal or absence of sexual education are prejudicial to women's health.

Inhumane Conditions of Work

The informal sector is characterised in its totality by the exploitation of women who are daily confronted with unlimited hours of work, punishing drudgery, low income, holidays without pay, lack of social cover in case of illness or break in activity, loss of leisure, etc.

Socio-cultural Constraints

Socio-cultural constraints exercised *vis-à-vis* women discriminate against them and maintain them in a state of dependence and inferiority. Since from birth boys are believed to be superior and girls inferior, there is a certain resistance to educating girls, and an inequality in educational opportunity between boys and girls above all in rural and poor regions. Girls are thought to be destined for marriage which is the essential goal of their lives. Early marriage, without the possibility of choosing one's spouse, persists in the rural zones. A woman's status in the family reinforces her inferiority. Wives are perpetually threatened by repudiation, or polygamy, and this impels them to have numerous children. A wife lives in a situation of moral insecurity to which is all too often added economic insecurity.

A negative cultural climate predominates in rural regions as far as women's work is concerned. Women accept their inferiority. They are not conscious of their rights as citizens, as wife, as mother, nor the value of the enormous amount of work they do. A survey of rural women and their work carried out by women sociologists ran into considerable resistance from rural women themselves in the first month. They always said that they were housewives. In their eyes, all the tasks and activities they undertook throughout the day away from home formed an integral part of their duties as mother. This reveals the fact that for them work is uniquely men's prerogative. Their activities and their toil are therefore not considered to be productive work by women themselves nor by their associates. Moreover, traditionalists preach that the break up of the modern family is provoked in great measure by the entry of women into the world of work.

Section 4: Future Perspectives

Our strategy should therefore be double:
(1) a radical transformation of the economic, social and cultural structures which tend to perpetuate the under-development of both women and men;
(2) direct actions enabling rural women and those of the less favoured classes to be considered as actors and beneficiaries in the development process, by planners and decision makers.

Structural Change

In order to identify the problems and evaluate the needs of a given form of development, one must base oneself on a critical overall analysis of the economic, social and cultural dynamic of a country in which the feminine dimension will not be forgotten. One must question not only the structures of production and of economic activity, but equally the forms of social, cultural and family life. That is to say all that conditions and constitutes a way of life. It is not possible today to respond to problems piecemeal; wholistic conceptions and visions of the future are more needed than ever. Economic and social change demand new regulations which must of necessity be supported by new cultural and social bases. One must:
(1) identify the structural characteristics which put a brake on the development of a society without forgetting the feminine dimension.
(2) identify the problems which make it difficult for women to participate fully in the process of development and equally the obstacles which, whether at the educational or cultural level, make it difficult for them to make progress within the world of work.
(3) examine the relationship of cause and effect between certain economic variables and the status of women.
(4) further develop the technical tools of planners and decision makers, who presently have at their disposal few measures or facts concerning working women, above all those in rural areas. This state of things makes any intelligent formulation of development policy impossible. Methods must be elaborated which allow women's problems to be taken into account and thereby ensure their better integration into the national process of development.

121

(5) conduct at the level of the national plan a lengthy period of
     careful thought and more general reassessment than is possible
     within each ministerial sector, and centred on the daily life of
     women, of families and of social groups. This will permit light
     to be thrown on relations and inconsistencies which sectoral
     approaches do not allow us to perceive.

Towards a Greater and More Efficient Participation of Women in Development

Within the framework of an overall political strategy, the condition
of women who work in the formal or informal sectors ought to be
treated with equal weight. Any adequate action in favour of women
can only be undertaken if there is the political will to face up to real
problems in all their dimensions. Only then can one anticipate an
effective participation of women in development. This political will
should become concrete by putting into action a series of dynamic
undertakings which will aim at eliminating all forms of discrimination which women suffer from, and factors which block their
promotion, both socially and culturally. A total policy ought to be
devised which presents the nature of the problems to be resolved,
determines the programme to be undertaken, the means to put it
into action as well as the areas where action should be undertaken.
A concerted approach by the different ministries should be undertaken with a view to bringing about a real change of structures and
elimination of negative attitudes as regards women's emancipation,
and to setting up the mechanisms necessary for women's effective
integration into sectors of productive life. These actions should
include:

(1) the creation of a favourable climate towards women's employ-
     ment: provoking changes in attitudes, behaviour, ways of
     thinking *vis-à-vis* women's economic activities; making
     changes not only in the image that women have of themselves
     but also of the role they play in society — the image women
     have of themselves often constitutes a major obstacle to their
     social progress; changing the stereotyped ideas people hold
     about women's role — these stereotypes are further exagger-
     ated in school texts and by the media; making clear that the
     development of a country is indissolubly linked to the fruit of
     women's work.

(2) widespread awareness and women's training campaigns. These

should be undertaken so that the dynamic of change will be started as rapidly as possible. In these campaigns it is important to underline the fact that work is one of the privileged means by which women can pass from the private to the collective sphere where power is exercised; to make clear that employment allows women to reach a minimum level of economic independence which is an indispensable condition for a certain autonomy of thought and decision-taking; to remind women that it is through paid work that women achieve social promotion; and further that by being involved in active life they will be able to learn how to undertake concerted actions. Work is equally the area of action where they can in an effective way have some influence over their own status, their own social representation, their own future. Women should be initiated into trade union activity and the importance of forming groups, organising, mobilising, explained to them. They must be helped to realise how necessary it is to speak out as men do already, and this on an equal footing, about their problems with life, with work and their specific needs. In this way they can change not only their lives as workers but also as women in general.

(3) the setting up of auxiliary services. These would help employed women to overcome the burden of the often excessive constraints which arise from the large amount of their family and work obligations. A social infrastructure dealing with children (creche, nurseries, etc.) should be set up in such a way that women can be freed from a certain number of constraints, and carry out their economic activities without break. These arrangements are all the more urgent if one considers the rapid transformation of ways of life which are being experienced in Egypt today.

(4) guarantees of women's equal opportunities relative to men as regards their careers so that they can achieve positions of responsibility and decision-making power.

Education and Employment

Literacy and education are the keys which will allow the conditions of life of men and women in Egypt to be modified and also changes to be made in the social structure. One can never insist too much on this fundamental point. Making women literate and bringing them education are prerequisites of development. As educators of the following generation it is through them that attitudes can be changed, innovations can be introduced which will help communities, above all rural communities, to take part more rapidly in modern life. An improvement in literacy rates and educational levels would give women the possibility of entering economic and social life with more assurance, and to control their difficulties better. Education and its quantitative and qualitative growth are essential for women's more effective contribution to development. Steps to achieve the above should include:

(1) ensuring that access to education and training for employment is without discrimination by sex. Although officially guaranteed by law, equality in access to technical and professional training is far from being a reality. Pedagogical and professional training should be systematically provided for all students and not channelled by sex. This would modify people's choice of disciplines and careers given that they would no longer be swayed by social streotypes.

(2) ensuring the coordination of education, professional training and the employment of women. Technical training needs to be harmonised with the real needs of the labour market and to develop a more positive attitude amongst employers towards women technicians.

(3) giving women access to decision-making positions. Although women in the teaching profession are mainly located in its lower ranks, they should be given access, in particular the most militant, to the higher spheres of the Ministry of Education where they could draw up plans and educational policies.

Adult literacy and training are essential particularly for women, given that they are fundamental agents of development: indeed they can be said to be privileged actresses in endogenous development. More than ever we have to pull the evil of illiteracy out by its roots: it is the source and multiplier of many ills. Adult literacy training should be integrated into a continuous process of general and professional training leading to promotion at work. In order to eradicate illiteracy and to strengthen women's activities in the informal sector a number of steps are needed:

(1) Literacy campaigns should be placed in those structures best adapted to the country's needs. Systems of education and training are urgently needed that are adapted to women's

situation. They must be guaranteed, through appropriate programmes of functional literacy, forms of training whose aim is to help them increase their incomes, satisfy their fundamental needs, and to permit them to participate actively in the social and cultural life of the community. From the psychosociological point of view, it is often through the education of women more than through that of men, that changes in attitudes and behaviour necessary for a better adaptation to the modern world are achieved.

(2) Women, particularly those living in a rural area, must be introduced to new techniques which will make their tasks less tiring and more humane.

(3) Training courses in community development should be organised for women.

(4) A social security system must be set up to liberate women from a number of constraints and to allow them to be integrated into the different sectors of active life.

(5) Collective structures should be introduced, above all in the rural areas, but care should be taken that these do not become the basis for new sources of exploitation of women. Pilot units should be established, both in the private and public sectors, which should be covered by the employment laws, so that the workers can benefit from social rights. This is not to argue for a uniformity of modes of production, but only to give them a structure. The example of Misr/El Mahllo, a large public sector undertaking, is revealing. The economic activity of women has been remarkably developed because the financial surplus of the unit is used both for its own expansion and the modernisation of its equipment.

Making the Informal Sector Count in the Sphere of Economic Activity

Organised and paid work will inspire women to want to change their attitudes and their behaviour *vis-à-vis* numerous social and cultural problems: high birth-rates, the education of daughters, fatalism, etc. For women the world of work, with all its inequalities and its discriminations, is the privileged place of political action. Politics being understood in its wider sense; that of being able to influence decisions which concern them, and the power to conceive of their position and that of their group in different areas of activity,

125

including that of the society in general.

A thorough assessment of the organisation of women's 'invisible' work should be undertaken at the level of national planning. New structures at the macro-economic level, incorporating the social dimension, should be devised to allow that sector, until now forgotten in the national accounts, to be managed and made more profitable. It is equally important to develop diversified activities at the local level because they favour women's autonomy. 'Feminist' activities and/or social activities in the traditional non-market sphere should be allowed to be balanced within the sphere of market exchange, still preserving the autonomy, initiative and liberty of women in their work. A strategy centered on the new order of women's situation should be adopted which permits them to be better integrated into the process of development. An assessment of the activities undertaken to better the conditions of work in the informal sector shows that the results are insufficient having regard to the depth and the gravity of the problem. As long as the initiatives are not taken within the framework of a well-defined overall strategy which has as its goal the totality of structures, their effect will be very limited. This strategy cannot be translated concretely other than putting into effect government planning which rests on a detailed knowledge of real facts and based on a vision of the future which envisages the bettering of the conditions of women's existence (family status, social rights, education, work, political participation, etc.) both in the urban and in the rural areas. A new world must arise in which both men and women together build their daily lives.

Section 5: Report on the Workshop on Women and National Development

Under the auspices of the Unesco Division for Socio-Economic Analysis, Sector of Social and Human Sciences, and the Centre for Social Science Research and Documentation for the Arab Region, Cairo, a two-day workshop was held to discuss 'Women and Development: obstacles confronting women in their struggle for development'. The purpose of the meeting was two-fold: firstly, to highlight major issues and concerns confronting women through the use of socio-economic indicators and research, and secondly to communicate to policy-makers and planners in the form of recommendations ways of improving the situation of Egyptian women through future planning.

A background paper was presented to all participants prior to the meeting. The paper highlighted the concept of development as that state of existence wherein all human resources and potential are totally liberated from all man-made fetters. The first day of the meeting focused upon the legal, political and economic structural constraining factors affecting women's participation in development, whilst presentations and discussions on the second day delved into the processes of socialisation and acculturation that reinforce discrimination against women, as well as preventing her from adequate participation in development. Discussions centred on the following topics:

Legal Discrimination and Constraining Factors

It was pointed out that legal discriminatory practices against women were especially pronounced in the area of personal status. However, a number of gaps existed between law and practice in labour and education laws. Moreover, women are not protected against legal circumvention, even when the law gives them a number of rights. The major obstacles lie not in the letter of various laws but in their spirit since, it was pointed out, in the final analysis men have absolute mandatory and protective responsibilities towards women. These rights and responsibilities are not necessarily supported by law, but are more in the way of customary practice.

Structural constraints; limited access to social and medical services. Budgets allocated to the building of nurseries are often very limited. Social security and pensions are available only to women employed in the formal sector which leaves a very large percentage of women out, since the majority of working women are active in the informal sector. Although medical services available to women, including nutrition, take up a significant portion of government finance, the quality is often unsatisfactory.

Limited Political Participation

Despite the establishment of women's political participation in the law, female participation lags behind male political participation in practice. This is largely due to the absence of consciousness, knowledge and education. Women are not sufficiently aware of the relationship between their everyday lives and public politics, nor are they aware of their potential bargaining power.

Recognition of Women's Economic Contribution

Research and observation ascertain the fact that the number of hours invested in daily labour is far greater for women than it is for men. This is particularly true of rural women who not only spend an average of 16–19 hours of daily labour, but their labour is in addition diversified and multi-sectoral; women carry out a number of productive activities simultaneously. Household tasks, child care and farming with all that it entails, can be subdivided into an indefinite number of tasks. Even though rural women, in contrast to urban women, suffer less from conflicting roles, they are however far more exploited and far less protected by the state. Urban women suffer more from their dual roles.

Socio-psychological Barriers

Rural and urban socialisation processes greatly reinforce discrimination against women. Women are from very early on taught to be weak and subdued creatures. Women's lives in the countryside are totally centered around men whom they serve and for whom they work. Women are often evaluated according to their child-bearing capacities. As independent creatures they are despised. Most of their effort is exerted in their struggle to please and keep their men. Heresy, sorcery, magic and other metaphysical practices are all employed to influence and have power over their men. Women's nutrition and health are neglected. The general inferiority imposed upon women by the patriarchal structure of society, is an added obstacle to the free development or their creative capacities.

The general inferiority of women is reinforced by the mass media which regards women as objects of consumption and male entertainment. Meanwhile the mass media provides a number of disfunctional female stereotypes which do not reflect the new image of serious and productive women. The mass media, which is but a reflection of the prevailing ideology, emphasises consumerism as opposed to productive values, superficial western as opposed to positive national values.

Even more serious than the above, is the whole area of psychic constraints. A number of women have in fact internalised and accepted their inferiority and do behave according to male defined assumptions about themselves. Many in fact identify with the 'aggressor'. As a result of all the above constraints women are very insecure. They are insecure physically, economically and socially, and thus they are not able to perform at their best capacity.

Cultural Constraints

Islam, the prevailing cultural and spiritual ideology, is often used to support reactionary views against women. The Islamic cultural heritage as interpreted by a male dominated patriarchal society places women in a disadvantageous position. This is a result of a static reading and understanding of Islam as a culture. An historical approach needs to be developed. The progressive aspects of Islam should be emphasised and placed in their proper historical context. Moreover, a new reading of Islam is necessary with the re-opening of female Ijtihad. Meanwhile women should also be able to define what they accept as their cultural identity and what they view as significant components of their overall cultural heritage.

The workshop participants spent some time discussing identification and elaboration of socio-economic indicators of women's participation in the development process. The general status of women and their participation in development was evaluated by looking at health, educational, political, mass media, labour and professional indicators.

Health indicators.   According to the national plan, the amount of money allocated to birth control, family planning and health centres should be an adequate indicator of proper existing services. It has however suggested that more research is needed to explore such areas of female health as nutrition.

Educational indicators.   Although the percentage of female school enrolment is constantly increasing, it is however important to look at the quality of education offered and the kinds of cultural expectations. Most women enrol in the faculties of arts, men in the faculties of science; men have markedly higher enrolment rate in the prestigious branches of engineering and medicine. Girls and women have higher drop-out rates.

Political indicators.   Female political participation in district politics seemed quite low. It was suggested that more data be gathered on recent national elections in order to map out female participation, the number of election cards issued to women, female party membership, and the number of individual identity cards issued to women.

Mass media indicators. Women's participation in the mass media was far below expectation. However this was not regarded as an adequate measure of the status of women in the mass media, since what is really necessary is increased numbers of enlightened men and women able to represent the plight of less fortunate women.

Labour and professional indicators. Some professions are almost exclusively reserved for men, such as the law. There are no women judges, and women lawyers are very scarce, all of which renders the area of legal practices and application totally male dominated.

Formal statistical indicators of female participation in the labour force are very misleading. Female housework and labour in the informal sector are not counted; unpaid labour is statistically unrecognised. According to research only a very small percentage of working women do in fact earn wages, the vast majority of women are involved in unpaid labour. This makes us question available data of female participation in productive activity.

Moreover the number of hours spent in productive activity by women is also statistically unknown. Research indicates that in some rural areas women may work an average of 19 hours per day. Moreover, existing indicators do not tell us when and why women withdraw from the labour market.

Workshop Recommendations

These focused on 6 areas and are discussed below:

(a) Women, law and social services. The meeting agreed that there were discrepancies between law and practice on the one hand and discrimination against women in some laws on the other hand. Since law was viewed as a reflection of existing socio-economic structures that reinforces inequality between men and women, it was suggested that societal value systems and ideology need to be changed.

Two strategies of change were suggested: one was more evolutionary and stressed the need to change existing norms gradually by dialoguing with men in their different roles of father, son and brother; the other was more radical and comprehensive and suggested that women become involved politically and confront their own problems.

A significant part of changes in values would have to deal with basic concepts, particularly those relating to women. Work and self-reliance would have to be reasserted as important values that not only increase their honour as human beings but also lead to greater maturity in marriage.

Another significant part of social change is to narrow the existing gaps between the various contradictory roles working women are expected to play in society. There appears to be a very real gap between the increase in female labour employment and the provision of social services and facilities by the State, which leaves the complete and total responsibility of making ends meet to women individually. It was the meeting's opinion that the State had to play an increasing role in narrowing the gap between conflicting social roles. In other words the State should be responsible for providing working women with basic services such as nurseries in working women's neighbourhoods; organising and facilitating housework through State supervision and organisation of such things as public laundrettes, prepared meals, restaurants, etc. Moreover, the State should encourage and develop the authentic customs which promote the position of women, such as communal informal banking systems and communal child care.

(b) Women, labour and political participation. Participants stressed the importance of developing and expanding women's access to employment in large modern and technologically advanced units. Such units would guarantee efficient and productive work, as well as protecting women's rights. It is only through large and modern productive units that women can acquire all their legal, social and economic rights. Also it is only within large productive enterprises that female labour is definitely remunerated. Most women are involved in unpaid labour and are totally unprotected by any social institution including the family, so it is therefore necessary for the State to pose as the protector of the male and female labour force.

It is very important that women become increasingly involved politically. In order to guarantee the first step in female political participation, all women should be encouraged to have identity and election cards. Political participation here has a much broader connotation. It is used to mean all decisions made by women on all levels of their daily lives. Moreover political participation is not exclusively the domain of political parties but may be also fulfilled through participation in rural councils and trade unions.

(c) Women and socialisation processes. The group suggested a number of research projects that needed to be carried out on women in all the various social classes with a special emphasis on rural women. Research should also aim at uncovering the existing different female cultures. Most past research focused on urban middle- and upper-class women.

In order to transcend rural underdevelopment, consciousness-raising activity was suggested by the group. It was pointed out that there should be greater concern to educate rural women. Women in the countryside should be able to see the link between their daily lives and public policies, and become more aware of their own rights. Female intellectuals of rural origin should be encouraged to participate in rural development. It was also suggested that more effort be exerted by social institutions such as the family and school, to abolish the discrimination and differentiation between sexes in the socialisation process.

(d) Women and the mass media. Workshop participants urged researchers to present their research findings to people working in the mass media in order to enable planners to change existing systems and programmes, and to select significant components for their future programmes.

They recommended that programmes presented in the media should be productive and have a sense of purpose. The content should carry social and economic messages and not simply be geared to pointless entertainment and consumerism. New media cadres should be trained and educated to understand the importance of the media's social responsibilities. It should portray women in their proper position as well as to educate and raise the consciousness of the female population. The media should promote an image of society which is closer to reality, take into consideration all the various social classes, and reflect the new roles performed by women.

As rural women constitute the majority of the population, they should be given more importance in the media.

There should be some form of supervision over the media in order to prevent it from propagating false information to the public.

(e) Women and cultural heritage. Islam should be placed in its proper social and historical context. There should be more emphasis on the spirit rather than the letter of the doctrine. Women should be allowed greater participation in its interpretation.

There should be greater emphasis on the values that promote the liberation of women and society in our cultural heritage. The media can play a vital role here. Women should have a greater chance to shape national cultural heritage.

Bibliography

Abdel Kader, S., *The Status of Egyptian Women: 1900–1973*, Ford Foundation, Cairo, 1973

Afza, N., 'Women in Islam', *Muslim News*, vol. 6, no. 8, February 1978, pp. 30–3

Al-Talib, N., 'Status of Women in Islam', *Islamic Literature*, vol. 15, no. 6, 1969, pp. 57–64

Anawati, M., *Conceptions of Relations Between the Sexes Among Urban Cairo Youth and Adults*, The American University in Cairo (Masters Thesis), 1973

Anonymous, 'Egypt: Jobs for the girls', *The Economist*, 8 April 1972

———, 'Islamic Tradition and Women's Education in Egypt', *Women and Education*, 1984

———, 'Self-Images of Traditional Urban Women in Cairo', *Women in the Muslim World*, 1978

Badran, H., 'Women, Population and Integrated Rural Development', a paper presented at the seminar on the role of women in integrated rural development with emphasis on population problems, sponsored by U.N. Food and Agricultural Organisation, 26 October–3 November, Cairo, 1974

———, 'Deliberations of the International Women's year conference and its relationship to the Arab Region', a paper presented at a seminar on the status of women in the Islamic Family, International Islamic Center for Population Studies and Research, Cairo, 1975

Dixon, Ruth, 'Counting women in the agricultural labour force', *Population and Development Reviews*, vol. 8, no. 3, 1982

Fergany, N., 'Egyptian Women and National Development: A Demographic Background', a paper presented at a seminar on Arab Women in

National Development, Cairo, 24–30 September, 1972

Frederick, P., *Tahia Nasser: The First Ladies of the World*, Meredith, New York, 1967

Gerzouzi, E., 'The Demographic Aspects of Women's Employment in the United Arab Republic', *The Egyptian Population and Family Planning Review*, vol. 3, no. 2, June 1970, pp. 93–8

GL Hamamsy, L.S., 'The Changing Role of the Egyptian Women', *Middle East Forum*, vol. 33, no. 6, 1958

Hammam, Mona, 'Women and Industrial Work in Egypt: The Chubra El-Kheima Case', *ASQ (Arab Studies Quarterly)*, vol. 2, no. 1, Winter 1980, pp. 50–69

Hussein, A., 'Status of Women in Family Law in the United Arab Republic', *Working Paper*, no. 2, for United Nations Seminar on Status of Women in Family, Lome, Togo, 1964

Jomier, J., 'Le Journal d'une doctoresse (Nawal Sadawi)', *Etudes Orientales du Cairé*, vol. 8, 1965, pp. 331–3

Kilpatrick, H., 'The Position of Women', in *The Modern Egyptian Novel: A Study in Social Criticism*, Ithaca Press, London, 1974, pp. 172–8

Mernissi, F., *Women in Islam*, New York, 1980

Mohsen, S., 'The Egyptian Women: Between modernity and tradition', in C.J. Malthiasson (ed.), *Many Sisters: Women in Cross-Cultural Perspective*, The Free Press, New York, 1974, pp. 37–58

Nelson, C. (ed.), *Women, Health and Development*, Cairo papers in Social Sciences, vol. 1, no. 1, Cairo, December 1977

——, 'From Seclusion to Emancipation: Social Change and Sexual Identity in Contemporary Egypt;', in G. Devos (ed.), *Responses to Social Change* Van Nostrand and Company, January 1978

Tomiche, N., 'The position of women in the United Arab Republic', *Journal of Contemporary History* (London), vol. 3, no. 3, 1968, pp. 129–43

——, 'La femme en Islam', in P. Grimal (ed.), *Histoire Mondiale de la Femme*, 4 vols., Nouvelle Librairie de France, Paris, 1967

Tucker, Judith, 'Egyptian Women in the work force' in *Merip Reports*, no. 50

Unesco, 1981, *Women and Development: Indicators of Their Changing Role, Socio-economic Studies 3*

Williams, N.U., 'Factory Employment and Family Relations in an Egyptian Village', University of Michigan (Ph.D. dissertation) 1964

Zaalouk, M.H., 'The Social Structure of Divorce Adjudication in Egypt', The American University in Cairo (Master's Thesis) 1975

4

WOMEN IN CHINA'S SOCIO-ECONOMIC DEVELOPMENT

Hou Di and Li Hong
  (All-China Women's Federation)
  and Lu Hengjun (Associate Professor of
  Economics of the People's University Beijing)

Section 1: Women and the National Economic and Social Development Plan

In China, the plan for national economy is formulated every 5 years. China is now in the fourth year of the sixth Five-Year Plan (1980–5), entitled The Five-Year Plan for China's Economic and Social Development (hereafter referred to as the Sixth Plan).[1] The Sixth Plan covers not only economic indicators concerning production and construction, but also those of social development: the enhancement of people's cultural and material life, including matters relating to the welfare of women and children, and women's life in general. Emphasis in the Plan is given to improving production of durable consumer goods, increasing provision of creche and nurseries, and hospital and medical services.

The specification of such indicators has an important bearing on reducing women's domestic chores, facilitating housework, protecting the mental and physical health of women and children and controlling the growth of the population. The inclusion of these new indicators in the Sixth Plan corrects the past policy of over-emphasising production and construction at the expense of the

---

1. The sources of the data used in the report are: (1) statistics issued by governmental and other national departments; (2) materials provided by the National Symposium of Social Research on and Theoretical Approaches to Women's Problems held in Beijing in September 1984; and (3) results of investigations conducted especially for this report by the authors.

people's living standards.

The national plan for socio-economic development serves the interests of the entire population; and so everyone, including women, is motivated to work together for the common cause of economic and social development. That is to say, in socialist China, the interests of women are the same as those of the nation and the rest of the population. It is, therefore, impossible as well as unnecessary to separate indicators for women's development from the common indicators for the entire population specified in the State plan. Whether certain women-oriented indicators should be included in future, is closely related to other factors such as the level of economic, political, scientific and cultural development.

In the initial years of the People's Republic, the economic base was weak, and most people lived in extreme poverty.

The Sixth Plan, however, was formulated and implemented under a totally different set of circumstances. The Third Plenary Session of the 11th Central Committee of the Chinese Communist Party (1978) re-established the ideological line of proceeding from realities and seeking the truth from the facts, and called for implementation of the policy of readjusting, reforming, consolidating and improving existing enterprises.

The results of the implementation of the Sixth Plan are heartening. Plentiful harvests have been recorded since 1980, with overall output increase in farming, forestry, animal husbandry and fishery. Light and heavy industry have developed in coordination; energy supplies have grown steadily, key construction projects have made rapid progress. The domestic market has been brisk, while the foreign trade, economic and technological exchanges with other countries have made good headway. The living standard of the rural and urban population has continued to improve. According to the State Statistical Bureau, the per capita income in 1983 of workers and staff members (RMB Y526) was 6.4 per cent higher than the previous year; the per capita net income of farmers (RMB Y309.8) was 14.7 per cent higher the previous year. In that same year, the value of the gross national industrial output increased by 10.5 per cent; the value of gross national agricultural output by 9.5 per cent. Many output targets in the Sixth Year Plan, including several items concerning the improvement of living standards, were reached 2 years ahead of schedule, and some even earlier. The output of electrical home appliances has increased greatly in recent years, which has helped to reduce women's housework and create the material conditions for the further emancipation of women and the development of the welfare for women and children. This example shows the direct bearing of national economic and social development plans on the interests of the entire population, including women.

Determining indicators for women's needs in the national plan is handicapped by the fact that China is a developing country with a vast territory, a huge population, but a low level of development of its productive forces. So it is difficult to provide for a substantial increase in women's and children's welfare. Although productivity in China has made big strides, progress is not sufficient to meet the needs in all fields. For example, heavy investment is needed to develop energy and transportation. As the State has to maximise the use of its funds, investment in some areas, including welfare for women and children, has to be adjusted to the overall plan and the level of production in general. None the less, the State has paid considerable attention to the needs of women and children. In 1981, for instance, the State Council designated 10 million yuan (RMB) exclusively for training child-welfare workers and pre-school teachers, and subsidising child care and education facilities in border, minority nationality, mountainous areas and poor areas. Statistics from 24 provinces, autonomous regions and municipalities directly under the central government show that in the past 3 years, 470 million yuan (RMB) has been designated by local financial departments at different levels for child welfare, and 150 million yuan (RMB) plus 24 million Hong Kong dollars have been donated by government bodies, people's organisations and individuals for the same purpose.

One main difficulty faced by the State is the control of population growth. The notable achievements already gained in this respect are the results of arduous educational efforts. However, centuries-old feudal ideas such as: 'men are superior to women' and 'more sons, more happiness' still linger on in varying degrees, particularly in rural families, despite years of educational and publicity efforts to counter them. They continue to stand in the way of planning childbirth and improving women's and children's welfare. More painstaking efforts have still to be made to spread knowledge about maternity and child health, and popularise the use of advanced contraceptive methods so as to promote the family planning programme and consolidate the gains in this important area.

However, since the women's issue is highly complicated and

involves many social problems, it cannot be adequately tackled through the nationnal socio-economic development plan alone. There are, however, several other major channels to protect the legitimate rights and immediate interests of women and children. They will be discussed below.

Laws and Regulations Promulgated by the State

In the Common Programme of the Chinese People's Political Consultative Conference and in the Constitution of the People's Republic of China, both promulgated in the early years of the People's Republic, it is explicitly stated that: 'Women . . . enjoy equal rights with men in all spheres of life, political, economic, cultural and social, including family life'. In the 1950s two important laws (Marriage Law and Land Reform) were passed, which had profound consequences for women. The Marriage Law abolishes the feudal marriage system in favour of freedom of choice in marriage, monogamy and equal rights between women and men. A nationwide publicity campaign about the Marriage Law informed millions upon millions of young women and men of the significance of the new law. Many women were encouraged to break out of arranged and mercenary marriages; and rural women, who had been the worst victims of long years of oppression, began to shake off the shackles of the old marriage and family system, and gain equal economic status with men.

The Land Reform Laws for the first time in Chinese history ensured women's right to land, which raised their economic status overnight and greatly strengthened their position. Meanwhile, women became more active in farm work. By 1952, nearly 60 per cent of the female population were engaged in agricultural production. In 1956, women from 120 million farm households joined agricultural cooperatives and participated in farming, animal husbandry and sideline occupations. In 1953, the first year of the First Five-Year Plan, the Government Administration Council[2] promulgated the Regulations concerning labour insurance, which stipulated that staff and workers should enjoy labour protection regardless of sex, and given women's physiological characteristics, made special provisions for them. In 1954, a law concerning the election of deputies to the National People's Congress and local

2. Replaced by the State Council in 1954.

congresses at various levels, stipulated that women and men have equal right to vote and stand for election. This was the first time in Chinese history that women had the right to participate in state affairs on an equal footing with men.

Since 1978, the government has passed a series of laws and regulations, and a number of amendments have been made to the Constitution, the Criminal Law, the Law of Criminal Proceedings, the Marriage Law and others. These provisions provide the legal basis for protecting women's and children's legitimate rights and interests and safeguarding matrimonial and family relations along socialist lines.

In 1983 and 1984, in the light of the principles laid down by the Central Government concerning the protection of women's and children's rights, similar laws and regulations have been promulgated by 12 Provincial People's Congresses.[3] These local versions are more detailed and are geared to the local conditions.

Functional Regulations, Notifications and Directives Originating from Government Departments

In the 30 years from 1953–83, at least 45 regulations, directives and circular notices catering for the special needs of women have been formulated by various government departments. The following are some examples:

— A woman staff or worker who is 7 months pregnant or who has been breastfeeding for less than 6 months must not work on night shift.
— A pregnant woman staff or worker whose current job is physiologically unsuitable, should transfer to a lighter job.
— A factory should provide rest rooms and other health protection facilities for its women staff and workers.

In 1980, the Ministry of Public Health circulated specific guidelines for raising the quality of health work for women and children, establishing additional health protection agencies in this field and perfecting existing ones, and the care and education of infants and children. In 1980, the Ministries of Light Industry, Commerce and Food Industry made a joint report on the problem of children's

3. Hebei, Liaoning, Sichuan, Fujian, Hubei, Jiangxi, Jilin, Guangxi, Gansu, Anhui, Guizhou, Yunnan, and the Municipal People's Congresses of Beijing and Tianjin.

food, which called for improvements in the organisation of the production of baby and children's foods, so as to increase their variety and output and raise their quality and nutritive value.

In view of the employment problems confronting women, the Ministry of Labour in 1980 and 1983 provided new sets of rules for the qualifying examinations for new factory recruits and applicants for vocational schools. The rules stipulated that attention should be paid to female applicants enrolling in vocational schools, taking into consideration the nature of the trades and actual conditions. As for recruitment, the rules specified that the male/female ratio should be based both on the production needs and the availability of labour, and that jobs suitable for young women should be filled by them as much as possible. In 1983 when the readjustment of enterprises created a problem of over-employment, the State Economic Commission and the Ministry of Labour ruled that of the surplus female personnel, pregnant women and nursing mothers should be given special consideration.

Women's Organisations

Women's organisations play a crucial role in identifying women's needs and bringing their views to the attention of the government and other related departments, making suggestions and actively canvassing for the solution of women's day-to-day problems. The women's organisations also do promotional and educational work among women, encouraging them to improve themselves constantly, to contribute to the task of building China into a rich, prosperous and strong country.

In the early post-liberation days when the feudal ideology of male superiority was still very much in evidence, women were barred from many public activities. To change the situation, the women's organisations came to the fore with the slogan: 'Get down to work, men AND women!' and persistently urged for the appointment and training of women cadres. As a result, 70–80 per cent of the agricultural cooperatives had women as heads or deputy heads. In cities, women were encouraged to go out to work: some of them participated in the productive activities of State-owned or collective-owned units, and some ran small businesses of their own. By 1956, the number of urban women workers and staff members[4]

4. This figure covers the workers and staff members in urban state-owned and

reached 13.48 per cent of the total working population (3.26 million); by 1983, the percentage had risen to 36.50 per cent. In the political field, women were called on to take an active part at the grass-roots level in the People's Congress elections in 1953 and 1955: more than 90 per cent of the women with the right to vote participated. Among the grass-roots representatives elected, women accounted for 17 per cent in 1953, 20.3 per cent (over 1 million in number) in 1956, and 21.2 per cent in 1983. Women's extensive participation in the elections was the result of the efforts of the women's organisations acting under the guidance of government policies.

In recent years, in response to requests from the female population, the women's organisations have decided to take more concrete steps to defend the rights and interests of women and children. At the initiative of the Fifth National Women's Congress, during the winter of 1983 and the spring of 1984, month-long campaigns publicising the legal protection of the legitimate rights of women and children were launched throughout the country. The campaign sharply criticised lingering feudal beliefs in male superiority, dealt a powerful blow to criminal violations of the women's and children's rights and interests, raised public awareness of the potency of the law, and reinforced the position that the Party and the entire society should pay attention to and respect the rights of women and children.

Women's organisations are found throughout the countryside and in cities at the district, county, provincial and national levels. Factories have their own women workers' committees. In places where the women's organisations do a competent job with the help and support of the departments concerned, women's problems can generally be correctly resolved. Because of the special role of the women's organisations in protecting the legitimate rights of women and children, they have deservedly earned the affectionate name, 'the women's home'.

At present, the entire Chinese population is striving to achieve the common goal of invigorating the Chinese nation, and of quadrupling China's annual industrial and agricultural output by the

---

collectively-owned enterprises and institutions, government offices and people's organisations at various levels. The figure does *not* include retired personnel, administrative personnel in rural people's communes (townships), workers in township-owned enterprises and institutions or self-employed workers in cities and the countryside.

year 2000. In order to attain this goal, China is reforming its economic structure.

Section 2: The Road of Reform — Rural Economic Reforms

In the last 5 years, China has experienced unprecedented agricultural growth and achieved encouraging changes. According to the April 1984 figures released by the State Statistical Bureau, our total grain output, its annual increase, the average per-*mu* grain yield, and the grain output per capita all hit new records; there was an all-round development of agriculture, forestry, animal husbandry, side-occupations and fishery; rural product markets were prosperous; peasants improved their standards of living. These successes are attributed first to the policy of enabling people to attain greater wealth, second to science and technology, third to rural women, and fourth to the peasants in general.

Since the general adoption of the *household responsibility system* in which rewards are linked to output, the encouragement of specialised households (households specialising in a particular product or operation), and the fostering of township and town enterprises, our rural economy has advanced rapidly. The rural economy is being transformed from a complete or partial self-sufficiency into relatively large-scale commodity production; traditional agriculture is changing into modern agriculture.

Under the household responsibility system the peasant household undertakes to cultivate a certain area of land and ensure a fixed amount of output by contract, and receives rewards linked to the actual output. The system integrates the producer with the entrepreneur. It not only overcomes the drawbacks of over-centralised management and egalitarian distribution, but closely interlocks the interests of the State, the collective and the individual. It has aroused the enthusiasm of the peasants, who say: 'The contract system is good for it ensures the part for the State, reserves enough for the collective, and gives all the rest to the household'. The adoption and spread of the system has brought tremendous changes in rural labour organisations and ways of production, and constitutes a fundamental reform of the rural economic structure.

The policy of establishing *specialised households* was adopted after the responsibility system. It promotes a division of labour in the rural economy and the growth of socialisation, specialisation and commodity production. There are now 24.82 million special-ised households or 13.6 per cent of the nation's peasant households. In some places specialised villages, markets and small economic zones have appeared.

Developing *township and town enterprises* is another policy designed to stimulate the rural economy. It should lead to the development of medium and small cities, the elimination of the differences between town and country, and promotion of exchange between urban and rural areas. Township and town enterprises absorbed more than 31 million surplus rural people in 1983, and the total output of commune- and production brigade-run industries accounted for 12 per cent of the value of all industries in China.

The implementation of the above policies has not only changed the previous situation in which China had to import grain, cotton, edible oil and sugar, but has also solved the problem of feeding and clothing 1 billion people, by basically relying on our own efforts and supporting the advances of industry and other economic and cultural undertakings. The reform of the rural economy and the rapid growth of all kinds of production provide numerous chances for women to take part in production. The wealth they have created for the State, the collective and the family as well as the economic benefits they have received has exceeded those of previous periods. Rural women are able to display their talents in various fields of production and have made big contributions to building the new socialist countryside. They enjoy an enhanced position in society and in the family and have substantially improved their standard of living. These changes can be discussed under the following 10 points.

(1) Liberated from the single grain-crop production, rural women are taking up *diversified management*. For many years, China's rural women were dependent on the soil and worked in the fields. Thanks to changes in production structure, labour organisation and ways of production, women are no longer confined to the fields and are active in handicrafts, side-occupations, industry and commerce, and service trades. They do weaving, embroidery and tailoring; cultivate cotton and hemp plants, tea bushes and fruit trees; breed chickens, ducks, pigs, sheep, cattle and bees; set up flower and seedling nurseries, catering establishments, hotels, barbers' shops and home nurseries. They engage in a wide range of trades using their advantages of nimble fingers, delicate skills and patience.

Of the 100,000 rural women in Wugong County, Shaanxi Province, 80 per cent weave corn husks into articles. Many households can earn 10,000 yuan annually from this handicraft; the county has earned more than 2.9 million yuan from this source alone and corn husk articles have become one of its major commodities. Many handicrafts — carpets, baskets and cushions — are sold abroad, in Japan, France, Italy and other countries, adding more than 16 million US$ to foreign exchange earnings.

Owing to the growth of household side-occupations, part of the surplus labour force, especially the auxiliary female labour force, may give free play to their talents. Longzheng Township of Haian County under Nantong City developed household poultry raising by using a large section of the auxiliary female labour force. The township now has 100,000 chickens and hens and produces 900,000 kilogrammes of eggs a year. With great satisfaction women say: 'We take care of household work while cooking and collect eggs with a child in the arms'. Thus, everyone is useful and does a suitable job.

(2) Many rural women become the *first generation of workers in township and town enterprises*, without leaving their home villages or going to the cities.

A survey of 3 counties — Shaoxing, Tongyang and Yiwu — in Zhejiang Province show that where township and town enterprises are developed, 70–80 per cent of the female labour force works in factories. Women of Tongyang County not only provide a major input in farm production, but also make up 70 per cent of the 80,000 workers and staff in the township and town enterprises. Shaoxing County's enterprises mainly produce textile and other light industrial products, and garments, and 80 per cent of their workers and staff are women. Of the 813 million yuan of output produced by the county's township and town enterprises in 1983, 552 million yuan came from textile mills alone. Dachen Township of Yiwu County is known for its tailoring skills, and women make up 78 per cent of the workers and staff of its garments enterprises. Their output amounted to 5.6 million yuan in 1983, accounting for 67 per cent of the total industrial and agricultural output in the township, and 96 per cent of the value of its total industrial output.

With the development of commodity production and township and town enterprises, many rural women have become the first generation of workers of a new type in China's countryside. The Xihe tapestry mill of Zhuoxian County, Hebei Province, produces beautiful and uniquely designed Oriental tapestries which are exported to 19 countries including the United States, Japan and Britain. These artistic products are made by ordinary rural women. Many rural women are also active in more than one kind of rural production, such as industry and farming, farming and side-occupations, or commerce and side-occupations.

The participation of rural women in township and town enterprises has liberated surplus labour from relatively limited farmland and lessened the imbalance between population and land. Moreover, it has also promoted a more rational use of the female labour force. Generally young women work in factories and middle-aged and old women take part in farming, diversified management and household processing jobs. This division of labour suits the respective skills, educational levels, age and physical strength of the women and helps raise labour efficiency.

(3) Large numbers of rural women take an active part in *commodity production* and there are many *specialised households* in which women are the main operators. From their practical experience, rural women learn that 'without agriculture, there is no stability; without industry, there is no affluence; and without commerce, there is no circulation'. Within the last few years, a large section of rural women have switched to commodity production and act as the main operators of specialised households.

According to surveys of rural conditions in 323 counties conducted by women's federations in 14 provinces, between 35 and 45 per cent of the rural specialised households are mainly operated by women and about 40 per cent of the value produced by all specialised households is created by women. Lianshui County, Jiangsu Province, is a good case in point. The total value of industrial and agricultural output rose by 112 per cent between 1978 and 1983 and the per capita outcome of its peasants quadrupled. More than half its 11,000 specialised households are mainly managed by women: of 19,400 households engaging in grain production (producing at least 5,000 kilogrammes of grain each annually) 9,000 are mainly operated by women.

Women are also taking part in all sorts of commodity production, ranging from planting, breeding, and processing to communications, transport and catering business. A survey by the Women's Federation of Langfang Prefecture, Hebei Province, indicated that in the first half of 1984 women made up 48 per cent of all those engaged in commodity production in Xianghe County and 85.4 per cent of the total female labour force. In over 4,700 businesses more than one-half of their workers and staff were women. Women created 43.63 million yuan of output in 1983, accounting for 35 per cent of the value of the county's total output of commodities. Rural women have also gone into the 'forbidden zone' of commerce: they set up stalls and stores in their localities, sell goods transported from other places, contribute to the considerable volume of purchases and sales and thus enliven urban and rural markets considerably.

(4) Rural women can take up various kinds of *production by contract* and make their own decisions in living arrangements. The principle of equal pay for equal work is widespread. Before the adoption of the household responsibility system, production management, form of labour organisation and working hours were all excessively centralised. If rural women wanted to take part in collective production in the fields, they had to work 3 periods a day like the men. They could not organise production in their own way and had little time to attend to their household affairs. Following the adoption of the system, rural women are able to take part in production, create wealth, earn an income and find time to take care of their children and household affairs. Given more freedom in living arrangements, rural women display unprecedented high levels of initiative and creativeness. For example in Heilongjiang Province at the end of 1983, the number of rural women taking part in production jumped to 4 million, 42 per cent higher than the previous record of 2.8 million. Many women over 50 years in age were not in the labour force, but played a major role in household management.

A sample survey by the Women's Federation of Jilin Province shows that most rural women have the right to make their own decisions in the following matters: to sign contract for cultivating farmland; to work out production plans; to arrange their studies and amusements; to take up projects of scientific farming; to buy high-grade commodities and furniture. Thus, they can plan the ways of using their labour, the time of production and the items to be produced in the light of their needs and their convenience. They skilfully take care of both farming and household work and still have time for side-occupations. They say with pleasure: 'Being bound to the fields, we lacked enthusiasm for production and could not expect much in improving living standards. Now the household responsibility system enables us to arrange our time flexibly and we have time to work, take care of household affairs, visit relatives and go to theatres'.

Because women can give full play to their talents and energy, income differences between men and women are narrow and equal pay for equal work is genuinely realised. The past practice of giving higher rewards to men without considering the women's work results has been changed. This further promotes equality between the sexes.

(5) Women have transformed their ideological outlook and are eager to *study science and raise their educational level*. In the past most rural women, especially those with children, were busy with cooking and childcare. As the countryside becomes more prosperous and commodity production steadily grows, women's ideological outlook has also undergone profound changes. They talk about effective ways to raise income and the scientific knowledge that can raise economic efficiency. For example, they use such scientific terms as multi-layer breeding and discuss the proper humidity for cultivating mushrooms. In short, they are devoted to gaining wealth through hard work.

In the past men largely mastered techniques, because the egalitarian distribution system failed to link techniques with the peasants' immediate interests and many women did not feel an urgent need for scientific knowledge and technology. Now rewards vary directly with output, and side-occupations are a major income source. More and more women understand that to become wealthy not only needs enthusiasm and diligence, but also scientific knowledge and timely market information. Shen Wenhui, a peasant woman, is a good example. She lives at Jinsha village, Maling Township, Gonxian County, Sichuan Province. When she heard that raising chickens and long-hair rabbits was very profitable, she decided to take up this activity. So she borrowed 2,326 yuan from the national bank and bought 30 long-hair rabbits and 320 chickens. But within a few days 12 rabbits died of disease and then a pest killed 100 chickens. This setback helped her to understand that the desire for higher income must be combined with scientific knowledge to produce results. From then on, she has studied science in earnest.

Now many women attend technical training classes and subscribe to scientific and technical periodicals and books at their own expense. For example Yin Yueli of Jiohe County, Jilin Province, began raising rabbits after she had graduated from a senior middle school. She has now become a specialist in this field after 3 years of hard study, and is writting 2 pamphlets entitled 'Answering Questions about Raising Rabbits' and 'Rabbit Raising'.

(6) A large number of able women have emerged in the rural areas who are adept at *making decisions and taking action*, are keen on study, skilful in operation and involved in pushing forward reforms. These women of ability have had to overcome the bias of looking down on women; they possess the pioneer spirit, believe in science, master certain techniques and show dexterous skills in management and operation. For instance, 38-year-old Yang Wechan of Pingyuan County's Guoyang Town in Shanxi Province blazed a way of getting rich by managing mobile food stalls as early as 1980. Then sensitive to the existence of local resources she imagined how they could be used in production and then transformed into commodities. She decided to learn about transport, and in 1983 she joined a motor company. Owing to her ability and determination to expand investment and business, she enjoys high prestige in the transport trade and has been elected vice-manager of the company. She is now one of the seven famous persons of ability in Pingyuan.

Wei Xiuping, a 35-year-old woman of Shenxian County, Hebei province, is director of the Daran village joint household garment factory. When some villagers first heard of her idea to establish a factory, they made rather unfavourable comments: 'With long hair but short wisdom, a woman cannot do anything with substantial results'. Ignoring discouraging opinions, Wei Xiuping persuaded her mother, husband and two brothers-in-law to become vice-directors and started the factory. Her mother is the designer and cutter; the two brothers-in-law are in charge of collecting commodity information, purchasing and marketing; her husband looks after the factory's administrative services and she is responsible for machinery maintenance and overall production in the factory. Having solved one by one the problems of getting funds, a workplace and sewing-machines she finally started the factory in 1983. In less than two years, the factory has expanded from 6 to 130 persons, from 6 to 20 rooms and from 4 to 60 sewing-machines; it has also bought a truck and a generator. It produced a range of high- and medium-grade garments which are sold in more than 40 stores in Beijing, Tianjin, Taiyuan and 3 other cities. Total value of output was 340,000 yuan in 1983 but reached 650,000 yuan in the first 7 months of 1984. Wei Xiuping is determined to make a still bigger contribution to meeting the people's demand for well-designed clothes in the future.

These women exemplify the orientation of women's advance and provide models for other rural women.

(7) Owing to rural women's *rising incomes*, their position in society and the household has been further enhanced. Thanks to the economic reforms rural women have doubled or trebled their incomes and some have even increased them more than tenfold. In many cases, women get higher incomes than men. A survey of 90 high-income women in 39 townships conducted by the Yiwu County Women's Federation of Zhejiang Province showed that 55 per cent of them made between 2,000 and 4,000 yuan, 27 per cent, 4,000 and 6,000 yuan, 10 per cent, 6,000 and 10,000 yuan, and 6 or 7 per cent 10,000 yuan or more. Women in the 164 households in Shentang Village, famous for its art and craft products, all do some knitting and this added 1.49 million yuan to their income in 1983, averaging 9,148 yuan per household. In that same year the value of the village's agricultural output doubled, as a result, the villagers' total income rose tenfold between 1980 and 1983.

Women are also exercising a bigger influence than before in household affairs. The Jiamusi City Women's Federation conducted a survey of 574 households to find out who takes the decision in the major family matters. The results showed that in 20 per cent of households the husband makes the decision; in 10 per cent the husband's parents; in 17 per cent the wife; in 53 per cent the husband and wife jointly after consultations.

Rural girls are changing their attitude towards love and marriage. Old ideas and traditions used to shackle youngsters in these respects: for example, marriage arrangements had to involve a marriage broker; otherwise, it was considered against custom. Nowadays, the number of youngsters choosing their own partner is steadily growing and cases of parents intervening in their children's marriage are gradually declining. In the choice of spouse, the stress is changing from economic position and family connections to ideological, moral and cultural factors. The practice of asking for betrothal gifts from the groom's family is being replaced by parents giving a dowry to daughters.

(8) *The functions of the family have expanded* in the rural areas and

more families have won the 'Five-Good' titles. In the wake of adopting the household responsibility system, the family has expanded its functions: it is not only a unit of consumption, education and propagation of future generations, but has become also a unit of production. Expanded production calls for family democracy and harmony, and family harmony and unity are beneficial to developing production. This has boosted the number of 'Five-Good' Families, i.e. families that are good at: (a) loving the motherland and abiding by the law; (b) raising production output, work and study; (c) practising family planning and educating children; (d) practising politeness and sanitation; (e) respecting the old, taking care of the young and uniting with the neighbours. Of the 9,889 nationwide 'Five-Good Families' in 1983, 5,449 were in rural areas. At the county or higher administrative divisions level there were 3.84 million throughout the country.

The 'Five-Good' conditions are continuously adapted to local needs. Recently many places have included scientific farming and eradicating illiteracy in the 'Five-Good' conditions.

(9) *Welfare provisions* for women and children *have expanded*. With improved living conditions and greater wealth, peasants want to give their children a good education. In the past, nurseries and kindergartens were set up at busy farming seasons and dissolved during the slack seasons; now peasants pool funds and invite educated village youngsters to run them. Households specialising in children's education and care have also emerged in many rural areas. Since 1978, rural kindergartens have increased their intake of children by 37.1 per cent. The government has also stressed the development of intellectual resources. For instance, Shaoxing County of Zhejiang Province has allocated 360,000 yuan in the last 5 years for expanding nursery and kindergarten capacity. Seven central kindergartens have been built or are under construction. The number of kindergarten classes rose from 392 in 1979 to 946 in 1983 and numbers went up from 11,516 to 24,894 children. The quality of education also enormously improved. The children's park has added new equipment and toys, diversifying children's activities.

Rural welfare is also expanding: there are now over 14,000 homes for the elderly in rural areas providing close to 170,000 childless people with a comfortable home. Almost 3 million rural Chinese enjoy the five guarantees (provision of meals, clothes, housing, medical treatment and a proper funeral), and they account for 96.18

per cent of all those who are entitled to these benefits. In the last 6 years rural collective economic organisations spent more than 1,100 million yuan on supporting the five-guarantee benefits. Shenqiu County, Henan Province, introduced a system of household responsibility for its 4,300 elderly people enjoying the five guarantees. Each of them received an average of 380 yuan (cash, grain and other things) in 1983, or 30 yuan more than the per capita income of the county's rural population.

A pension system has been adopted in rural places with better yields; men start to draw pensions at 60 and women at 55. Statistics from 13 provinces and municipalities show that 530,000 peasants in over 6,000 production teams receive pensions.

(10) The *life style* and demands of rural women are also undergoing changes. An increasing number of rural women are paying more attention to 'fixing nutritious food, wearing better clothes and living in spacious rooms'. Large numbers of peasants live in brick houses; in many economically advanced villages, blocks of two- or three-storey buildings have been erected. Rural middle-aged women and girls wear similar dresses to those worn by their counterparts in cities. In places of higher output, ownership of watches, bicycles and sewing-machines — formerly sought by peasants as a symbol of richness — is common. Peasant families are now able to buy high-grade consumer goods such as colour television sets, tape-recorders, electric ovens and electrically warmed matresses. In some villages every household has a colour television set or a refrigerator. To help expand production, some specialised households have installed telephones or bought trucks, motor-cycles and minicomputers.

Rural women are no longer confined to working in the fields and cooking. They lead a rich cultural life and make new demands for their material and cultural life. Many women say they want to become wealthier, to study and to have amusements. As life improves, rural women need more electric appliances to relieve their household chores and like to buy attractive and stylish clothes. No longer content with two braids fastened with red woollen thread, rural young women also go to hairdressers' shops. Even young mothers like smart hairstyles. Rural women are interested in seeing films, photography, planting flowers and participating in recreational activities; they also set higher standards for their leisure time cultural life. Well-off peasants now tour different parts of China.

Newly married couples are beginning to spend their honeymoon travelling to places of scenic or other interest. Many peasants visit Beijing at their own cost — seeing the Forbidden City, tasting Beijing roast duck and taking snapshots of each other before Tian An Men. Such activities were once inconceivable for Chinese peasants and particularly rural women who never used to leave their native villages.

Problems Still to be Dealt With

This description of 10 major changes helps us to understand the influence the reform of rural economic structure has had on China's rural women. The changes in production and quality of life are of historical significance, as are advances for women. On the other hand, rural women still have their weak points and still face a number of critical problems.

(1) The educational, scientific and technical levels of rural women fall behind the needs of modern agriculture. China is a developing country with a weak economic base and relatively backward in education and science: 235 million people are completely or semi-illiterate, of whom 72 per cent are women. Levels of productivity and mechanisation in China are low; many operations are still done by hand. As a result some women do not feel an urgent need for general, scientific or technical training. To increase incomes, some short-sighted parents only want their young daughters to work and won't let them go to school. This problem is rather serious in mountain, border and national minority areas. Unless this is quickly tackled by effective measures, what are now women's strengths will change into their weaknesses. Women's educational disabilities not only cannot meet the needs of agricultural modernisation, but will hamper the further progress of equality between men and women, and women's emancipation.

(2) Insufficient attention has been paid to protecting women workers. For instance, in some town and township enterprises using simple equipment, women workers do high labour intensity work for long hours. The enterprises neglect labour protection measures for their women workers. Some enterprises do not know what the necessary steps are to protect women's and children's health. A number of women who

strive to raise their incomes pay insufficient attention to taking proper rest and protecting their health.

(3) The traditional bias of looking down on women still exists to a certain extent. In some places, women giving birth to girls are maltreated or discriminated against; there are still cases of arranged marriages and asking for betrothal gifts. Prolonged efforts and education are needed to wipe out these practices completely.

Heated discussion of such problems took place at the meeting on theoretical studies of the women question (discussed later). Participants agreed that of the three problems the most urgent one is raising women's educational and scientific levels. Women have lagged behind in their educational and scientific levels for several reasons. First, recent efforts to eradicate illiteracy were not consistently carried out as in the 1950s. Second, given the previous long-term stagnation of agricultural production and lack of mechanisation, peasants felt little need for education, science or technology. Third, women still shoulder a heavier burden of housework than men, and therefore have less time to study. Fourth, rural schools are not distributed rationally. There are also few agricultural or vocational schools, and the education offered by regular middle schools cannot be directly applied to farming. This affects women's enthusiasm for study.

The situation is however changing: economic reforms have led to rural women demanding better facilities and this has highlighted the question of raising women's scientific and educational levels. The government departments concerned and women's federations at all levels have adopted various measures to solve the problem. For instance, to help women learn to read and write quickly, the Women's Federation of Zhuzhou County in Human Province in cooperation with township government and educational departments sponsored a study campaign of 'learning 1,000 characters, making 100 sentences and writing 10 compositions in 100 days'. The county established 368 women's literacy classes and enrolled 1,683 women grass-roots cadres and practically all the illiterate or semi-illiterate women below 40. The classes helped 12,820 women to become literate and proved a big success. According to the Ministry of Education, 21.26 million people have learned to read and write in the last 5 years and most of them are women.

In places where women already have achieved a certain educational level, scientific and technical classes and evening schools are established to offer courses on production techniques to women. In Hebei Province 34.4 per cent of all those attending scientific and technical classes in 1983 were women. Many women also passed the entrance examinations to the Central Broadcasting Agricultural School, and there are more than 5,400 women students of the schools in Heihe Prefecture of Heilongjiang Province, Hanshou County of Hunan Province and Dalian City alone.

To meet women's needs, some places have set up study groups to learn techniques such as chicken raising or training classes; it is anticipated that those attending the classes will spread what they learnt to others in their villages. Zhenan County of Shaanxi Province first trained 56 women in silkworm breeding; they then passed the technique on to women in their villages and in this way the numbers of silkworm breeders jumped to 15,000. There are also places where the masses are encouraged to teach each other. Sometimes one person spreads a particular technique to the whole village so as to help all villagers take the road to common prosperity. In Shahezi of Shangxian County, Shaanxi Province, Yang Caixia and her husband breed martens and earn 10,300 yuan a year because the fur is of high quality. Yang Caixia explains how to breed martens to her fellow villagers once a week. As a result, there are 28 households specialising in marten breeding in the village and they have achieved high survival and multiplication rates. There has also been an upsurge in women running private schools in Luyang County, Hunan Province. Xu Tongsheng, a retired staff member of Chengguan Town, set up 4 private classes, 2 evening schools and 1 sewing class in several remote places in less than 4 years. There are 175 graduates from her classes and schools, and her efforts are praised by the local people. Liuyang County now has 335 private classes and schools with an enrolment of 8,510 of which 2,592 are women. These establishments provide a chance of further study to women who have just learnt to read and write, to those who missed their primary- and middle-school education and to youngsters who want to continue their studies.

As for protection of women workers in places and enterprises where production goes smoothly, it is mainly a question of lack of relevant knowledge. In the rural areas many cadres at the primary level and the masses in general including women do not know how to protect women's and children's health adequately. Therefore, the problem should be solved in two ways. First, various labour regulations should be produced which take into account women's productive jobs such as transplanting rice seedlings and fish breeding which involves working in water. Second, hygiene education should be promoted so that grass-roots cadres and women can learn and thereby improve women's labour protection.

In summary, the rural economic reforms in the last 5 years have led to tremendous achievements, which have brought many benefits to women and also given rise to new demands. These will be gradually met with the further growth of agricultural production and deepening of structural reforms.

Section 3: Experiments in Urban Reform

In recent years much experimentation has gone on with a view to reforming China's urban and industrial structure, and many important measures have been adopted. These include the policies of replacing the profits enterprises used to deliver to the State by taxes; reorganisation and consolidation of enterprises; extension of the enterprises' decision-making power and introduction of various forms of the economic responsibility system; implementing the principle of 'distribution according to work' and overcoming the egalitarian practice of 'eating from the common pot' which prevailed in the relations of enterprises to the State, and of workers and staff members to their enterprises; reforming and opening up channels for the circulation of commodities; encouraging the development of collective and individual economy; opening to the world; setting up special economic zones, opening up 14 coastal cities, etc. All this has motivated the workers and staff members of enterprises to achieve conspicuous results, and brought a vitality and vigour to urban economic life unknown for many years.

These urban reforms are, however, only in the initial stage. Many defects hindering the development of the productive forces in the urban areas have yet to be eradicated. According to the decision of the CPC Central Committee on China's Economic Structure Reform passed on 20 October 1984, fairly extensive urban reforms shall soon be put through in many fields. Judging from the results of recent experiments in the cities of Chongqing, Shashi, Changzhou and in a number of enterprises of different sizes, these reforms also have the warm support and approval of the women workers and staff members, intellectuals, engineering and technical personnel, who have gained new skills and experience.

The central intention of urban reform is to enhance the viability of enterprises by expanding their autonomy; and providing by a system of enabling the enterprise directors or managers to assume full responsibility for decision making. The choice of the right people for these and other leading posts is hence of paramount importance. The reforms are having particular impact on women.

Women's Participation in Reform and Leadership

According to a survey by questionnaire and discussions organised by the Women's Federations of the 8 cities of Tianjin, Chongqing, Harbin, Zhengzhou, Shashi, Changzhou, Taiyuan and Fuzhou in over 50 factories, enterprises, shops and neighbourhood factories, the majority of the women surveyed wholeheartedly want these reforms. The Shanxi Women Cadre School, for instance, sent out 1,800 questionnaires entitled 'Women and Reforms' to 7 enterprises including the Taiyuan Steel Co., the Shanxi Knitting Mill's Spinning Factory, the Shanxi Wireless Broadcasting Equipment Factory and the Taiyuan Department Store. Of the 1,000 questionnaires returned, the majority showed that women feel these reforms will bring prosperity to China. Only a few expressed some misgivings.

There is no shortage of women with entrepreneurial spirit and ability in China, however, due to faults of management, their talents and abilities were not discovered and utilised in the past. Through the reforms, many capable women have either been elected by other workers or staff members, recommended by the leaders, or volunteered themselves to assume posts of leadership. These are women with vision and spirit: young, capable, energetic, educated and knowledgeable. They neither give arbitrary and impracticable directions nor work conscientiously but lack initiative. The women who have become new factory directors, managers, workshop chiefs and foremen are pragmatic, efficient and well-informed. In the Dongli District of Harbin, for instance, two-thirds of the total number of workers and staff members in the commercial field are women. Before the reforms, 33 per cent of the leaders at various levels were women, now 62 per cent are.

The aim of the reforms is to develop the productive forces of society so as to satisfy the people's growing material and spiritual needs. Whoever can bring vigour and vitality to the enterprises and turn losses into profits deserve to the leaders, regardless of sex. A number of talented women have come to the fore under these circumstances. An illustration is Zou Hong, the manager of the Friendship Restaurant in Shenzhen Special Economic Zone. She started in business at 27 by providing a fast food service and was hugely successful. She went on to form a joint venture with Hong Kong businessmen, bought land at high cost and built Shanzhen Restaurant. In less than a year, she was able to make 20,000 yuan in profits. Modernising management methods and keeping well abreast of market demand, she helped restaurant employees to upgrade their culinary skills and expand and improve service quality. She hired people by contract and brought in a wage system paying most workers a variable salary, which depended on performance: this changed the employees' attitude of not caring about quality of service because their salary was fixed regardless of performance. As a result, the restaurant's business boomed. In 3 years, the restaurant has increased its tax payments from several hundred thousand yuan to several million yuan. Not satisfied with these successes, she is going on to build an international standard restaurant, 70 times larger than the present one. People call her a woman with far-sightedness and business acumen, a 'modern entrepreneur'.

Increased Income

In China today, people say that the rural areas are spurring on the cities, the enterprises are spurring on the government departments, and the rank and file are spurring on the leaders. The rural responsibility system is now coming into town. In enterprises, everyone's responsibilities are clearly defined, and only when workers perform well can they benefit: income is thus in direct proportion to efficiency. This has provided the necessary motivation to workers to fulfil or overfulfil their work quotas and turn in quality performances.

The reforms have driven home the idea of respect for and acknowledgement of the fruits of labour. Whoever wants to earn more has to work more: more pay for more work and less pay for less work. At the Changzhou Sox Plant, people used to get the same bonus regardless of performance; now bonuses are based on individual work performance. In July 1984 the lowest bonuses were 6 yuan, the highest 13. Some younger workers are getting higher bonuses than older ones, as in the case of a newcomer of 2 years in the plant who received over 90 yuan a month, more than many long-service women workers. At the Qunlin Market in Chongqing, the salesgirl Lu Qingli received a bonus of 1,900 yuan for her marked ability to sell motor-cycles. At the No. 1 Construction Co. of Chongqing, a young woman mason Han Shiying took part in a city-wide masons' competition last year and got the full score for laying brick walls. She received the same amount of bonus as some of the men — 450 yuan — and has now been promoted to a 9th grade worker.

Employment

One of the important objects of urban economic reform is to solve the employment problem, which largely affects young women. Government statistics show that in 1979 there were 6 million youth waiting for employment in the country, of whom 70 per cent were women. At its 3rd Plenary Session in 1979, the 11th Central Committee of the Communist Party of China, starting from facts of a large population, abundant supplies of labour but slow growth of production and uneven economic development, made the important policy decision 'under the prerequisite of maintaining the superiority of the socialist public ownership of the means of production, to implement a policy of long-time coexistence of diversified economic forms and different methods of management'. At the same time, the system of unified employment and distribution of the labour force was changed into a combination of creation of jobs by labour departments and through voluntary organisation for employment and individual employment. This has opened up wide opportunities: from 1979 to 1983, the State has arranged for the employment of 10.71 million young women, swelling the ranks of women workers and staff members in the country from 31.28 million in 1978 to 41.99 million in 1983, and their proportion in the total number of workers and staff members from 32.9 per cent to 36.5 per cent.

In the course of urban reforms, employment for young women has been expanded and changed in a number of ways. Changes in the economic structure and development of textiles, service and light industries: the development and expansion of the cultural, educational and health fields, and economic and financial departments have all expanded women's employment.

The State has readjusted the former imbalance between heavy industry, light industry and trade. The amount of investment in light industrial capital construction has risen from 12.6 per cent during the First Five-Year Plan to 20 per cent in the Sixth Five-Year Plan. This has brought greater numbers of people to the light industrial departments. Since 1978, of the 9 million personnel added to the industrial departments, 68 per cent went into the light and textile industries. At the end of 1983, the number of trade, food and other service outlets has reached 6.98 million, employing a total of 22.26 million people, an increase of 12.89 million over 1978. Most of these were women. Labour departments at various levels have also widely publicised the State's employment policies and stressed the development of the collective and individual economy as the main solution to employment of young people. This has changed the attitude that all employment comes from the State and helped foster the idea that a variety of solutions can be found, that State organisations and enterprises, neighbourhoods, the young people's parents and young people themselves can organise for employment and for self-employment.

State enterprises and departments in the past few years have opened many service companies to give employment to the grown-up children of their workers and staff members. Such companies absorb between 20 and 30 per cent of the youth waiting for jobs. A new pattern of youth employment has appeared in Chaozhou, Guangdong Province. In the past 5 years, the city has arranged employment for 50,000 people, of whom 92.1 per cent formed collective or individual businesses and only 7.9 per cent went into State-owned enterprises.

In the past few years, many young women have also set up businesses on their own; shops run by couples or mother and daughters have mushroomed. Between 1979 and 1983 the number of individually employed women has grown rapidly — from 30,000 to 2.31 million. For example, a young woman, Zhang Zhanying of Beijing, and 9 other young people started by selling tea on the streets. In the past few years, they have developed into a collective enterprise embracing trading, food and services employing 1,700 people. Of these 1,200 were young people and, in turn, 80 per cent of these are women.

In many cities, youth are no longer unemployed and new labour force entrants can generally get employment in the same year. At present, the problem of employment among young women has been basically solved; this has not only brought security to the life of the young women but also invigorated urban economy and brought convenience to the residents. In Guangzhou, over 100,000 individual businesses are active in the 1,000-odd streets, 36 per cent of which are in food services, the rest in repair and other service trades. Roasted chickens, ducks and geese, big favourites with Guangzhou people, are in plentiful supply thanks to individual businesses, which get their supplies straight from the individually owned poultry farms in nearby rural areas.

Continuing Education

Large numbers of women workers and staff are now going in for continuing education to meet the challenges of the technical revolution. At present, men and women in every field are faced with stiff competition in respect of qualifications. The elimination of the inferior is unavoidable. Whereas before people relied on physical labour to improve economic results, now more intensive labour and longer hours can no longer give them the competitive edge that technical expertise and knowledge of modern management methods will bring. For this reason, more and more women are going in for continuing education. 30 per cent of those enrolling in workers' and employees' schools or courses run by factories and enterprises are women. In 1983, of the 7,148 students enrolled in the economic department of the Beijing Television School, 50 per cent were women. In Shanghai, 30,000 women workers and staff members were studying in various spare-time television or correspondence universities or colleges in 1983. Of the 130,000 students registered in intermediate level spare-time schools, 55 per cent were women. The salesgirl Wang Juanhua, a national Advanced Worker in the commercial field and a deputy to the National People's Congress had only completed a junior high-school education. Perceiving her lack of education, she attended the senior high-school culture and science courses run by the State for Advanced Workers, and, with excellent grades, was admitted in 1984 to the Shanghai Management College for Financial and Trade Cadres.

Women intellectuals of China have not only thrown themselves into the technical reforms but are eagerly mastering new knowledge and the new disciplines of science and technology to meet today's challenges. The woman engineer Li Yuxiu, graduated in 1963 from the electrical department of Fudan University; she devoted herself for 20 years to research on corrosive cleaning agents. After overcoming many obstacles and with the support of the municipal Party

Committee of Langfang, Hebei Province, she set up a service-manufacture-research company. The company contracted to clean the underground sewage system of the old Beijing Hotel; originally the hotel management had planned to shut down the hotel and spend 200,000 yuan on the project, but Li Yuxiu completed the work at a cost of only 60,000 yuan and without the hotel having to suspend operations.

Since 1982, 832 women have been awarded doctorates or masters degrees. In 1951, there was only one woman academician in the Chinese Academy of Sciences; in 1981, there were 15.

Goods and Services

The reforms have resulted in the socialisation, electrification and professionalisation of household duties. Home duties have long been heavy burdens for millions of Chinese women workers and staff members. One survey showed that shopping for groceries and preparing meals alone took up an average 3 hours daily, or 60 per cent of the time spent on housework.

In the reforms, the State has put much stress on the development of the service sector, to provide a great many daily necessities that used to be prepared at home. To meet this need, the Chinese food industry is developing rapidly. Many fast foods such as cooked noodles, bread, cleaned and prepared groceries, cold meats, canned foods and so forth are now on the market. In Beijing alone, prepared meats sales from January to September 1984 reached the total amount sold in the entire year of 1979. A new fast food plant is under construction, which will be able to provide consumers with 200 kinds of fast foods. Shops selling grains, vegetables and other groceries, and snack shops are now supplying all kinds of prepared or half-prepared foods. This has helped to alleviate inconveniences in shopping and food preparation. The garment industry is also developing fast and is providing consumers with better styling and a variety of styles. Ready-made clothes are now the main source of family clothing.

Due to the errors of the past, the expansion of State commercial networks was very slow. In some areas, small shops and other outlets were merged into larger ones, which was inconvenient for the consumers. Since 1979, 256,000 new State retail outlets for consumer goods, foods and services have been set up. Since 1980, the State has encouraged individuals to go into business, and now, not only have a number of collective and individually owned shops, food stores and service companies been opened, but the peasants have also opened department stores on their own. By 1983, the number of collectively owned stores and shops had increased by 56 per cent over 1978, and stores owned by individuals by 26 times. This has promoted the socialisation of housework and lightened women's burdens.

Home electrical appliances have come on the market in large numbers. Whereas 5 years ago, very few Chinese families had a washing-machine or a refrigerator, now they are becoming much more common, although the supply lags behind demand. In 1983, the number of washing-machines and refrigerators owned by Beijing families was respectively 290 times and 21 times that of 1978.

The reforms have also expanded the fields of social labour and promoted the professionalisation of home duties. In many cities service companies have burgeoned, providing much needed home services to the old, sick, disabled, pregnant women and children. Many retired workers and staff members and other idle manpower have been encouraged to set up home nurseries to supplement regular nurseries and kindergartens. The Home Service Company of Chaoyang District in Beijing, after giving its personnel the necessary training, sent out 1,000 people from December 1983 to April 1984 to sign contracts with 1,040 local households for various services. I have personally seen an aged, bedridden professor thanking one of these personnel with tears in his eyes. Thanks are due indeed to these advocates of professionalising home duties.

Marriage

The reforms have helped women to develop in a civilised and progressive direction in all realms of social life. Economic reforms have not only enhanced social productivity but have brought profound changes to the women's life in other ways. On the question of love and marriage, ideas of marriage for the sake of position and gain have further weakened. A survey of young people under 35 seeking a marriage partner showed that the primary consideration now is the 'character' of the other person; other considerations include 'common interests', whether the other person is 'understanding', and whether he or she is 'enterprising'. Family status and financial conditions are no longer stressed as they were before. As for parental choice of their grown-up children's marriage partners: a survey of 790 married women in urban areas in Anhui Province reveals that 83.7 per cent of marriages are self-determined. Nowadays too many couples spend about the same length of time sharing housework. Family planning has become a basic policy in China. More and more urban women want fewer children. In 1983, 99.9 per cent of the non-rural populaton in Beijing had one child only. This gives parents more time to educate their offspring and to devote to their careers.

Chinese women are also paying more attention to presenting a good appearance and dressing well. For the first time since Liberation in 1949, body-building courses and beauty parlours have opened. High-quality clothing and cosmetics are in great demand, as are other good things in life. Women now want a richer and more colourful life. To have a career and a good life — this has become the goal for millions of Chinese women.

Women's Welfare

The reforms have promoted more welfare for women and children. With the larger revenues resulting from the reforms, enterprises can now provide their workers and staff members with benefits which they could not afford before. The Qunlin Market in Chongqing, for instance has adopted many new welfare measures including improvements in the staff cafeteria, addition of baths and hairdresser shops for the women workers and staff members, and is spending 15,000 yuan in the building of a new creche for their babies. At the Changzhou Tractor Plant, the welfare fund in 1984 amounted to over 100,000 yuan, which went into expansion of the plant's nursery and women's rest-rooms, and a consumers' cooperative store providing many services.

In enterprises where reforms are being carried out, the lawful rights and interests of the women workers and staff members are protected. The Colour Printing Plant in Yichang, Hubei Province, for instance, made 4 new rules against unreasonable phenomena which had appeared in the course of the reforms. These rules are: women workers who are breastfeeding babies should be given below-norm work quotas and be exempted from night shifts; those who are sick should get 60 per cent pay according to labour insurance: and women after 5 months of pregnancy should be given light work. These measures have the full support of the women. Many enterprises are also experimenting with new work schedules.

The Acheng Relay Factory in Heilongjian Province, for instance, is trying out 5 days of work and 1 day of study a week. This has been very helpful to the intellectual development of the women there.

The Beijing Women's Federation, in addition to showing how existing State-run nurseries in the city and enterprises could take in more infants, also organised many youths who are waiting for jobs and retired women workers and staff members as well as other idle manpower to set up 15,000 home nurseries taking in another 20,000 children. The Guangdong Opera Troupe and the Beijing Children's Art Theatre cooperated to hold a number of benefit performances in Shenzhen, the proceeds of which, amounting to 600,000 yuan, went into the building of a Children's Welfare Centre in that city. Many cities have also set up after-school instruction centres and home instruction centres for school children and give school children dietary supplements between periods. The Tianjin Women's Federation, in cooperation with related departments, jointly set up a 'San Mao Restaurant', which specialises in giving birthday parties for children.

New Problems Arising in the Course of Experimental Urban Reforms

Although experimental urban reforms have brought many changes and benefits to women, some new problems have arisen which need to be studied and solved.

(1) Improvement of the quality of women workers and staff members: one major problem urgently needing solution is how to improve the scientific-cultural level of the women workers and staff. According to a survey of 12,885 women workers and staff members made by the Shanghai Textile Bureau, 75 per cent have only had an elementary education and only 1.3 per cent have had a college education. In Sichuan Province as a whole, the percentage of technically qualified female personnel is low, as is the percentage of women engaged in scientific and technical work. The majority are in heavy physical labour jobs and service jobs. In Shanxi Province, 70.7 per cent of the answers to the questions 'What bothers you most and what difficulties do you have?' on 1,000 questionnaires sent out, centered on a low educational level and lack of job skill. The women were troubled that their educational and technical levels fell short of the demands of the reforms. This shows that improving

the quality of the education and training of women is a problem that deserves serious attention.

On the question of how to raise the cultural-scientific-technical levels of all workers and staff members, China's Sixth Five-Year Plan explicitly stipulates that 'workers and staff members shall be trained on a rotating basis to reach an intermediate education level'. In accordance with this stipulation, mines, factories, and enterprises everywhere have set up spare-time schools of intermediate or college level for technical and other workers and staff members. Some have opened cultural and technical schools and correspondence schools. All such schools specialise in line with their own needs in production. According to 1983 statistics, 19,084 million workers and staff members studied in school of various types at various levels. However the heavy burden of housework which falls on women workers and staff members with children has often been an impediment to their studies.

(2) The problem of housework: recently, as discussed above, these duties have been somewhat lightened. However rising standards and varied diets have added time to food preparation. According to a survey made by the Tianjin Statistical Bureau among 759 workers and staff members (of whom 234 are women), women workers and staff members spend on an average $3\frac{1}{2}$ hours a day on food preparation and other housework. On holidays and weekends, this time can increase to 7 hours. A survey by the Beijing Statistical Bureau showed similar results the Shangai branch of the Chinese Academy of Sciences surveyed 86 women scientists and technical personnel and the results showed that 70 per cent spend over 3 hours daily and 55 per cent spend more than 4 hours.

The conflict between home and social labour has become sharper since the reforms when higher demands are set on the employees and the tempo of life has quickened. In Shanxi, of 2,000 women surveyed 65.8 per cent answered the question 'In what way do you want the Women's Federation to help you?', that they wanted the Women's Federation 'to help relevant departments provide more home services' and 'set up more nurseries and kindergartens'. This demonstrates how acute the problem is. The solution lies obviously in the direction of socialisation, modernisation and professionalisation of home duties. With the present level of production and workers and staff members' incomes, however, it will be hard for modernisation to happen overnight and for professionalisation to meet all needs. Our present policy, therefore, is to promote modernisation and professionalisation actively, but to focus mainly on socialisation to satisfy the varied needs of different families, so that the largest number of women workers and staff members can be released from home duties.

One important way to relieve the problem is to develop the home service professions. Shopping and food preparation take up most time; therefore, the main problem to be solved right now relates to meal preparation. That is, there should be a more rapid development of the food industry and the processing of farm and subsidiary products; the number of shops and stores should be increased and the quality of their services improved. Shops and stores should not keep the same hours as workers and staff members, making it difficult for them to buy things; the number of self-service markets and agricultural markets should be increased.

Another urgent demand of women workers and staff members is that the number of nurseries and kindergartens be expanded. At present, 40 per cent of all pre-school children in urban areas are already in nurseries or kindergartens, but this is not enough. We must continue to open up more channels and adopt more flexible ways to expand this number. At the same time, we must give better guidance and management to personnel working in home nurseries and service centres to improve their quality of service.

(3) Organising women in a more scientific way: although the problem of employment, including that of young women waiting for jobs, has basically been solved, a new problem has appeared. With the reshuffling of work in factories and enterprises in the course of the reforms, surplus labour has appeared, in the main female. As the technical revolution will continue to develop, this problem will not be solved in a short time. The reasons for this are manifold: firstly the past practice of enterprises employing the grown-up children of their own workers and staff led to overmanning. Secondly, irrational categories of work are now being readjusted. Thirdly, the low educational level of the women workers makes them fall short of the needs of expanding production.

Enterprises and Women's Federations everywhere have adopted a positive attitude to solving this problem. The Tianjin Civic Construction Engineering Company, for instance, had a surplus of 350 women formerly engaged in heavy manual labour. The company decided to expand its service undertakings: it invested 300,000 yuan and got help from the Women's Federation and other departments to train these women in the necessary skills, so that they were smoothly transferred to a sewing factory. In this way, not only was labour productivity raised as a whole but reorganisation of work effected.

Another example is the Chengdu Municipal Engineering Company, where women workers and staff members made up 29–32 per cent of the total number. During the reforms, many women workers had to stay out of team contracts because of their lack of physical qualifications. The company leadership transferred the surplus women partly to its own service departments and partly to jobs more suited to them in other enterprises. Forty women of the prefab plant formerly working in the open were transferred to the Tuanjie Electric Motors Plant. Those nearing retirement age or in weak health were allowed to request early retirement with full labour insurance. However, some factories and enterprises have not paid enough attention to this problem.

The State Council recently issued a call for developing the service sector in China. This will not only provide jobs for new entrants and surplus women but also enliven the economy, lighten women's home duties and protect their health.

In conclusion, with the progress of urban reforms, other problems will crop up. The constant attention of the relevant departments and women's organisations is needed to ensure that they are looked into and solved in good time.

Section 4: A Bright Future for Chinese Women

The achievements in economic reform in the past 5 years have greatly encouraged women, who have not only benefited from them but have seen their own bright future. The aspirations of Chinese women for a fine future life have grown along with the development of production and with the passage of years. People still remember the early period after Liberation in 1949, when, during the land reform, a popular doggerel ran: '30 mu of land and an ox, a wife, children and a heated brick bed . . .'. This was the simple yearning of male peasants who were content to have land of their own to use, to clothe and feed their families and give them security. With time, the rise in production and living standards, people are demanding better things from life. A more recent doggerel called for 'a house with an upstairs and downstairs, electricity and a telephone; to plough without an ox and see without an oil lamp'.

After decades of efforts, some of these wishes have come true, others are coming true. A good life, however, will not come from nowhere or the bounty of other people but from common efforts and constant innovation and advance. At present, the women, together with the entire population, are single-heartedly devoting themselves to creating a fine future. Starting from these aspirations and hopes and the problems that need attention, two further questions arise: how can the cause of women and children be incorporated better in the economic planning of the State and how can labour protection of women be improved?

1985 is the last year of the Sixth Five-Year Plan and the country will soon go into the period of the Seventh Five-Year Plan. In this new plan, we believe that, firstly, in addition to national goals, goals in regard to women and children should be expanded, and secondly, new objectives based on women's needs and the State's ability to meet such needs should be included.

Great efforts should be made to increase the production of electrical appliances since demand outstrips supply. The supply of gas to urban areas should be expanded for the convenience it brings to people's life, the time it saves, the improvements on the environment, and, in particular, the relief of women's home labours. The supply of nurseries and kindergartens must be expanded. The crux of the problem lies in training the teachers in child education: at present, there are only 33 such institutions in the country. This number is far from adequate and improvement must be made.

On the question of contraceptives, the results achieved from many years of family planning should be consolidated and improved. In the past, China invested huge sums in this area and had supplied contraceptives free: the quality of such contraceptives was not of the highest and it needs to be further improved. The problem awaits solution by relevant government departments, which are now studying them.

The question of improving the quality of women's educational level likewise merits serious attention. If this is not solved speedily, it will affect genuine equality between men and women, and will slow down the progress of the 4 modernisations. Solutions have already been suggested in this paper. In future, the role of the grass-roots organisations should be enhanced, especially those at the county level, including cultural and education departments and people's organisations. The women's organisations should actively cooperate with other departments to mobilise women to participate in all kinds of training and study.

There is still a large gap between women's health needs and availability of health care. The Sixth Five-Year Plan included regulations and measures on this, which helped the situation in regard to hospitalised births and medical attention for the children. But in future, beside additional targets in State plans, particularly as regards expansion of maternity and pediatric wards and the training of midwives, an important innovation is the setting up of sick beds at home with care from the hospital and medical personnel. Such care is much more convenient to the patients, and given the large numbers of retired medical personnel whose talents can be put to good use, it is quite feasible.

The question of how to improve the labour protection of women has always been given a good deal of attention by the government and mines, organisations, factories and enterprises. Given the widespread incorporation of women in the labour force and their varied job structure, the 1956 Labour Regulations are no longer entirely suitable to present conditions and should be revised and amended. At present, a number of Ministries, the All-China Federation of Trade Unions, the All-China Women's Federation, have jointly formed a group to draft new regulations. When their work is completed, they will submit a proposal to the Standing Committee of the National People's Congress for ratification. Before the new regulations are passed, however, things need to be done:

— women workers and staff members should be exempt from jobs not suited to them, especially those that might harm them physically and mentally;

— the period of maternity and breastfeeding leave should be expanded to protect the health of women and their babies, and problems related to the length of this extension and labour benefits and wages to be paid should be studied;

— the theoretical study of the question of women should be strengthened. In recent years, some well-known people and women workers have been paying much attention to women's questions and have written a great deal about it. In some provinces and cities, research and theoretical discussions have been conducted on women's role, marriage and the family, women's psychology, family budgeting, as well as on the building of a civilised, scientific and healthy way of life. A research society on the question of women has been established in Beijing and a number of provinces and cities have founded or are forming research societies into marriage and the family. Societies on family education have also been formed in a dozen provinces, autonomous regions and municipalities directly under the central authority, and in over 300 prefectures, municipalities and counties throughout China. Women's cadre schools at different levels, women's colleges and vocational schools have sprung up everywhere. All this has laid the foundations for more theoretical work on women. This work should be strengthened, and a national research organisation should if possible be set up.

5

WOMEN'S PARTICIPATION IN DEVELOPMENT: THE CASE OF TOGO

Togolese Federation of Women in the Legal Profession[1]

This paper is based on the results of a national survey of women's actual participation in the economic life of the country, and what women of different occupational groups and ethnic backgrounds express as their most urgent needs. The paper is divided into 4 sections. In the first the authors describe the steps taken by the Togolese government to respond to international initiatives such as the International Women's Year and the Decade of Women. In Section 2 it looks at the actual situation of rural and urban women in Togo, and in Section 3 gives some results from the National Survey conducted by the multidisciplinary team in charge of carrying out the Unesco project. In Section 4 general conclusions are drawn from the survey and a number of recommendations are presented (Editor's note).

Section 1: Politico-administrative Actions

Before the Proclamation of International Women's Year

In 1972 the Togolese authorities decided to create the National Union of Togolese Women (UNFT), as a special wing of the Assembly of Togolese People (RPT). It was to the Constitutive Congress of the UNFT that the President of the Republic, conscious of the political force which women represent, said: 'Women should be intimately linked to the life of the nation because any delay in their advancement and their education cannot but translate

1. The paper was written by members of an interdisciplinary team under the leadership of the Togolese Federation of Women in the Legal Profession. Writers were: Mesdames Kekeh, Ametepe, Bouamey, Kuevi and Messieurs Aziaha, Figah, Kenkou, Sokpor and Sossah.

itself into an impediment for the development of the country'. The aim of UNFT was 'to enable Togolese women to play fully their role as citizens in all the areas of the nation's activities and to give them an adequate political education which would imbue them with the ideas of the RPT and the principal objectives of the New Togo.' The UNFT has a national bureau of 19 members, which plays the role of the executive organ. Nine specialised Committees were set up to undertake studies of the problems facing both the Union and women: General Policy Committee; International Relations Committee; Economic and Financial Affairs Committee; Social Affairs Committee; Press and Propaganda Committee; Legal Affairs and Status of Women Committee; Cultural and Artistic Affairs Committee; Festival Organisation Committee; Young Women's Committee. The UNFT, like the RPT, has branches in all villages and urban wards in the country, which act as women's sections of the RPT.

International Women's Year in Togo

In Togo a National Committee was established by ministerial decree in 1975 to design and carry out the national International Women's Year (IWY) programme for the year. This programme included: (1) providing information and education for both men and women on the themes of the year: equality, development and peace. Chat shows, lectures, debates, films on radio, press and television were organised to raise public awareness of the issues; (2) organising seminars in every region of the country. These gave women the chance to meet and not only to get to know each other, but also to concentrate on their common problems based on the experience of each person and on the way of life in each region. In the course of the seminars a number of themes were discussed: women and employment; women and the home; social and educational support for women; family budgeting; birth spacing; improvement of handicrafts and marketing; education of children; tools and technologies; establishment of small industries; functional literacy for women. A documentary film about Togolese women was made within the framework of the IWY, which showed the role of women in both town and countryside in commerce, agricultural and handicraft production, and women's political and religious roles.

To ensure continuity of activity, a National Women's Commission was also set up in 1975. The main aim of this Commission is to design the government's strategy in support of women's advancement, by utilising the skills of the Ministries and Organisations involved in all the aspects of women's advancement and protection, and after an in-depth analysis of women's needs. This important interministerial body sets the priorities needed for women's full integration into various sectors of society, and should also continuously evaluate all the actions taken on behalf of women. The commission also serves as the framework for the coordination of government and NGO activities. Its duties are as follows: (1) to estimate the present and potential contribution of women to various sectors within the framework of overall development plans and programmes; (2) to encourage or to undertake studies which can orientate or re-orientate the efforts of government and NGOs with regard to the status and the advancement of women, and to define the measures and priorities needed to ensure women's complete integration and a flowering of their capacities; (3) to make a methodical and continuous evaluation of the actions undertaken in support of women and to recommend any necessary changes; (4) to coordinate the efforts of government and NGOs regarding the protection of women.

By the end of the decade a number of structures in Togo had been set up to deal with women's concerns: The National Union of Togolese Women; The National Commission for Women's Status; The Directorate of Women's Advancement which later became part of the Ministry of Social Affairs and the Advancement of Women. Have these institutions in fact contributed to the evolution of Togolese women?

During the Decade: Structural Innovations

1. The National Commission for Women's Status. From April 1975 to August 1977 the Commission functioned within the Ministry of Public Health and Social Affairs. Its task was to draw up a programme of action to integrate Togolese women rapidly into different sectors of political and social life of the nation. The Directorate of Social Affairs acted as the Secretariat of the Commission.

2. The Secretariat of State. In January 1977, a Secretariat of State of Social Affairs and the Advancement of Women was set up within the government, and headed by a woman.

3. The General Directorate of Women's Advancement. This was set up in August 1977 and has 4 sections: the division of Social Education; the division of Research, Documentation, Information and Training; the division of Legal and Social Status of Women; the division of Employment, Vocational Guidance and Professional Training. These sections are responsible at the national level with devising and implementing different programmes relevant to their respective areas of action. The General Directorate for the Advancement of Women is responsible for: defining a national policy for the protection and the advancement of women; ensuring and overseeing its implementation; promoting all actions regarding the betterment of the legal, cultural and political status of Togolese women; ensuring full access of women and girls to education, vocational training and employment; assisting rural and urban women to improve their productivity; encouraging studies which can orientate or re-orientate the efforts of government and NGOs as regards the status and advancement of women; reviewing and proposing laws and regulations regarding the protection of women; planning, supervising and evaluating all the programmes regarding the advancement of women; coordinating at all levels all the activities regarding the protection and advancement of women. It is clearly recognised that the protection and the advancement of women must include their education in general and their vocational training in particular so as to permit them to participate better in the national development effort. For this reason the Directorate of Social Affairs drew up an ambitious programme of functional literacy for Togolese women which won the Unesco prize in 1984.

4. The Ministry of Social Affairs and the Advancement of Women. In November 1978, thanks to a ministerial reshuffle, the Secretariat of Social Affairs and the Advancement of Women became a Ministry still with a woman at its head. It was also the first time that the Advancement of Women was elevated to a Ministry. It should be added here that the UNFT is always ready to work with the administrative structures for the protection and the advancement of women.

Activities Undertaken

1. Participation of women in political life. If the quality of a democracy is measured by the place women occupy within it, the advancement of Togolese women rather than being signalled by the accession of a few privileged women to civic responsibilities, is manifested by their collective participation at all levels of public life. In fact Togolese women were not content to have their National Union where they could discuss their problems, but also formed an integral part of various bodies of the country's political system. In the Central Committee of the National Political Movement, the RPT, women's representation was 18.51 per cent in 1979 as against 12.12 per cent in 1971. At the government level, participation rose to 5.88 per cent in 1979 from 0 per cent in 1971. Women are also members of municipal councils; they participate without fear of losing their jobs in the trade unions of their occupations. They also sit on the Economic and Social Council, and the Chambers of Commerce, Agriculture and Industry.

2. Information and research. At the beginning the Department for the Advancement of Women had to inform Togolese public opinion about women's problems and above all to raise awareness. A number of regional seminars were held in March 1978 on the traditions and customs regarding family law in traditional Togolese societies. This made the collection of customs and usages of the different ethnic groups in the country possible. The observations of the evaluation committee of these seminars contributed to bringing the family code up to date. In December 1978 a National seminar was held in Lome which brought together women and men from different social strata and all ranks of the national administration, to think about the concept of the advancement of women for 5 days. This national seminar had as its aim to promote collective recognition by Togolese society of the actual situation of women, and to analyse the ways and means by which to work for women's betterment. Within the framework of civic education of women, and thanks to well-known speakers, it was possible to go quite deeply into a number of issues: the integration of women in rural development; Togolese women and national commerce; the civil status of women; the rights and the duties of women; education, training and vocational guidance; health of mother and child; the concept of women's advancement.

In March 1979 a second National seminar on women's integration into Togo's economic development was organised by the UNFT in collaboration with the General Directorate of the Advancement of Women and held in Lama-Kara. The purpose of this meeting was to make a wide range of professional women more aware of the importance of their role within the nation.

Since that time the mass media (radio, TV and press) have been frequently used to inform women of their rights and their duties, and to discuss different problems affecting them. Daily radio programmes in a number of national languages tell women about such topics as professionalism, children's education, family health. The national press devotes several pages weekly to the Togolese woman. Various themes are covered to inform women about ways in which they can better their living conditions and those of their families.

The Legal Status of Women and Legislation

The Constitution, the fundamental law of the country, as well as numerous legislative dispositions, enshrines the principle of equality between men and women and guarantees women's right to employment, to equal pay, free access to all the professions, giving regard only to the vocation, aptitudes and training of each person, and the exigencies imposed by the need for development and the growth of the national economy. Many special articles of the employment code assure these rights as well as the necessity to protect pregnant women.

In January 1980, the government proclaimed a new Family Code. This was the culmination of a number of coordinated efforts and constitutes the chief weapon in the battle for women's rights. Before the proclamation of the Code the status of women was covered by a mosaic of customs which impeded the advancement of Togolese women. In such a situation, women were generally considered to be minors. Rather than painting a sombre picture of the inequalities from which women suffered before the Code, we will concentrate on the gains made with the Code which has brought about structural reform as far as the recognition of women's rights is concerned. In certain respects, the Code goes against custom and traditional law; in others it improves on the humanitarian principles in our customs and thus makes possible a fruitful symbiosis between Togo's past and its future. The dominant idea of the Code is to seek the improvement and gradual change of the situation of women who for centuries have seen their rights flouted. The Committee responsible for drawing up the Family Code considered that it was better to bring customs up to date, adapting them to present-day conditions rather than attack them fundamentally. This allowed new rules to be established which take into account the needs of the present without sacrificing Togolese originality or African character.

A number of political and social organisations in the country were then involved in detailed discussions of the Code. The essential ideas of the code turn on certain fundamental inequalities in the traditional system:

— women were kept in a state of strict dependence on the family and their husband because tradition obliged a woman to respect, obey and submit to her husband;

— as a minor, a woman could be deprived of the goods acquired during the marriage even though she had contributed to the prosperity of the household. A woman could not sign a contract; the payment of bridewealth restricted a woman's choice of partner and prevented her from recovering her autonomy at the death of her husband;

— only a woman's adultery was punished. A woman was obliged to accept in the conjugal home the children born of her husband's adulterous unions and could be repudiated unilaterally by her husband.

The following are some of the Code's dispositions governing the marital rights and obligations of all Togolese:

— *bridewealth* is reduced to a symbol and its upper limit is fixed at 10,000 F CFA (roughly £ 540).

— *marriage* is subject to certain conditions as regards its recognition: as a public act, the spouses need parental consent if under 21 years of age and receive it only when the bridewealth is paid.

— *marital obligations*: spouses have reciprocal obligations, i.e. fidelity, aid, mutual support, joint obligation to feed, maintain and educate their children, and they can be forced to do so by law.

— *divorce and separation*: spouses are now subject to the same rules of divorce and separation which allow either party to obtain a divorce by invoking a limited number of causes foreseen by the law; in case of divorce because of the husband's wrongdoing, or of reciprocal wrongdoing, the tribunal can allow the wife some damages for the material and moral prejudice that the dissolution of the marriage will cause her.

Women have acquired full legal capacity and thus either spouse can represent the other either by express mandate or by authorisation of the law. Although the husband remains the head of the family, his powers are limited. He may not use his prerogatives other than in the common interest of the household and children. A husband cannot impose the presence of a child conceived in adultery on his wife. If he does not tell his wife about his illegitimate children, his recognition of them is legally nullified. In the regulation of matrimonial arrangements, the Committee insisted on the equality of rights of both spouses. The husband's recognised prerogatives are above all subject to the fulfilment of his duties and involve limitations which prohibit the possibility of abuses which could be prejudicial to his family or wife. Each spouse can administer and enjoy her/his own goods; goods acquired during the marriage form a common property which are divided in half on the dissolution of the marriage. As for inheritance, each child inherits an equal amount from their parent; the Code thus affirms the equality of all children without distinction. On the death of her husband, a wife will inherit as a minimum one-sixth of his estate.

The Family Code has established legal protection of women's rights on an equal footing with men, an equality guaranteed by the relevant national tribunals. The State recognises women's equality with men before the law: they have the same legal standing as men and the same possibilities of exercising this, particularly as far as signing contracts and the administration of property is concerned. Women are given the same treatment as men at all stages of the legal process.

In summary it can be said that the Decade has been marked by a growing awareness on the part of women and the authorities of the need to incorporate women into all areas of social life because their isolation runs the risk of aggravating the human problems which society is experiencing. In Togo the problem of women's situation is no longer posed in terms of race, or sex, ethnicity, power relations or beliefs. Women are integrated in various economic, political and legal institutions. They are not at a disadvantage in comparison with men, for in Togo discrimination in terms of salary does not exist: 'To those with the same diplomas, the same salary'. Given that women are also agents of development and thus indispensable complements to men, it is time that they no longer suffer any type of discrimination. Fully aware of this, the government of Togo on 26 September 1983 signed the United Nations Convention on The

Elimination of All Forms of Discrimination against Women.

Section 2: The Situation of Rural and Urban Women

Rural

In many regions of the globe, rural zones appear as those settled spaces characterised by the predominance of socio-cultural values solidly grounded in the survival of traditional rules and social practices. This is particularly true in Africa where almost 90 per cent of the population is rural and subsists essentially on a traditional self-sufficient agriculture based on the use of rudimentary technology and family labour.

Togo is no exception to this general picture despite considerable efforts undertaken in the rural area and particularly in agriculture since its independence in 1960. The population of Togo is concentrated in the rural area and 75 per cent of all women are rural. Women occupy an important place in agriculture: it has been estimated that they supply 40 per cent of all field labour, 80 per cent labour in sowing, 70 per cent in weeding, 70 per cent in harvesting, 90 per cent marketing and 95 per cent in processing foodstuffs. However none of this work is recorded in national statistics or taken into account in development programmes. There is a social division of labour in most ethnic groups, characterised by a rigorous division of tasks according to sex and age. This defines the occupational and behavioural norms appropriate to each social activity.

For example a study[2] in North Togo noted that the sexual division of labour covered the whole of daily life. In the household, the man was in charge of the weekly distribution of foodstuffs to his wife or wives and was also responsible for the construction or the repair of the huts. For her part, the woman was concerned with domestic tasks such as cooking (preparation of food, provision of the ingredients for the sauces), fetching water and firewood, educating the children, cleaning the huts and the yard, whitewashing the walls and repairing earth floors. Women also raised small

2. J.-C. Froelich, P. Alexander, R. Cornevin and P.J. Delord, *Les Populations du Nord-Togo* (Collection 'Monographes ethnologiques africaines'), Presses Universitaires, de France, Paris 1963.

livestock. In the field, men did the work of clearing and preparing the plots, while women sowed and harvested the grain. Apart from cultivation and domestic work, men and women also carried out other types of activities, especially handicraft production. Weaving, smithing, basket and jewellery making were men's main handicraft occupations; pottery, dyeing, and the preparation of local beer were women's activities. Women were entitled to dispose freely of the products of their labour. This sexual division of labour has tended to disappear in rural areas of Togo with the reinforcement of women's multiple roles.

The household. The woman in the conjugal or family home is a housewife occupied with a number of domestic tasks: the maintenance of the house, preparation of cooked meals, provisioning it with water and wood, washing clothes and dishes, raising small livestock, looking after the kitchen garden, education and care of children, transformation of foodstuffs. In certain of these tasks women can count on the help of other children (those over 5 or 6), boys or girls, but usually girls are more socially indicated to carry out certain tasks (preparing the fire, the ingredients for the sauce, fetching water, washing dishes, etc.).

It is important to stress the arduous nature of the majority of these tasks. In particular the need for water generally forces women to get up extremely early (4 or 5 o'clock in the morning) to walk several kilometers (on average 3 to 5) to get water in jars, buckets or large 20 litre tins. This trip is generally done several times in the morning before the other members of the family or the household head wake. As for firewood collection, women ordinarily dedicate an afternoon or a whole day to this, depending on the abundance or scarcity of wood in the immediate vicinity of the village. In this case the round trip may be as much as 20 kms and on her return a woman will be carrying a large bundle of firewood on her head.

Handicrafts and commercial activities. Traditional rural subsistence societies have developed a mode of existence marked by the pursuit of self-sufficiency by means of multiple activities which ensure the production of the principal goods needed by the family or village community. Handicrafts represent one of the areas of economic activity where this aim of self-sufficiency is rigorously pursued following the criteria determined by the sexual division of labour. Originally a woman's handicraft production focused on making certain tools or foods which were needed to help her fulfil each of her domestic tasks. These have rapidly been extended with the growing monetisation of the economy and the development of urban centres. Thus activities have developed such as pottery making, processing of palm oil, palmetto or karite, production of soap, local beer, manioc and yam flour, etc.

Moreover the opening of local markets for agricultural products and other things linked to the life of the family or community unit has facilitated the women's entry into the circuits of commercial exchange introduced and organised around the market economy. In other respects the need for cash introduced by the new type of economy leads rural women to become more visible in public places and within the local community through petty vending of various articles, cooked food and drinks.

Within the local community. The social stratification of lineage societies which characterises local rural populations is based on social structures derived from a system of kinship which varies slightly from one region to another. The kinship system in rural communities determines the social status of individuals and of groups by means of the network of rights and duties which underlies it. In this context a person's social status is relatively predetermined; it evolves in accordance with the passage of an individual from one kinship status to another. This is particularly true for a woman when she leaves her life as a young girl to be incorporated into the conjugal household. In this sense marriage plays a privileged role in the evolution of women and of the community. It reveals the social relations of kinship or friendship which exist among the various groups and which form the basis of the rural community. It also reveals the strategic place which women occupy in social equilibrium.

None the less in the customary transactions linked to marriage a woman plays no direct part in the decision about her fate. She submits to the outcome of the discussions between the two families and more precisely between the heads of the two families who belong to specific lineages or clans. As guarantee of the transaction, bridewealth is demanded and the amount is determined according to customary social rules. It is made up of a number of things, both material goods and sometimes even money, as well as a number of obligations which the groom's family has *vis-à-vis* the bride's family during the betrothal period. The groom may have to provide a certain number of services to his bride's parents; these generally involve a certain number of days of agricultural or construction work in the household of his future parents-in-law. These obligations remain in force until the ending of the period of betrothal or the celebration of the marriage.

The demands and social obligations linked to the payment of bridewealth have as their aim to test the groom's seriousness and capacity for work; they are an index of his future level of support for the bride in the conjugal home and of his allegiance to his in-laws, who have been responsible in the community's eyes for all the care given to the development of his future wife. They indicate the progressive integration of the groom into the bride's family and vice versa, and are a sign to the local community of the coming together of the two families as a result of the marriage of their children. The new Family Code discussed earlier has replaced many of these traditional marriage practices.

As for community work, women take part in all sorts of activities linked to the economy and social life of the collectivity, their participation varying with the objectives of the community. At the village level women periodically clean public places, participate in the preparation of ritual feasts on the occasion of important religious ceremonies and agrarian festivals; they are active in the organisation of funerals (laying out the corpse, carrying out the funeral rites, greeting funeral participants, etc.). Women also take part in the politico-legal domain. In fact, the disputes which are the object of lawsuits frequently are linked to problems about land or women. While rural women do participate fully in the different activities of the local community, they appear to be more intensely engaged in domestic work and economic activities whether of production or of exchange. Women are also present in the socio-cultural or religious domain but particularly so in more collective types of activities (mutual aid orientated to collective interests; religious rites and agricultural festivals).

In the Urban Area

Urban women's active life seems to be orientated more to occupations taking place outside the household. At the same time, a certain degree of professionalisation of domestic tasks is developing, in particular in Lome and in towns which are administrative headquarters and important entrepôts. This indicates that progressively as one category of women is absorbed by economic activities outside the home, another category of women replace them within the home to ensure that the task allocated to women by the sexual division of labour are carried out. Originally a young kinswoman of one of the couple came from the village to provide these services: although she was treated like an adopted child, she was rarely sent to school. Those thought to be faithful and serious however were sometimes given vocational training towards the end of their stay with a view to their future marriage and role as housewife. Nowadays a new professional category of personnel paid to carry out household tasks is developing.

The urban housewife. The sexual division of labour between spouses in the urban areas takes much the same form as the rural division described earlier: water collection, meal preparation, care of children, cleaning, washing, shopping for the basic foodstuffs are allocated to women. Generally women start their day between 4 and 5 in the morning. With the help of younger family members (girls and boys of between 7 and 10), the courtyard is cleaned, water collected and the breakfast prepared. If the husband is an employee or self-employed with fixed hours of work, the wife must organise her activities around this constraint. A number of morning domestic tasks are repeated in the afternoon and the evening — preparing food, water collection, buying foodstuffs, washing and the care of children. In fact one frequently encounters women who on leaving the office make a detour to the market to buy food for the midday or evening meal. Once at home they then have to start cooking for the family. Urban life in general is characterised by a series of activities programmed by the clock: school, office, administrative services, markets, workshops, etc. If the woman works outside the home, she is more pressed by time because of her own hours of employment. This is the case of employees, government officials and traders. Women traders, the most important category in the urban milieu, must also take account of the time their clients will arrive at their stalls.

None the less women in the urban area have a number of conveniences which lighten the burden of domestic work: water standpipes near the house or even in the house itself, local markets which sell all the basic cooking ingredients, local schools, health centres in the residential area or in its vicinity. The existence of infrastructure does not of course eliminate the laboriousness nor the time spent on certain tasks such as cooking. Even the supply of water poses a certain number of problems because of the inadequate number of standpipes in relation to the urban population's needs. In many of the urban quarters, the majority of households have neither running water nor drinking water within the home; thus much time is wasted by women standing in line. Such households need to keep a reserve supply of water for their various daily needs in jars, buckets or 20-, 60-, and 200 litre tins. In other words, conditions are somewhat similar to those in the rural areas.

Outside the home. Outside the home, the urban woman usually is involved in a money earning activity or perhaps a secondary activity which may take the form of involvement with an NGO with social and humanitarian aims, or political activity whether in a political party or movement.

The social division of labour at the level of the urban economy is marked by a process of specialisation both of areas of activity and forms of activity in the productive, service, or commercial sector. It is characterised by a number of economic activities regrouped into socio-economic, socio-professional activities divided between men and women. The predominant socio-professional categories for both men and women are wage employment, commerce, handicrafts, liberal professions and agriculture (flower raising, market gardening). The small craft sector orientated towards manufacture, repair or technical adaptation generally has a large number of male workers: in contrast cloth and clothing have equal numbers of men and women, as does the services sector; hairdressing, for example, is rather popular among both sexes. None the less over the last decade, women's hairdressing has better adapted itself to the needs of the urban population who are liable to time constraints and willing to pay the price for speedy service. The desire to overcome such constraints is central to a process of specialisation which provides a variety of services to meet the needs of those people for whom looking smart is essential to their job and even their leisure.

Although urban women are found in all the main socio-professional categories mentioned above, the majority engage in trade. In general, the rate of participation of the female urban population (based on the proportion of women present in each socio-professional category), could be considered as one of the main indicators of the integration of women into the modern, urban economy. In the urban centres there are a great number of women's associations: traders associations — usually differentiated by the different type of goods sold (cloth, foodstuffs, fish, oils, etc.) — as well as dressmakers' associations; religious societies both Catholic and Protestant; the Red Cross Association (headed by a woman), etc.

Section 3: The Results of the Survey

The Survey

Unesco approached the Togolese Association of Women in the Legal Profession to carry out research on socio-economic indicators which would show the integration of women in the development of Togo. A multidisciplinary team was recruited locally and divided into three sub-groups to carry out specific tasks. Sub-group 1 was in charge of the critical analysis of the National Development Plans; Sub-group 2 was in charge of the survey itself; Sub-group 3 (further divided into two sub-groups) studied methodological questions and edited the final document.

The Methodological Approach

It was decided to carry out a country-wide survey and to sample each of the country's 5 economic regions. Lome, given the cosmopolitan character of its population, was surveyed separately. Research into women's integration can be done in two ways: through the classic type of survey using written questionnaires administered to respondents within the setting of formal interviews; or by means of unwritten, unstructured interviews. Although we had prepared a survey using the first method, the innovative and unusual nature of the research posed serious methodological problems and obliged us to supplement this approach by using unstructured interviews.

Questionnaires and survey schedules, however well designed methodologically and theoretically, if developed within a particular socio-economic reality, cannot be applied without change to a different situation. A methodology has to be designed which is both rigorous and takes into account the social reality to be captured. The particular situation of African women requires methods of approach rather different from that used in the industrialised countries. In this case wide-ranging discussions were held with women

185

leaders from both rural and urban areas. These informal discussions in the African manner helped to develop confidence and to make known the wishes and the ideals of women. The research was carried out by an interdisciplinary team of economists, jurists, planners, sociologists and statisticians. The methodological difficulties had a considerable effect on the results of the research. The lack of time available to carry out the study did not allow us to train interviewers properly; as a result the research instructions and the recommendations regarding applying the questionnaires were not carefully followed by a number of interviewers in both the rural and the urban areas. None the less the survey results allow us to grasp the principal characteristics of women's participation in the economic and social development of the rural or urban community from the perspective of bettering the situation of particular women and of the furtherance of women in general.

As Togo is divided into 5 more or less different economic regions, these were made the basis of the sample.[3] The aim was to interview 50 women in each region: a total of 250 interviews in all. Two sociologists directed the team of 25 interviewers, who visited hamlets and villages and in all covered over 3,021 kms throughout the whole of Togo and interviewed a total of 262 women. A special questionnaire was designed for Lome because it constitutes a melting-pot of the country's various ethnic groups, and because it suffers from specific problems because of its high rate of urban growth (7 per cent per annum). Although the Lome questionnaire is somewhat different to the one administered in the rural areas, its intention is the same, to capture indicators concerning women's economic participants. It also aims to get the views of women, wage workers, civil servants and government cadres who are differentiated from other women by their social status.

Analysis of the Rural Surveys

Table 5.1. (below) gives the sample by region. Weight was given to those regions which can be considered socio-economic wholes and group a number of relatively well integrated zones that are subordinated to the same ecological constraints which determine the be-

---

3. This was unfortunate given that the aim of the survey was to measure women's participation in development, but time and budget constraints did not allow for a larger sample.

haviour of the local population. Local groups were characterised by kinship systems based on geographic proximity and numerous joint undertakings and exchanges in the exploitation of natural resources. They formed a socio-demographic and regional ensemble which included ethnic specificities as to the way in which each of the main human groupings assured their mastery over the natural environment.

(a) Ethnic origins of the sample. Togo is a multiracial country where all ethnic groups live in harmony. More than 58 dialects are spoken in the country as a whole. The dominant groups are the Ewe, Mina and Ife from the south; the Kabbye, Cotocoli and Moba from the north. All of them were interviewed as well as some members of the Peuhls and Mossi which are nomadic.

(b) The age range of the surveyed population. Only women between 15 and 65 were interviewed of the sample. The average age of the women interviewed was 31 for four of the regions. In the fifth region, the Savannah, about 54 per cent of the women interviewed were between 25 and 39 years of age against 10 per cent between 15 and 24, 30 per cent between 40 and 54, and 6 per cent over 55.

(c) Educational level of the women interviewed. More than half the women interviewed (51.4 per cent) in the first 4 regions had received no education at all; about 24.5 per cent said they could read and write French, and 20.8 per cent said the same for their own language. The latter seems unlikely given the experimental character of the transcription of a number of local languages — only Ewe and Kabbye benefit from a national programme. Thanks to missionaries and to the influence of British indirect rule in the old Gold Coast where the use and teaching of local languages was quite well developed, the Ewe language appears to be spreading to some of the majority national population living in the Ewe area. In the Savannah roughly 96 per cent of the women interviewed had received no education at all against 4 per cent who had.

These findings underline the importance of illiteracy which characterises the rural population in general and rural women in particular. Illiteracy is more marked in the older age brackets; women between 20 and 29 years of age, 7 out of 35 (i.e. 20 per cent) had been to primary school as against 10 out of 177 (i.e. 5.6 per cent) aged between 30 and 55. The difference in educational level of

Table 5.1. Geographical spread of the research zones

Economic regions	Prefecture	Headquarters of the Prefecture	Numbers interviewed	Regional totals
Maritime	LACS	Aneho	28	
	VO	Vogan	13	
	ZIO	Tsevie	20	61
Plateaux	HAHO	Notse	28	
	KLOTO	Kpalime	12	
	OGOU	Atakpame	15	
	AMOU	Amlame	6	61
Central	TCHAOUDJO	Sokode	14	
	TCHAMBA	Tchamba	10	
	SOTOUBOUA	Sotouboua	5	29*
Kara	KOZAH	Kara	40	
	BASSAR	Bassar	11	
	ASSOLI	Bafilo	10	61
Savannah	OTI	Mango ⎱		
	TONE	Dapaon ⎰	50	50**
Total			262	262

*In this region the survey was undertaken during the harvest time and few people were available.
**Because of timing and other difficulties the results from the Savannah region are given separately in the analysis of the survey.

women between 20 and 29 reflects the changes at the national level which education for young girls has undergone. The figures also give some idea of the magnitude of the effort needed to lessen the gap between the rates of education of boys and girls, of men and women and also between the urban and rural population.

(d) Women's main socio-economic activities. About 71 per cent of women are engaged in agriculture as against 29 per cent in other sectors of economic activity in the 4 regions. In the Savannah almost all the women interviewed were involved in agriculture; in the 4 other regions almost 18.4 per cent of women had commerce as their main activity, 6.6 per cent wage work and 3.8 per cent handicrafts. Among women involved in agriculture about 60 per cent gave commerce and 12 per cent crafts as their secondary activity. In general, about 47 per cent of the women interviewed gave trade as

their secondary activity as against 15 per cent for whom agriculture was secondary. This double activity of women is witness to their dynamism and their desire to better their individual cash incomes and to solve their subsistence needs. In other respects these results also underline the importance of trade for women given that trading is quite developed in the rural zones and that the subsistence economy is shrinking in the face of the market and cash economy.

Comparison of the educational levels of women farmers with those of women in other economic sectors shows that a certain degree of literacy is not incompatible with working the land. In fact of 17 women who had attended primary school, 11 were farmers. The survey showed that although women are also involved in cattle raising, they mainly care for small livestock (sheep, goats, pigs and chickens), the average number of animals owned by women being between 6 and 11. The majority of women acquire land by inheritance or gift (about 36.5 per cent and 35.5 per cent of the sample respectively), the rest through buying it or renting it (5.9 per cent and 12.4 per cent respectively.) Those women who acquired land through inheritance or gift did so generally through the mediation of a kinsperson (inheritance) or their husband (gift).

The survey reinforces the importance of married women in farming activities: of the sample 77.3 per cent were married women, 13.2 per cent widows, 7.1 per cent divorcees and 2.4 per cent single women. Of the married women, about 71 per cent were principally occupied with farming. About 24.5 per cent of the women farmers were involved in conflicts over ownership of land for cultivation as against 27.8 per cent over land for housing. Access to land was similar in the Savannah but almost 92 per cent of women had got land through inheritance.

(e) The principal productive tools. Women generally use traditional tools; around 98 per cent used only a hoe against 2 per cent using animal traction and a tractor. These results underline the rudimentary character of the working tools used by the majority of rural women (including those in the Savannah). At the national level agriculture is characterised by the use of production techniques which are both traditional and archaic. Most women possessed enough working tools: on average they had 2 dabas, 2.7 hoes, 1.6 coupe coupe, 1.2 axes. However the number of working tools at women's disposal appears to be totally inadequate when their rhythm of use and the process of wear and tear is taken into

account. However judging by women's own priorities, this situation does not appear to worry them.

(f) Rural women's needs. For the majority of women, health comes at the top of their priorities: nearly 48 per cent of those interviewed shared this view as against 26 per cent who rated food and 14 per cent land highest. In second place comes food, followed by housing, clothing, land and lastly tools.

An examination of these priorities shows women's clear understanding of the main inadequacies of their living conditions and their socio-economic environment. It also reveals that their priorities are in line with the behavioural norms for women in a society defined by customs. For example, health. Although health is an essential preoccupation of human beings and, in particular, rural people with a low life expectancy, it also represents an area allocated to women by the social division of labour. When a member of the family group or of the community falls ill, a woman generally cares for that person. The care of children assigned by the social and traditional division of labour to women is generally extended to all members of the household or of the community. As a result, the absolute priority given by women to health appears both as an individual and a collective need.

The importance given to food is also justified by the sexual division of labour which allocates the nourishment of family members and food preparation to women. It is equally explained by the spectre of hunger which has appeared during the last few years of persistent drought and irregular rains which prejudice the growth of cultivation in general and food crops in particular. As for the preoccupation with housing, this is determined by habits born of women's attachment to domestic life and the delegation to women of the maintenance and cleanliness of the home by the sexual division of labour. However this concern is not restricted to the house site (made up of a number of huts) alone, but includes the entire social environment in and around the home. We came to the conclusion that many rural women want to have a place of their own, because of the number of women who had invested in building a house. Around 17 per cent of the women who responded to the question about investment priorities had built a house for themselves against 14 per cent who had invested in clothing and toiletries, 14 per cent on the family, and 29 per cent who had made no investments. The priority given to clothing is related to the natural flirtatiousness of women and their taste for toiletries. Being able to meet this need is seen as reinforcing a woman's social status in the community above all *vis-à-vis* other women.

The relegation of land and tools to the lowest levels of priority appears rather contradictory. It might be explained by arguing that customary means of access to land are not particularly unfavourable to women. Women obtain access to land generally through the mediation of men. In our survey 12.7 per cent of the women interviewed are the primary occupiers of the land; for 40.2 per cent the head of the family is, and for 19.8 per cent the village chiefs are. State action appears insignificant as far as allocation of land is concerned: only 2 per cent of women mentioned this source in the survey. However, the traditional system of land ownership, while ensuring that women do get access to land, systematically denies them ownership and appropriation of land. Women are effectively excluded from land inheritance which is traditionally reserved for men, who can then give use rights to wife, sister or others. The attitude of rural women shown by the survey could be interpreted as showing their awareness of this situation. This could indicate that rural women are no longer willing, given the customary rules of appropriation and exploitation of land, to invest either in land or the improvement of their tools. They prefer to accept poor returns on their labour for fear that the benefit of their investment will be enjoyed by the real owners of the land.

(g) Principal problems of rural women. The main difficulties the women interviewed referred to fall into the following categories:
— financial problems (especially those linked to ill health and famine);
— the organisation of work (the survey asked respondents to indentify their main problems and also the principal difficulties experienced in their work);
— sickness;
— hunger;
— lack of shelter/housing;
— lack of land.

Financial problems predominate: more than half the women in the 4-region sample emphasised this type of difficulty. Around 10 per cent of the women had to face general financial problems because of their health as against 3 per cent whose financial worries were related to conjugal problems.

When asked about specific difficulties encountered by respondents, a slightly different list of concerns was generated which included:

— lack of labour;
— delays in supply of improved seeds;
— cost of transport;
— financial difficulties;
— the lack of production inputs;
— sickness;
— climatic risks;
— slump in sales.

Although almost 33 per cent of the women appeared to have experienced no difficulties (against 8 per cent poorly defined responses and 8.4 per cent who did not respond), around 15 per cent of the sample encountered financial difficulties and 10 per cent difficulties linked to the lack of inputs, 9 per cent delay in receiving supply of seeds and 8 per cent to shortage of labour. These results reflect the principal difficulties encountered by women in carrying out their economic activities. They indicate the predominance of problems associated with a shortage of cash, the state of their health, shortage of labour power and production inputs in general. This latter also has financial implications given the relatively high cost of agricultural labour and chemicals used to protect the crops from parasites in the field or after harvest.

As far as labour is concerned, the participation of the majority of women in systems of mutual aid (around 52 per cent of the sample) helps to lessen the effects of labour shortage. However the existence of work organisation problems mentioned by about 2.3 per cent of the sample indicates the relative persistence of the problem of labour in the rural area. Women in the prefectures of Lacs, Amou, Haho and Ogou seemed particularly troubled in this respect. In contrast the women of the prefectures of Kozah, Kloto, Haho and Lacs were more worried by financial problems, while those of Zio were more concerned by harvest losses due to attacks by parasites and rodents.

(h) Rural women's incomes.   About 33.4 per cent of the women interviewed made less than 5,000 F CFA per month, 25.5 per cent and 11.5 per cent of the sample made between 5,000 F and 10,000 F

Table 5.2. Income of rural women in Togo

Income (in F CFA per month)	Percentage
up to 5,000	33.4
5,000–9,999	25.5
10,000–14,999	11.5
15,000–19,999	5.0
20,000–24,999 } 25,000–29,999 }	8.1
30,000–34,999	7.5
over 35,000	9.0

respectively. Of the remaining 30 per cent, 5 per cent earned between 15,000 F and 20,000 F, 7.5 per cent between 30,000 F and 35,000 F, and 9 per cent earned 35,000 F per month or more. Those with the lowest earnings were concentrated in agriculture: farmers represented about 86 per cent of those who earned less than 5,000 F against 10 per cent in trade and 4 per cent in handicrafts. This same tendency is found among those earning between 5,000 F and 15,000 F. Of those women who earned more than 35,000 F per month, 35 per cent were traders, 30 per cent wageworkers, 30 per cent farmers and 5 per cent artisans. In analysing our survey results, it appears that the lowest income are found in agriculture and handicrafts and the highest in commerce and wage work.

The survey showed that in agriculture the commonest pattern is for both husband and wife to be farmers — around 81 per cent; 10.4 per cent of women farmers had husbands who were wage workers, and 4 per cent husbands without work. In contrast, spouses are rarely both traders: of 36 married women traders 47 per cent had husbands working in agriculture, and 28 per cent husbands who were wage workers. This tendency was also observed amongst artisans. Women in wage employment, tended to have wage-earning husbands.

The high proportion of rural women with low incomes reflects the overall socio-economic situation of the rural population whose income is generally inadequate. A number of rural studies underline this aspect of the economic life of villagers. This explains the importance of financial problems indicated by most of the women interviewed. It also explains the participation of rural women in more than one activity. None the less it must be remembered that rural women (like urban women) not only participate in paid

Table 5.3. Daily routine of Togolese women in the North

4.00	get up
4 – 7.00	fetching water in a number of round trips between the house and the source of water
7 – 8.00	cleaning, meal preparation
8 – 13.00	comlecting wood, washing clothes or field work
13 – 15.00	cooking midday meal and eating
15 – 16.30	grinding millet in a mortar (if no mill in the area) to make flour for the evening meal
16.30 – 17.00	rest time
17 – 18.00	collecting water
18 – 20.00	cooking the evening meal and eating

activities, but also carry out many tasks which are not directly remunerated in economic terms. In other words, they do domestic work which is absolutely necessary to household life and the harmony of the community as a whole.

(i) Other unpaid activities. Rural women spend a good deal of their time on domestic tasks. The survey allowed us to establish carefully the daily routine of women in the North (see Table 5.3). This indicates that most women have a 16-hour day with little leisure time. The situation of women in the South is little different: they also get up extremely early, go to bed around 8 or 9 p.m. and do much the same work as their sisters in the North.

Urban Survey: The Case of Lome

Aims. The aims of the Lome survey were:
— to provide data which would enable women's participation to be measured;
— to study a sample of women by means of an appropriate questionnaire;
— to use the questionnaire to provide statistical data in tabular form.

The survey. The survey focused on Togolese women between 20 and 65 who lived in the commune of Lome. The limits of the town used were those conventionally defined. As a result, the field of study was the urban territory of Lome with the exception of the hospital, the gendarmerie, the military zone, the university, the embassies and the administrative quarter. It should be noted that there are 60 residential quarters in Lome of different sizes and population densities.

The sample. Given the limited budget and time allowed for the survey, we were obliged to choose a small sample, and anticipated interviewing between 150 and 200 women representative of the total female population of the commune. The sample was drawn at random as follows:

— first, the town of Lome was divided in a certain number of quarters, 9 of which were selected at random;
— second, 3 residential blocks in each quarter were randomly chosen;
— third, one house in three in each block was chosen all the women in it between 20 and 60 were systematically interviewed.

The final sample was of between 150 and 180 women. The female population (on 15 March 1985) between 20 and 65 in Lome was estimated to be 99,700; so our sample covered between 1.5 and 2.0 per 1000. Lastly, the size of the sample did not permit us to include all the socio-professional categories in which women are to be found.

The collection of information was undertaken by 7 interviewers under the supervision of a statistician, a sociologist and a demographer. The survey took only 3 days, not counting 1 day spent on training and in getting to know the areas to be surveyed. Although we used experienced interviewers it must be said that the training period was very short. And, while we did not encounter any major resistance to taking part in the survey if we had been able to sensitise the target population they might have answered a number of the questions more accurately, notably those about income, time use, participation in decision making in the household, economic activity, etc.

Analysis of the Results of the Survey

(a) Ethnic distribution. Lome being a cosmopolitan town, the dominant ethnic groups (the Ewe, the Mina, the Kabbye, the Ouatchi and the Cotocoli) are found in the sample, which covered 8 ethnic groups: Akposso, Ana–Ife, Cotocoli, Mina, Anhlan–Ewe,

Ouatchi, Fon, Kabbye, Moba. The results show that of the 180 women sampled, there were 69 Ewe–Ouatchi (38.3 per cent), 53 Mina–Anhlan (29.4 per cent), 19 Fon (10.6 per cent), 11 Kabbye (5.1 per cent). The 4 other ethnic groups represented 15.6 per cent of the total of women interviewed. The Lome sample is quite representative of the other large urban centres of Togo.

(b) Marital status. Of the 180 women interviewed, 151 were married (84 per cent), 6 were divorced, 16 widowed and 7 concubines or separated. Of the married women 58.1 per cent were married according to customary rites; in other words celebrated according to ethnic group traditions and not registered either at the registry or the Mairie. This shows that the Togolese population does not give up its traditions lightly. Of the 86 customary marriages, 65 were in three ethnic groups — Mina–Anhlan, Ewe–Ouatchi and Fon — the rest spread evenly among the other ethnic groups. These 3 ethnic groups are not necessarily the most dominant in other Togolese towns. In addition, it is often in such towns that western practices such as monogamy or free choice of partner are born; therefore it is likely that the same proportions of marriage types would not be found elsewhere. The new Family Code now leaves the choice of marriage form up to the spouses: they can opt for monogamy or polygamy. Traditionally the number of wives a man had was source of prestige, above all in the rural areas as well as a source of labour power. The survey showed that in Lome half the women interviewed were in monogamous marriages the rest in polygamous ones. These findings can probably be applied to other urban populations in Togo. Of the monogamous marriages (91 in all), 67 of the women were either Mina–Anhlan, Ewe–Ouatchi or Fon, while 24 were from the other ethnic groups. Again, 68 of the women in polygamous households were mainly from the 3 main ethnic groups. In 43 cases out of the 180, the parents had played an important role in the choice of husband for their daughters. Of the 118 women who had freely chosen their husbands, 41 were Mina–Anhlan, 55 Ewe–Ouatchi, 13 Fon and 9 Kabbye. As far as religion is concerned, 27 per cent of the women interviewed were Catholic, 27 per cent Protestant, 7 per cent Muslim and 39 per cent animist. Of the 98 Catholics 83 were Mina–Anhlan, Ewe–Ouatchi, Fon or Kabbye.

A notable finding of our study is the relatively high percentage of believers in animism, which is considered in Africa as the ancestor of all our other religions, and which is increasingly attracting converts. The animists were largely Ewe–Ouatchi or Fon. Animist rites and customs are dominant factors holding back the emancipation of African women in general and Togolese women in particular. The most striking example of this is the food prohibitions for women initiates in the Afan cult[4] or Voodoo. A second example is that of a young girl obliged to give up her studies to join a Voodoo cult because its preacher told her that a supernatural force was in possession of her soul. These examples illustrate how much traditions and customs weigh against the total liberation of African women. It should be noted that these practices may well be on the increase in the towns because the heavy migratory flow from the countryside to the urban areas is leading to a ruralisation of towns.

(c) Age spread. The target population of the survey was between 20 and 65. More than half the women interviewed were under 39 (70 per cent), those between 40 and 49 represented 18.4 per cent and those between 50 and 65 11.6 per cent. From Table 5.4 it can be seen that the Lome sample differs from that of the population census of

Table 5.4. Comparison of the Lome & sample and the population census of 1981

| Age | Survey population | | 1981 population census | |
	Number	%	Number	%
20–24 years	33	18.3	23,589	28.8
25–29	34	18.9	20,274	24.7
30–34	34	18.9	12,282	15.0
35–39	25	13.9	8,601	10.5
40–44	19	10.6	5,866	7.1
45–49	14	7.8	4,548	5.5
50–65	21	11.6	6,903	8.4
Total	180	100.0	82,063	100.0

1981, under-representing women between 20 and 29 and over-representing those between 30 and 39.

Of the women surveyed between 20 and 39, 91.7 per cent had had more than one live birth, 8.3 per cent had had none. Of the former — 28 had had 2 live births and 51 had had 3 or 4; the remaining had

4. Afan is an animist cult.

had 5 or more. The fact that over 30 per cent of the women had had more than 5 live births suggests that knowledge of contraception is not widespread. 87 per cent of those who had had more than 5 live births were over 35.

The fertility of women is an important component in the quantity of human resources produced and thus in the labour force supply. It is fundamental that women must be at the centre of the debate about population and development.

(d) Women's health and the quality of health provisions. Our survey showed that Lome has a modern medical and social infrastructure, and that the quality of care is adequate. Most women interviewed showed willingness to attend the Maternal and Infant Protection clinics (PMI) because they felt the health of their children depended on it; only 19 did not attend the PMI for a variety of reasons: ignorance, distance from the centre, etc. One of the advantages of attendance at the medical centres is the improvement in the health of both mother and child, and its effect on infant and child mortality. The proportion of infants who died of the women surveyed was 6.9 per cent showing the quality of care in the urban area.

One problem is that of language, but as the number of Togolese doctors increases, local doctors will be able to communicate better with illiterate women in their own language which will allow them to diagnose their illnesses better.

(e) Educational levels and professional activity. The female population of Lome just as that of the rest of the country still has a high proportion of illiterates. Our study showed that of our sample 36 per cent had no schooling, 33 per cent had attended primary school, 22 per cent had the equivalent of *lycée* or college, and only 5 per cent had reached higher levels. In addition 7 women (4 per cent) had received literacy training which shows that functional literacy programmes are having some impact. This improvement of the level of education among women will have favourable effects on their way of life and their economic activities. Most of the women (71 per cent) belonged to the economic sector of traditional trade; of these 59 were illiterate, 22 had reached the equivalent of *lycée* or college, the remainder had some primary schooling.

School wastage. For some time the drop-out rate among school-children had been more pronounced among girls than boys. A number of factors explains this: parents' lack of financial means as a consequence of the economic crisis; problems linked to the social environment such as the refusal of certain parents to educate their daughters because they think it is a waste of money since daughters will marry and leave the paternal roof. In other regions of Togo, daughters have to go through a number of initiation rites before being able to leave home. These practices hamper girls' schooling. However the greatest obstacles to girls' education are premature pregnancies and their lack of motivation because of the lack of employment opportunities.

(f) Professional activities and incomes. Although women in Lome are found in all economic sectors (public, private, modern and traditional trade, gardening and market gardening), the majority are in trade. The women in our study preferred trade and dressmaking to other occupations. Almost 71 per cent were in trade and 14.4 per cent in dressmaking; the majority were self employed (74.4 per cent). In all, 55 women indicated that they would like to train for an occupation other than their own. Their greatest preference was for a training in dressmaking, an occupation which has always attracted women because of rapidly changing fashions. This desire of Togolese women to learn a trade is an index of their participation, and of their response to changes in their social and professional life.

As far as giving information, on income, the women were reticent and distrustful. None the less some data were obtained which suggest that their average income is low — around 15.000 F CFA per month. The majority of women earn between 500 and 10.000 F; only three women earn more than 10.000 F. Women's incomes represent a not insignificant economic contribution to the household budget. In those homes where the husband enjoys a high income, that of the wife is not essential, but when the husband's income is lower than or near the level of subsistence the economic contribution of the wife becomes very important. In some cases the wife is the main economic agent and often the head of the family.

Many of the women, almost 75 per cent, stated that the housekeeping money given them by their husband is inadequate. A good number of women bear the financial burden of their children themselves (buy their clothes, shoes, etc.). The financial contribution of the woman to the smooth functioning of the home is considerable: honest husbands recognised that 'without the financial help of my wife, we would have to face problems'.

Table 5.5. Togolese women's contribution to the economic life of the nation

Period	Essential unpaid work	Paid work	Description of work
	Hours		
4.00	0	0	WAKE UP
4 – 5.00	1	0	Housework, various preparations
5 – 6.00	1	0	Helping the children get ready for school
6 – 7.00	1	0	Preparing for work
7 – 12.00	0	5	Paid employment
12 – 12.30	$\frac{1}{2}$	0	Shopping in market
12.30 – 14.30	2	0	Housework
14.30 – 17.30	0	3	Paid employment
17.30 – 19.00	$1\frac{1}{2}$	0	Shopping at market for evening
19 – 20.00	1	0	Food preparation
20 – 21.00	0	0	MEAL
21 – 21.30	$\frac{1}{2}$	0	Helping children with homework
21.30 – 22.00	$\frac{1}{2}$	0	Getting children to bed
22 – 4.00	0	0	SLEEP
Total	9 hours (essential unpaid work)	8 hours (paid work)	

(g) How urban women spend their time.   Making a study of urban women's daily schedules helps us to understand concretely their activities. After working at 4 a.m. they busy themselves with household chores between 4.30 and 6.30 when they leave for work. Although this is the pattern for salaried women, that of traders varies only slightly, and one can say it corresponds to the average use of time by women who earn money. Employees spend 8 hours doing paid work — 5 hours in the morning and 3 in the afternoon — and nearly 9 hours a day on unpaid work. Of our sample, 15 women employees had no domestic help. A Togolese woman's contribution to her family's budget and to the national economy is therefore important.

Yet, despite the absolute necessity of domestic work and therefore of the housewives' input, society does not always consider women to be performing indispensable economic social tasks. As a result women themselves are not always clearly aware of their role in society.

(h) Women's needs. Most women interviewed felt that credit was absolutely essential for the smooth functioning of their businesses; this is particularly the case of the traders, many of whom have rather limited resources. The problem of financial resources is so acute that Togolese people have partially resolved it through the system of *tontine* (a mutual aid and savings association with funds distributed equally among members in rotation). *Tontine* probably existed even in the precolonial period, our ancestors having discovered this practical method of saving. It is more widely practised by women than men and without it many women stated that they would not have been able to acquire goods such as sewing-machines, beds, etc. Given the fact that the system of *tontine* has survived until now and forms part of our traditional economic inheritance, it deserves formal recognition and efforts to modernise it, because as a mechanism to mobilise savings or encourage saving it is inadequate. Through recognition and modernisation, it will be able to take its place among the banking practices of our country.

The women interviewed also wanted to receive good vocational training so as to better their conditions of life, and rightly so, since what is the point of having decent financial resources if one lacks an adequate and practical training? In the last resort, women hope that equal educational training opportunities will be given to both sexes. In Togo a particular effort in this direction has already been made because of educational reforms. As mentalities change, so do myths.

As for personal needs, food is considered top priority by farmers (7 out of 10), employees (6/12) and artisans (2/12). None of the categories enjoy high incomes except for the traders. Housing was an urgent need for employees; often they rent their home and dream of buying their own.

(i) Ranking of women's occupations. We asked our respondents to rank occupations in order of their contribution to the economic and social development of the nation. Women farmers, employees and artisans suggest that traders should be ranked first because they contribute a great deal to the economy. Among active women, traders have a higher buying power than all the others. Traders and employees also thought that they made an important contribution to the national economy. No one, including the farmers themselves,

Table 5.6. Answers to the question, 'What are the main difficulties you experience in your work?'

Type of difficulty	Category of women	Number of responses
(1) Sparseness or lateness of rainfall	Market gardeners	10
(2) Lack of knowledge of management	Traders	3
(3) High cost of transport	Traders	4
(4) Slack seasons	Traders	3
(5) Money given by husband insufficient	Employees	8
(6) Means of transport to work	Employees	7
(7) Lack of credit	Traders	5
	Employees	12
	Market gardeners	10
	Artisans	2

ranked farming high. Yet the nourishment of Togolese households depends above all on agricultural production: many of the goods the traders sell in the towns come from the agriculture sector.

(j) Principal problems of urban women. The women were asked what difficulties) they experienced in their work. Their answers are given above in Table 5.6.

The Traders

Despite the fact that the majority of farmers are also traders because they sell the foodstuffs they themselves produce, they do not properly fall within the category of those specialising in trade in general. There are in fact two types of traders: those who sell imported goods (12 per cent of our survey) and those who sell local produce (78 per cent). The latter leave Lome to go to the countryside where they buy products either at a weekly/monthly market or direct for resale in Lome. Although these traders are quite satisfied with local trading they also encounter a number of problems in the following areas: transport, conservation of food, turnover, lack of credit, poor profit margins, insolvency.

Transport: traders complained about the high cost of transport which reduces their profit margins. Their main complaint is not about the fares which are government regulated but the charges imposed by the drivers for bags and other articles. Drivers are often inflexible about the price charged despite the nature of the merchandise.

The conservation of products: how to conserve perishable products is one of the toughest problems suffered by traders. Many women avoid trading in goods such as fish, fruit or vegetables because they are difficult to conserve. They suggest that the authorities should install cold-storage rooms near the markets which they could rent.

Turnover: many of the traders say that trade is not as good now as in the past; many products remain unsold and spoil easily. The traders feel that this is due in part to the permeability of certain borders, for example that of Nigeria.

Lack of credit: many traders have problems of access to credit, yet the latter acts as a stimulus to their transactions. They suggest that credit should be made more general.

Reduced profit margins: 50 per cent of the traders noted a drop in their profits. We consider this due to the difficulties noted above.

Insolvency of clients: every trader has a network of clients who generally buy to resell and only after they have sold the goods do they pay the original trader.

Section 4: General Conclusion

The participation of women in economic and social development at the local, regional or national level represents in principle a normal process of the contribution of the principal social actors to the realisation of the development aims of society. Why then does this question arouse such particular interest at the international and national level? The response to this question seems to lie in the general situation of women and the evaluation of their participation in those activities in the home and in the heart of the community which coincide with socio-economic development.

This study has shown the diversity and the volume of women's activities in the home, the community and the nation. It also indicates the complexity of the problem which is related to the situation of women and the contradictions created by the imbalance between the intensity of women's participation in society and their socio-economic status. The analysis of women's socio-economic status reveals an imbalance between women's strong participation in the development of society and their weak position with regard to access to the benefits of their productive activity and to social prestige derived from social recognition of this participation. It indicates the existence of a relationship between the determination of women's economic status and the evaluation of women's participation in economic and social life by the rest of the community. In other words, women's weak socio-economic status is the result of an inadequate evaluation of women's participation in the socio-economic life of the society under consideration. This could also result from a social group deciding that certain types of tasks or activities should be more important or more noble than others. This latter argument seems to be justified by the existence of the sexual division of labour, which is characterised by a more or less rigid division of tasks between men and women. The results of the survey have shown that this social division of labour is an essential mechanism of the social stratification of rural and urban communities.

The impact of traditional customs is greatest in rural areas where the difficult conditions of life accentuate the punishing character of the tasks assigned to women in particular those in the arena of domestic activities. In the urban areas, the existence of a certain number of services (provision of water, cooking or heating materials) lessens this burden. Urban women's difficulties lie more in the conflicting demands on their time due to the importance of their socio-economic activities outside the home and their need to carry out the main domestic tasks. This double burden is a source of nervous tension which is accentuated by the problems of travel and the cost of transport. This in turn aggravates financial problems and leads to a desperate search for more lucrative economic activity or employment.

In other respects the observations drawn from our survey show that both urban and rural women are seeking to adapt themselves to the modern economy by relying on traditional social structures. This tendency is confirmed by the high proportion of women who undertake those activities customarily reserved for women by the traditional sexual division of labour: agriculture, trade, handicrafts, transport, selling of cooked food, etc. In the rural areas the main occupations of women other than domestic work are agriculture and trade; in the urban area the majority of women are in trade, handicrafts or wage work.

Whether in town or country, women do not appear to be active in the formal sector which is based on modern socio-economic structures. Available statistics show that the participation of women in the modern professions is rather weak. This is probably in part due to the national educational policy which, before its reform in 1975, only encouraged boy's education. As a result the structures of the modern economy are dominated by men with adequate levels of education and appropriate socio-professional training. Today this gap may be decreasing because of the progress in women's education at all levels.

Women have also become aware of the marginal position in which they have been trapped, and are beginning to organise themselves. They are doing this in ways defined and recognised by society so as to avoid all possible conflict, which would risk their search for peace and the liberty of action necessary to achieve their multiple tasks. Women have remained outside the 'official paths' of development which benefit from systematic State support and a whole range of actions destined to promote the development of the modern economy in the medium term. None the less actions of the State in favour of the economic and social promotion of women do exist in a diffuse, varied and multiple form. In the course of the present decade women have benefited from greater degrees of planning to correct the inadequacies of the previous period in which the 4 main Five Year Plans for social and economic development were implemented. The initiatives taken at this level are aimed at women working in the rural sector so as to enable them to respond to the need to adapt to the possibilities created by the monetisation of the national economy and expansion of the market. This orientation seems pertinent in as much as three-quarters of the national population and two-thirds of the female population live in rural areas; and that women's participation is essential not only in production but above all in achieving the aim of food self-sufficiency promoted by the government in 1977. All these considerations lead one to privilege this sector, the true heart of the economy of the country, in which the rural population still use traditional low-productivity tools. The behaviour of the rural population is also more deeply influenced by traditional values whose impact appears to be weakened in the urban milieu. The towns in fact are characterised by a radical process of acculturation and widespread diffusion of modern socio-economic and cultural values.

In any attempt to introduce support for women's active participation in the socio-economic development of the community, the region or the nation it would be interesting to start from the norms and structures favoured by rural women and adopted by the majority of urban women. Local particularities should of course be taken into account, but this should not prevent decisions being taken on the main areas of action which will bring appreciable benefits to a large majority of rural and urban women. The sectors of economic activity which largely interest rural women are crop and livestock production, handicrafts, trade in all its forms and in all its branches. These same economic interests, except agriculture, are shared by urban women. Consequently, the participation of women should, to begin with, be improved in those activities linked to agriculture, handicrafts and trade. To do this, the degree of participation of rural or urban women in each of these areas of activity must be identified so as to introduce appropriate improvements to meet women's expressed needs within the framework of a rational planning of national development.

Recommendations

Indicators, however elaborated, will never entirely take into account the role of women in the development of Togo. As a result, planners must not depend on the use of indicators alone during the design of development plans. They must also use other non-qualifiable parameters such as children's education, the household, etc.

As for the information collected, we would make the following recommendations:

(1) The principle of non-discrimination by sex and the equality of the rights and responsibilities of men and women should be strengthened by constitutional and legislative means.

(2) Women should be provided with a suitable education to help them participate in the development of the country because:
    — it is clear that, despite some progress, women do not enjoy total equality of status. The problem of attitudes still remains;
    — the majority of women are still illiterate.

(3) Young women should be encouraged to take up scientific and technical careers.

(4) The collective provision of basic services should be increased so as to facilitate women's tasks in the home and in their professional life. In particular:

   — the programme to provide piped water to rural villages should be expanded;

   — transport costs should be lowered and developing better means of communication should be given priority;

   — a system of storage and conservation of agricultural products should be introduced.

(5) Reafforestation should be encouraged not only to fight against desertification but also to ensure that women have sufficient supplies of firewood.

(6) The distribution of tasks by sex has to be re-examined so as to correct the imbalances in traditional social division of labour.

(7) Research should be undertaken into the characteristics of the tasks carried out by women in the home, the local community, the region and the country.

(8) Women should be asked to collaborate in the conception and design of development programmes and projects.

(9) Women should be given the chance of seeing how new technologies could be used in their productive undertakings.

(10) Human and financial resources should be mobilised to

   — create a system of credit for women;

   — improve the system of *tontine*;

   — set up women's productive groups or cooperatives;

   — encourage women to save and to invest in productive sectors other than real estate.

(11) A methodology should be established by which the participation of women can be measured and their performance improved. The following elements should be taken into account:

   — women's use of time and volume of activity in the course of a 24-hour period;

   — the nature of the tasks undertaken and the degree of toilsomeness;

   — the contribution women make to promoting socio-economic well-being and to the development of the family, the local, regional and national community.

(12) A system of evaluation of women's participation in economic and social development should be set up.

(13) A strategy should be designed to integrate women's participation in regional planning. To ensure this a system of permanent evaluation should be set up which would make available a whole range of information about women's participation

and the results achieved in this area.

(14) A data bank should be set up which would permit the publication of information about women to be organised; this should lead to a growing rate of execution of projects undertaken.

6

REFLECTIONS ON A METHODOLOGY FOR INTEGRATING WOMEN'S CONCERNS INTO DEVELOPMENT ACTIVITIES

Isabelle Deblé (Head of the Centre for Comparative Development Studies)

In this article I will sketch out a potential methodology by which women's concerns could be incorporated into development activities.* I hope that this will help to stimulate further discussion on methodological approaches and the elaboration of more effective measures. The paper starts from three premises which appear to be broadly accepted at the national and international level:

(1) that women play an important role in society in all its aspects — economic, social, cultural and political;

(2) that women's lives are different from men's and often they have to cope with particularly difficult circumstances;

(3) that many development activities have had negative consequences for women, such as excluding them from the benefits of their participation in production; their partial or complete exclusion from access to new technologies, which in turn makes it more difficult for women to participate in dynamic social activities; the increased competition between men and women for access to education and employment; and the deterioration in their status.

The model we have devised includes a number of dimensions.

---

* This article was translated from the French by Francoise Read and was then edited for inclusion in this book. The original, entitled 'Guide de réflexion méthodologique pour intégrer la dimension féminine dans les opérations de développement' was presented at the second Unesco meeting, held in Paris 5–9 October 1987 on meeting women's needs at the local, regional and national level.

Firstly that of three separate perspectives for action: those of the international and the national institutions, and of the actors themselves. Secondly it incorporates three critical needs:

— to take into account the crisis in development planning
— to improve women's education at all levels
— to improve the tools enabling men and women to understand the key mechanisms and dynamic processes of contemporary societies.

The model can be portrayed graphically (see Figure).

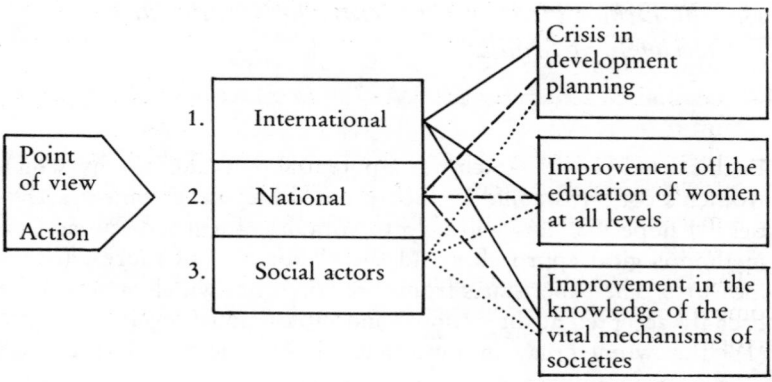

We now turn to look at the major components in the model and then outline some of the actions that could be undertaken by the three central actors of the model — international and national institutions and the populations of developing countries themselves.

Section 1: The Crisis in Development Planning

Development planning is today greatly criticised. If we follow Hugon and Sudrie,[1] criticism focuses largely on the facts that:
— plans remain very formal. They are documents which are not integrated into a permanent process of planning:

1. See Philippe Hugon and Olivier Sudrie, 'La crise de la planification africaine', in *Revue Tiers-Monde*, no. 110, April–June 1987, pp. 407–37. The article can also apply to other parts of the world.

— they are drawn up at the centre;
— there is little or no mobilisation of social actors;
— information is scarce and unreliable;
— the package of projects and programmes envisaged are:
    inadequately assessed
    not ordered in terms of priorities
    dependent on outside sources of finance
    lacking in real macro-economic perspective;
— there are no real planning bodies or institutional mechanisms to:
    coordinate short-term financial controls with long-term policies
    maintain a permanent process of negotiation and agreement;
— a large number of indebted countries are subject to outside supervision;
— centralised structures are linked to omnipresent State apparatuses;
— there are a variety of approaches to market regulation: codes for the domestic sphere, rules and policies aimed at those who make decisions about national and international trade.

The crisis is almost unanimously acknowledged. Each one of its components can be discussed from the point of view of our three actors.

(a) The Role of International Institutions

Since international institutions have come to dominate the financing of development activities, it is essential to initiate or to continue the process of making these bodies aware of the role of women in their respective areas of competence.

It is therefore necessary to ask the United Nations, the World Bank, ILO, FAO, Unido, Unesco, WHO, etc.
(1) to compare the results which they have achieved in the course of the last twenty years in incorporating women into their projects and programmes;
(2) to investigate the criteria used when setting up and financing activities affecting the integration of women into the development process.

In a study detailing the means by which a development project is decided upon, identified, conceptualised, implemented and

211

assessed,[2] I showed that some projects set out from an apparently satisfactory problematic, which takes as a prerequisite an understanding of the situation of women based both on what can be observed and what can be perceived in a given field of intervention, and uses an analytical framework which allows identification of the data needed to calculate and measure the observations to be made. However others are less carefully designed. Deciding on the suitability of a project on the basis of inferring from direct (that is to say visible) observations is a risky business. Projects will almost inevitably fail to achieve their aims if they are built upon observations which do not capture the structural factors which influence conduct.

The role of international and non-governmental organisations in the choice of projects has also to be questioned. Firstly, given that they claim to embody the aspirations of the world community, they should offer a general framework encompassing both equity and efficiency, and take into account both components — male and female — of the population. This is an indispensable prerequisite for any policy of international cooperation, but depends on the way in which the role of women in society is envisaged. In fact women's activities in more than the economic sphere should be recognised, given value and made known to the wider public. Operational aid — except in emergency situations: famine, catastrophe, epidemic — should also endeavour to seek the conditions of success both at the national level and at that of the actors.

Given this, it is advisable:

— to assist in setting up planning bodies and systems of information adapted to the economic, social and cultural realities of the country concerned;
— to train the necessary staff, both female and male, capable of maintaining a permanent process of negotiation and agreement.

(b) The Role of National Institutions

Given the wide variety of empirical situations, generalisation is rather difficult. However a few desirable interventions should be mentioned:

— Political will must be clearly expressed at the highest level, such as the constitution, the government and all ministries. (One can

2. Isabelle Deblé, 'Lévaluation des effets de quelques opérations mises en oeuvre par l'Unesco sur la situation des femmes', ref. 6661353, March 1983.

anticipate a debate over the means to be used: specific organisations? control bodies ensuring that the population of both
sexes has been taken into account? use of the mass media for a
permanent campaign to make people aware of the problem?).
The role of the planning ministry requires precise definition
and strengthening.

— There should be implementation of legal instruments indispensable to development planning. (A list should be drawn up
covering a whole range of activities, not just economic but also
cultural and social.)

— The organisation of information systems which take into account the reality of the country in question is needed. This
must involve expanding the set of indicators currently used:
GDP — yes but how is subsistence production to be recorded
or dealt with? Salaried and wage-earning population — what
segment of the population is involved in non-salaried and
non-wage-earning work? School population — how is the
non-school population assessed? Rather than averages, figures
should be disaggregated. In short, the existing system of social
indicators should be reorganised and problems of definition
raised. What is a household? Is it more appropriate to record
them according to their actual characteristics (single-parent
families, polygamous families, etc.).[3] It may be necessary to
make bilateral or international assistance available for countries
which want to develop appropriate concepts and indicators,
which will enable the real mechanisms at work in a given
country to be better understood. This should avoid the present
situation in which essential aspects of the phenomena are
pushed into the background or into the category of the informal.

— Depending on the case in question, the choice of a variety of
tempos for planning[4] and the integration of the short and
medium term[5] are necessarily national, or even regional
choices.

— The role of the State is a determining factor in the definition of
development policies and the prioritising of them. However,
this assumes that the State is able to manage its external

3. Recent university research shows that it is impossible in secondary schools to
record the number of 'brothers and sisters', the 'occupation' of the 'parents' (the
quotation marks indicate terms devoid of any content in certain contexts).
4. Hugon and Sudrie, 'La crise'.
5. Ibid.

relations on the one hand, and to establish a dialogue with the various existing social groups on the other. The State may itself be led to create, or to instigate the organisation of this twofold action.

(c) The Role of Social Actors

Currently, the way that the bulk of the population survives in many countries depends increasingly on the unregulated and the informal. The discrepancy between ideals, plans and facts, and these different forms of adaptation are an expression of the vitality of various social actors. It is essential to identify the different groups which show initiative and creativity and which intervene in civil society. Here too, the situation varies widely. In addition it might be thought that the political complexion of a country whether it inclines more towards capitalism or socialism would probably alter the nature and intensity of the role played by the various social actors. However certain studies suggest that this is not so and that in many cases economic and political crises reflect social factors.

If social actors are to be taken into account, women as much as men should be integrated in the development planning process. There are various ways in which this can be achieved:

— identification of female elites and promotion of awareness of women's problems

— organisation of women's associations, groups and trade unions if these do not already exist

— where such groups do exist, campaigns should be organised to make them aware of the need:

to take an interest in overall development projects and programmes. These should be presented to them and discussed by them.

to articulate their needs in response to the changes taking place in their way of life, distinguishing between collective, family and individual levels.

to explain how they experience the existing changes from an intergenerational point of view — how do mothers prepare their daughters for life today? How do they imagine the future will be?

— without recognised organisations, women's actions as social actors remain marginal. However the role of a small number of women in the fields of literature, art, and audio-visual production, is likely to have unexpected consequences such as the creation of 'role models' or 'reference points' which are currently lacking in developing societies.

Section 2: The Improvement of Women's Education and Training at all Levels

The aim of the previous discussion was to point to the necessity for the active participation of various social actors — but particularly women — in development planning. In this section we want to highlight the principle that education is an indispensable prerequisite for developing the capacity to participate. The relationship between education and development is widely accepted and acknowledged in theory but it is often denied in practice for two main reasons; firstly the high cost of investment in education and secondly the time factor which is often not taken into account when forecasting results. In addition emphasis on the economic aspects of education tends to obscure those beneficial aspects which are not directly translated into monetary or productivity gains.

This necessarily brief reminder partly explains women's great inequality in all aspects of education in developing countries.[6] Discrimination in women's access to education has in the past been continuous and relentless.

— inequality of access is very strong and often begins at a very early stage,[7] condemning a high proportion of women to illiteracy. It is particularly pronounced in the 12 to 17 age group,[8] which is a critical period in life with respect to enhancing one's knowledge and preparing for adult existence. Differences between regions and between rural and urban areas need further investigation

— unequal achievement in school is less pronounced than inequality of access. However, girls' prospects of reaching secondary and, more especially, higher education are very dependent on the wider economic and social context. Estimates by statisticians and demographers suggest a significant increase in the number of uneducated girls in the world

6. Which account for three-quarters of the world population.
7. Differentiation shows up from the age of eight years.
8. Often rising from a factor of one to a factor of two.

Table 6.1. Percentage of male and female illiterates in the over-25 population of selected countries

Country	Year	% Male	% Female
Mozambique	1980	50.3	72.8
Togo	1981	62.9	87.3
Tunisia	1984	53.8	79.0
Cuba	1981	3.3	4.1
Haiti	1982	72.3	81.3
Brazil	1980	30.5	35.2
Ecuador	1982	21.1	29.6
Peru	1981	13.5	34.2
Venezuela	1981	20.5	26.4
China	1982	27.6	62.3
India	1981	60.6	85.2
Indonesia	1980	27.8	53.9
Korea (Rep. of)	1980	12.0	26.9
Kuwait	1980	27.8	62.7
Pakistan	1981	68.7	90.4
Philippines	1980	10.1	13.3
Thailand	1980	14.3	26.3
Turkey	1980	36.3	68.3

— unequal representation of the sexes in technical education and professional training is very pronounced and reflects discriminatory practices as regards access to the different forms of educational opportunity. Discrimination is either direct (engendered by the system itself) or indirect (the result of the student's own choice, itself shaped by the wishes of the family, social restrictions etc.)

— the consequences of unequal access are that 60 per cent of the world's illiterates were female in 1980. The percentage of illiterates over 25 years of age in a few selected countries in 1986 was as shown in Table 6.1.

In the light of this, what action should be taken by the three principal agents of our model?

(a) The Role of International Institutions

The need to avoid compartmentalising the responsibilities of international organisations is very obvious. While Unesco should undertake to:

(1) set a clear example in the area of non-discrimination;
(2) pursue with the same determination the equally important task of spreading information and;
(3) assist with the definition of education at all levels and the implementation of specific projects;
it is essential for the other international organisations to:
— identify
    points of intervention
    the populations to be targeted
    the content of preliminary training — for instance, taking the example of productive labour at rural primary schools, how do the ILO, FAO and the EEC define the productivity of the particular types of activities carried out by girls and boys? From what age? What implications does the implementation of irrigation projects have on the tasks expected of girls and boys, or women and men? With respect to better nutrition, what information should be spread by means of the radio, television, schools, and so on.
— establish correlations between levels of general education, of specialised qualifications and of employment;
— identify differences in ethical norms which make cultural transfers difficult whether they are written or, more frequently, visual (T.V. programmes by satellites etc.);
— be attentive to:
    linguistic aspirations
    the aspirations of ethnic minorities

As the role of financial backer is most frequently played by international organisations, the latter also take a major part in deciding whether to use non-governmental organisations in a supporting or even an executive role, given they are often more closely in touch with the populations concerned.

It is also important within international organisations to make sure that programmes are coordinated and that different phases of an intervention are properly timed and ordered, that available information is related to missing data, etc. In short, in both cases, only coordination can ensure that partial points of view are brought together to reconstitute the whole and that women are adequately taken into account.

Crises may well arise in the selection and implementation phases of projects in the following conditions:

— when projects are based on partial and disjointed perceptions and analysis focusing on immediate goals
— where there is insufficient knowledge of the specific characteristics of the condition and role of women in a given place
— where there is insufficient awareness of the fact that any project necessarily has consequences for both men and women
— where there is no clear vision of the role of education in an appropriate form for the group concerned. No intervention should be financed if it lacks an educational component, and the resources necessary for education must be provided by grants, not loans.

(b) The Role of National Institutions

Again it is necessary to point to a number of possible actions, given the wide diversity of actual national situations:

— political will at different levels of the State is necessary if equality of access to education is to be achieved;
— the formation of high-level commissions — comprising both men and women if possible — responsible for giving the government a complete account of the cultural codes which regulate the life of different social groups, together with their historical background, and of their attempts to open up to the contemporary world;
— regulations should be devised appropriate to a variety of situations with respect to the posting of female teachers, housing of school-teachers, and the encouragement of husband and wife teams;
— establishing boarding-schools or centres which give priority to female students;
— devising a system of scholarships for girls to create incentives;
— setting up a system of vocational guidance which makes a clear distinction between girls and boys;
— stressing the importance of education for girls and the role of female teachers by means of posters, newspapers, radio and possibly television;
— devising presentations which show the range of roles and opportunities of women who have received some education;
— review of school text-books;
— promotion of educational projects bringing together women who have received different types of education: midwives,

teachers, farmers, shopkeepers, etc. to further public awareness
of the advantages of educating girls;
— in the various types of teacher training institutions, development of staff training programmes according to the principles
of equity and equality of the sexes; the setting up of working
parties to integrate the female dimension in all activities; the
introduction of basic knowledge of demography, of statistics
relating to education and employment, of educational planning
and the potential role of educational institutions in their spatial,
human and cultural environment.

(c) *The Role of Social Actors*

As there are considerable differences between actual situations, it is
advisable to seek the means necessary to:
— get families to agree to the education of girls taking into
account the different positions of young and not so young
parents, grandparents, older siblings;
— mobilise associations — not just female ones — in order to
bring training projects to a successful conclusion;
— communicate between the different elements of the social
strata;
— give value to the different roles played by the sexes in everyday
life and the impact of education on the quality of these roles;
— when female groups or associations exist, make them aware of
the need to support a variety of educational activities for girls
and women;
— make use of groups and representative women to work out the
content of training programmes and methods of apprenticeship
which would vary according to age and type of activity;
— endeavour to make use more successfully of girls coming out of
various levels of education and training by facilitating their
integration into social, family and economic life (creating networks of qualified females in a particular region, sharing projects, mutual knowledge of failures and successes).

Section 3: Improvement in Understanding the Key Mechanisms of Society

This third point intersects the previous two and could well have provided the starting-point for our reflections. It is precisely because we have little understanding of the mechanisms of social life in developing countries, and because we are ignorant of the real roles of both sexes — but those played by women in particular — that development planning is going through such crisis.

Planning all too often cannot engage with the actual processes of real life. Furthermore it is channelled through a dominant State which is more concerned with short-term economic and administrative problems than with its relationship to civil society and social and political structures.

Nowadays, awareness is growing of the lack of attention paid to the repercussions at the global level of the problems of developing countries whether capitalist or not. The World System, as some economists call it, has generated a whole set of concepts and intellectual tools but these have proved incapable of providing greater understanding of the key processes of development. They are particularly deficient in the face of demographic explosion and accelerated urbanisation which alter power relations and value systems, and which give rise to new mechanisms of survival generically referred to as 'informal'. To enhance our understanding, the observed facts need decoding. This is made less likely where education is lacking. Even in those countries where education is widespread, the content of education constantly needs feedback from research. Ignoring one phase of this incessant interaction may cause the whole system to grind to a halt.

(a) The Role of International Institutions

International bodies can play a decisive role since they have the best overall knowledge of existing malfunctions and deficiencies in the development process. The following actions are among those that should be taken:

— intersectoral groups should be formed (on their own initiative? at the request of national institutions?) to provide a centre for the modelling of various scenarios based on approximations of the supposed situations of various countries — in other words devising models which can integrate hypotheses on all the observed, doubtful and unknown quantities

— new indicators should be devised and discussed with relevant practitioners

— before financing new projects, the direct or indirect effects on

the female population should be estimated and if these turn out to have negative outcomes, alternative options sought
— in addition to operational aid, the following activities should be undertaken:
  systematic appraisal of the effects of the operation in question
  setting up many more educational projects to benefit both sexes which should always include follow-ups and continuing support
— assistance should be given to set up coherent and comprehensive systems of information of social situations, together with mechanisms of assessment and control
— charts illustrating the results by sector — divided in terms of female and male beneficiaries not just populations — would help identify new instruments of analysis; for instance, if the figures for those who have and have not attended school are disaggregated by sex, differences between the boys and girls become clearer. The same applies for non-wage-earning or non-salaried people, for degrees of health, for non-entrepreneurs, etc. This points to the need for a more thorough and detailed analysis.
— financing of projects should be dependent on this new data being obtained.

(b) The Role of National Institutions

The degree of credibility of governments and planning ministries depends largely on the extent to which they consult and agree with the policies of international institutions. Credibility is not so much a function of the omnipotence of the State as of the existence of reliable tools of information and analysis. In this, governments can be aided in a number of ways:
— setting up of high-level groups to research into the functioning of contemporary society and focusing on questions around men and women's relation to the land, to work, to citizenship, to education and to culture
— knowledge of the ways of life of differing social groups ranging from the highest authorities to the less privileged, and the interpretation of these ways of life in their various aspects can result in growing sensitivity to and consciousness of women's differing roles in society
— the use of existing research facilities should be strongly encour-

aged. Universities should be urged to take part in this campaign to raise awareness, and to undertake joint action with other groups and organisations. Fieldwork supported by proper resources,[9] giving value to concrete knowledge, exhibiting caution in drawing conclusions about 'what is real', and a concern to comprehend the substructure of social behaviour will permit a much richer understanding of contemporary society

— use of the media to present research results recognising women's responsibility for various areas of social activity and seeking direct contact with social actors

In short, a study of the knowledge of the mechanisms of national life needs to be perfected and made known widely.

(c) The Role of Social Actors

An analysis of concrete situations is not possible without the support of social actors. A great step forward was taken when the participation of women in the economy was acknowledged and quantified. But a much wider range of women's needs should also be taken into account. For example, women should know about:

— the legal and institutional means at their disposal
— social legislation and the health and education system
— the variety of social, family and economic systems
— the degree of freedom of individuals, and of women in particular in the different arenas of their lives — in cities and rural areas; polygamous or monogamous circles, as a single parent — with respect to:
marriage
the birth of children
the exercise of a trade
access to credit, to land
— knowledge of the real tasks carried out within the family unit by each one of its members. If we follow the methodology of some research on food systems in West Africa,[10] the following should be included:
the compilation and analysis of existing data and information

9. The number of serious research works on the realities of countries which can be found in their national libraries is too small.
10. United Nations Research Institute for Social Development, *Women in Food Systems in West Africa.*

on the theme being studied and on women

the analysis of the evolution of the sexual division of labour in the areas selected for study by means of biographies and secondary data on the political and economic history of the village

the study of the impact of socio-economic transformations on the role and status of women on the basis of a representative sample of family farms

— knowledge of the world of labour should bring out the real roles played by everyone, girls and boys, women and men. These activities should be valorised and steps taken to widen progressively the choices and distribution of roles between the sexes.

The methodology put forward in this article represents a first step towards systematising our knowledge of social and development processes and women's roles within them, and to providing a means of integrating a number of key elements in the measures adopted to promote women's concerns within development.

Further Reading

ACCT (Agence de coopération culturelle et technique), *A la recherche du temps des femmes: communication, éducation, rythmes de vie*, collected work, Paris, ACCT, ed. Tierce, 1985

Deblè, Isabelle, *La scolarité des filles. Etude internationale comparative sur les déperditions scolaires chez les filles et les garçons dans l'enseignement du 1er et du 2nd degrés*, Unesco, Oct. '80 (published in English, French, Spanish, Arabic and Russian)

____, *L'évaluation des effets de quelques opérations mises en œuvre par l'Unesco sur la situation des femmes*, Paris, Mar. '83

____, 'Population et besoins scolaires', in *Revue Tiers-Monde*, 'Demain le Tiers-Monde: population et développement' (under the direction of Ph. Bourcier de Carbon), no.94, vol. XXIV, Apr.–June '83, pp. 349–66

____, *Analyse de l'action menée depuis 1975 par l'Unesco pour favoriser l'égalité des chances de jeunes filles et des femmes en matière d'éducation*, Paris, July '84

____, *La décennie des Nations Unies pour la femme et l'évolution de la situation dans le secteur de l'enseignement*, Paris, Sept. '84

____, 'La deuxième stratégie de l'Unesco à l'égard des femmes', in *Revue Tiers-Monde*, no. 102, vol. XXVI, Apr.–Jun. '85, pp. 283–97

――, *Egalité d'accès à l'éducation et alphabétisation des femmes*, working paper for a multidisciplinary consultative group, Paris, Sept.'86

――,'Lécole publique dans le pays d'Afrique noire francophone', in 'Administrer l'école', *Revue française d'Administration publique*, no. 39, July–Sept. '86, pp. 449–61

Dury, Raymonde (under the direction of), *Femmes et nouvelles technologies*, Papers from a seminar organised in Feb. 1985 by the Centre européen de Bruxelles et l'Institut de Sociologie, ed. Labour, Brussels, 1986

Revue Tiers-Monde, (under the direction of Y. Mignot-Lefebvre), *La sortie du travail invisible : les femmes dans l'économie*, vol. XXVI, no. 102, Paris, 1985

――, *Industrialisation, Salarisation, Secteur informel*, vol. XXVIII, no. 110, April–June '87

――, (under the direction of Y. Mignot-Lefebvre), *Transferts des technologies de communication et développement*, vol. XXVIII, no. 111, July–Sept. '87

UNRISD (United Nations Research Institute for Social Development) (under the direction of M.A. Savané), *Femmes et développement en Afrique de l'Ouest*, Geneva, 1986

Weekes-Vagliani, Winifred, *Les femmes dans le développement, quatre études de cas*, Centre de développement de l'OCDE, Paris, 1980

RECOMMENDATIONS OF THE SAN MARINO MEETING

Various Participants

The participants* divided into two groups for detailed discussion of two main areas of concern:

(a)   methods of sensitising planners and incorporating women's concerns into national planning;

(b)   raising women's awareness and quality of life.

The following recommendations were made:

Section 1: Recommendations to Member States:

Methods of Sensitising Planners and Incorporating Women's Concerns in National Planning

(1)   Development is a social, cultural and economic process. Planning is thus not merely a technical exercise, but a political process which involves making choices between different social and economic options. The planning process is thus open to political directives as well as to pressures from various groups in society. Women's organisations have therefore an important role to play as advocates of women's causes, in exerting legitimate pressure on those politically and technically responsible for planning. This is one way in which women can contribute to national planning and policy making.

(2)   For women to be able to make a significant contribution to policy definition and to planning, it is of the utmost importance: (a) that a greater number of women planners be involved in the significant centres of decision and policy making; (b) that members of women's

---

* See List of Participants at the end of this Appendix.

groups get a basic understanding of planning at the local, regional and national level, so that they can evaluate planning proposals and suggest viable alternatives; (c) that more women take up planning as a career. Only by these means will women's needs, viewpoints and contributions have a better chance of being taken seriously into account.

(3) Governments should draw up, in consultation with women's organisations, policy criteria which would clearly set out priorities and objectives regarding women's participation in development and means to enhance this. With each section of the National Plan, these priority criteria and the activities and programmes derived from them, should be identified and the ministries and technical departments responsible for their implementation be named. All these initiatives should be summarised at the end of the Plan in a separate chapter. This will permit a rapid evaluation of the actions undertaken. At the same time a coordinating commission comprised of institutions working with women should be established to coordinate all these efforts and monitor progress in Plan implementation. This Commission should include members of women's organisations and other NGOs, persons working in ministries and technical departments with special responsibility for women's concerns. The Women's Bureau (if such exists) can act as the Commission's secretariat.

(4) There is an ever growing awareness that planning for development includes but transcends mere economic goals; planning must satisfy people's needs, and this means taking into account the needs of different social groups not all of whom have common problems or goals. This requires the planning process to be more decentralised than is the case in many countries. Decentralisation of planning permits much greater attention to be given to the needs of different social groups at the regional, district and even the local level. To ensure the effectiveness of decentralisation, the planning process must integrate people at the grass-roots level, and this in turn implies a greater degree of democracy in planning and in the definition of national policy. Women's active participation must be promoted at all these levels. One successful way to ensure more democratic planning is to use an iterative process by which planners listen to local groups' immediate demands, draw up a programme/policy, which is then fed back to the local group and modified according to their suggestions. The end result of this process is a programme/ project that observes the basic technical rules of planning, while incorporating the local groups' demands. This methodology, if used with women's groups, could enhance the quality and effectiveness of the planning process.

(5) Planners have to be sensitised to women's issues, but for maximum effectiveness efforts must not be restricted to planners. Society itself needs to be sensitised. This can be done in several ways, such as: organising regular discussions between planners, researchers, academics, lawyers, jurists and women's representatives in the mass media; broadcasting regular programmes on the situation of women in all social groups in the country and abroad running phone-in programmes on women's issues; organising seminars and workshops where members of women's organisations can meet with planners, State administrators, ministry officials, etc.; organising workshops at the local level for planners and ministry officials to meet with working women (rural or urban) to discuss their needs.

(6) Development strategies which emphasise the satisfaction of the basic needs of the population will inevitably have to resolve many of women's most pressing practical needs, as will strategies which emphasise quality of life issues in all their dimensions since these meet women's fundamental concerns: Both strategies will help promote women's active participation in the development and planning process.

(7) Planners must understand the importance of training local people as survey or census interviewers so as to improve the quality and accuracy of data collection, to avoid the possible negative impact of using interviewers from a different background to the female population interviewed.

(8) Planners should make a social map of women's contribution to non-monetary production, in order to evaluate its importance and its place in the national productive structure, and should design techniques to analyse, monitor and evaluate the impact of rural women's participation in development.

(9) Planners must include in an employment policy provision for training women for new occupations to avoid undue unemployment as a consequence of the introduction of new technologies.

(10) Planners and women's organisations need to improve the effectiveness of women's contribution to the development planning process. To achieve this: (a) research should be promoted which responds to immediate operational requirements without neglecting research which has longer term and structural focus; (b) all relevant national statistical data should be disaggregated by sex, at the same time the collection of statistics by the State should be improved both in terms of range of data collected and of the concepts used; research centres and women's organisations should themselves carry out data collection and research which is both quantitative and qualitative, and which defines new areas of interest; (c) the development of appropriate indicators pertinent to evaluate women's development and the

effectiveness of planning in meeting their needs is a fundamental requirement. In many countries greater effectiveness would be promoted by giving planners, women's organisations, members of technical departments easy access to a wide range of existing information on women. Research results should be centralised in a documentation centre for women's concerns.

Raising Women's Awareness and Quality of Life: Actions

Women's participation at all levels

Women, even when illiterate, have a well-defined vision of their future. Therefore:

— existing networks and official structures should be used to promote women's active participation (development of civic education, functional literacy, etc.);

— women should be encouraged to discuss their problems and wider social issues at first within women's groups and then in mixed groups.

Mass media and audio-visual means

— Record life histories, pilot projects, case-studies, etc.
— Encourage popular theatre.
— Record the personal histories of successful women whether rural or urban.
— Make videos of pilot projects whether rural or urban.
— Promote the publication of women's newspapers and magazines and encourage women of all social classes to write for them.

All these undertakings should encourage women to express themselves without inhibition. It is important to create a space in which women can express themselves and where they are active.

Technology

— Women should be given the means and be taught how to maintain and repair the technical tools and machines which they commonly use.
— In each community, women leaders should be identified who could introduce new techniques so that if successful they could be adopted by the community.
— Research on energy sources should look for practical applications which are cheap and usable at the local level.
— Existing technology should be upgraded.
— Women should be encouraged to participate in the evaluation of existing and new technologies to see whether they meet their needs.

— Networks of women extension workers should be created to promote the introduction of techniques to improve crop production and livestock raising.

— These extension workers should wherever possible help to diversify family production so as to create new sources of income.

Improving the productivity of small family production units

In general, help the planners and decision-makers to recognise the importance and the preponderance of subsistence in family survival strategy. Convince planners and decision-makers that the subsistence economy is a fundamental part of macro-economy. In particular:

— Help women to get access to agricultural training.

— Respect, retain and reinforce informal credit structures, e.g. *tontines* in Togo.

— Finance and reinforce the solidarity networks and initiatives of women.

— Take the necessary steps to prevent intermediaries from exploiting women's production.

— Raise the prices of rural products in order to increase the buying power of the rural population.

— Create cooperatives.

— Oblige the banks to change their credit regulations and lower interest rates for rural women working in the informal sector.

— Insist that the State or official organs guarantee pilot projects.

— Encourage women to organise themselves and become more involved in management.

Training

— Organise evening courses and radio programmes of functional literacy.

— Give women access to training by setting up childcare centres which are open after working hours or by providing a service of family help (employing older women, etc.).

Women's economic status

— Women's work within the household should be recognised as a social and economic function.

— Divorce, the conjugal property should be divided equally between spouses; on the death of the husband, half the conjugal wealth created during the marriages should go to the wife.

Research

It is recommended that wherever possible research in this subject should be carried out by multidisciplinary teams, so that research results can be used

with greater ease by development planners and decision makers.
— Research should be undertaken to find out where women's initiatives
   are most visible so as to help those making audio-visuals or working in
   the mass media.
— Both successes and failures in modernisation should be evaluated in
   order to draw the appropriate practical lessons.
— An analysis of women's traditional working practices and techniques
   should be made in order to evaluate their effectiveness.

Section 2: Recommendations to Unesco

Unesco should play an important role together with other agencies (e.g.
INSTRAW, ECLA, UNDFW, etc.) in the development of methodologies
of integrated planning taking into consideration women's concerns.
   Unesco should:
— Continue to finance methodological research and pilot projects.
— Distribute the results as widely as possible.
— Make available to member states, NGOs and women's organisations
   materials which give examples of ways in which sensitisation activities
   have been carried out in different countries.
— Facilitate the setting up of documentation centres on women's concerns at the national and possibly the regional level.
— Provide member states, NGO's and women's organisations with
   audio-visual and other materials for raising awareness of women's
   concerns.

List of Participants

Mme Paule Bouvier, Institut de Sociologie, Université Libre de Bruxelles, BELGIUM

Mrs Fabriola Campillo. Minesterio de Agricultura, Bogotá, COLOMBIA

Mme Nadia Chellig, Chargée de Cours, Institut de Sociologie, Algiers, ALGERIA

Mrs Saisuree Chutijul, Secretary-General, National Youth Bureau, Bangkok, THAILAND

Ms. Carmeta Fraser, President of the National Organisation of Women, President Officer of the Caribbean Women's Organisation, St Michael, BARBADOS

Mrs Maria Herczogh, Institute of Sociology, Hungarian Academy of Sciences, Budapest, HUNGARY

Mrs W.W. Ikua, Assistant Secretary, Ministry of Finance and Planning, Nairobi, KENYA

Ms Chandni Joshi, Chief, Women's Development Section, Ministry of Panchayat and Local Development, Kathmandu, NEPAL

Mme Biyémi Kekeh, Cour Suprème du Togo, Lome, TOGO

Mme Jacqueline Ki-Zerbo, Consultante, Fonds de Développement des Nations Unies pour les Femmes, Dakar, Senegal (from BURKINA FASO)

Mr Francisco Pareja, Centro Ecuatoriano de Investigaciones Sociales (CEIS), Quito, ECUADOR

Mrs Sonia Abadir Ramzi, Consultant auprès de l'Unesco, Paris, France (from EGYPT)

Ms Kate Young, Institute of Development Studies, University of Sussex, Brighton, ENGLAND

Unesco

Mme Maria Luisa Nitti, Division of Socio-Economic Analysis, Sector of Social and Human Sciences

Observers

Mme Francisca García-Sicilia, Conseil International des Sciences Sociales, Paris, France

Avv. Enrichetta Somalvico Bevilacqua, Conseil International des Femmes, Pesaro, Italy

Mrs Maria Luigia Baldini Nitti, Membre du Conseil Municipal de la Ville de Raverne, Italy

List of Unesco Socio-economic Studies

Currently available:

Socio-economic studies — No. 1. *Evaluating social action projects : principles, methodological aspects and selected examples.*

Socio-economic studies — No. 2. *Socio-economic indicators for planning methodological aspects and selected examples.*

Socio-economic studies — No. 3. *Women and development : indicators of their changing role* (published also in French).

Socio-economic studies — No. 4. *Planning methods and the human environment.*

Socio-economic studies — No. 5. *Quality of life : problems of assessment and measurement.*

Socio-economic studies — No. 6. *Evaluation manual.*

Socio-economic studies — No. 7. *Applicability of indicators of socio-economic change for development planning.*

Socio-economic studies — No. 8. *Social science methods, decision-making and development planning.*

Socio-economic studies — No. 10. *Evaluation in Latin America and the Caribbean : Selected experiences.* (Published also in Spanish.)

Socio-economic studies — No. 11. *Planning integrated development : methods used in Asia.*

Socio-economic studies — No. 12. *Socio-economic analysis and planning : critical choice of methodologies.*

Socio-economic studies — No. 13. *Women's concerns and planning. A methodological approach for their integration into local, regional and national planning* (published also in French and in Spanish : the present volume is a revised and augmented edition of this issue).

Socio-economic studies — No. 14. *Innovative approaches to development planning*